MAGICK CITY:
TRAVELLERS TO ROME
FROM THE MIDDLE AGES
TO 1900

VOLUME II:
THE EIGHTEENTH CENTURY

D1451775

BY THE SAME AUTHOR

Pharaonic Egypt in Victorian Libraries
University of Melbourne, 1970

The Unification of Egypt
Refulgence Press, 1973

Zosimus: New History, translated with commentary
Australian Society for Byzantine Studies, 1982

Gibbon's Complement: Louis de Beaufort
Istituto Veneto, 1986

The History of Rome: A Documented Analysis
Bretschneider, 1987

The Historical Observations of Jacob Perizonius
Accademia Nazionale dei Lincei, 1991

*The Eagle and the Spade: The Archæology of Rome
During the Napoleonic Era*
Cambridge University Press, 1992

Jessie Webb, A Memoir
University of Melbourne, 1994

Melbourne's Monuments
University of Melbourne, 1997

*Napoleon's Proconsul: The Life and Times
of Bernardino Drovetti (1776-1852)*
Rubicon Press, 1998

The Infancy of Historiography
University of Melbourne, 1998

The Pope's Archæologist: The Life and Times of Carlo Fea
Quasar, 2000

(ed.) Raymond Priestley, *The Diary of a Vice-Chancellor:
University of Melbourne 1935-1938*
University of Melbourne, 2002

*The Emperor's Retrospect: Augustus' Res Gestæ in
Epigraphy, Historiography and Commentary*
Peeters, 2003

What an Historian Knows
University of Melbourne, 2008

The Prince as Poisoner: The Trial of Prince Sigismondo Chigi (1790)
(with Dino Bressan), Tipografia Vaticana, 2015

(ed.) *Fifty Treasures: Classical Antiquities in Australian
and New Zealand Universities*
Australasian Society of Classical Studies, 2016

Rome, Twenty-nine Centuries: A Chronological Guide
Gangemi, 2017

The Prince of Antiquarians: Francesco de Ficoroni
Quasar, 2017

Akhenaten: An Historian's View
American University (Cairo), 2018

MAGICK CITY

TRAVELLERS TO ROME
FROM THE MIDDLE AGES
TO 1900

VOLUME II:

THE EIGHTEENTH CENTURY

BY RONALD T. RIDLEY

PALLAS ATHENE

CONTENTS

The Eighteenth Century..1

TRAVELLERS...1

INTRODUCTION..9

BASILICAS, CHURCHES AND CATACOMBS...25

PALACES...57

VILLAS...88

ANTIQUITIES...108

COLLECTIONS OF ANTIQUITIES...142

CONTEMPORARY ROME..146

WITNESSED EVENTS...185

PORTRAITS..198

SOURCE NOTES..228

List of Popes...237
List of Illustrations...238
Note on Leading Illustrators..242
Sources..243

NOTE ON MODERN WORKS OF ART

Travellers often mention modern paintings in various collections. Every effort has been made to trace these; they have often been moved. Where a new location is known it is indicated; where nothing of any such work can be found in modern catalogues of the artist in question – and the attributions are often fanciful – nothing more is said; where the work is still in the same collection, it is asterisked.

CURRENCY

One other thing is indispensable for understanding the many references to prices: the CURRENCY system. For most of the time the following is valid:

10 *bajocchi* (copper) = 1 *paolo* (silver) = 6d Eng.
100 *bajocchi* = 1 *scudo* (silver) = 5 *livres* / francs
2 *scudi* = 1 sequin (gold) = 10/- stg = 1 ducat
4 *scudi* (4.5 by 1780s) = £1 stg.

THE EIGHTEENTH CENTURY

THE TRAVELLERS

The eighteenth century saw the heyday of the British and Irish travellers in Italy. JOSEPH ADDISON (1672-1719), later a leading literary figure and a Whig politician, visited Rome from June to October 1701 with a Treasury grant in order to prepare for a diplomatic career. GEORGE BERKELEY (1685-1753), the Irish philosopher and churchman, travelled while fellow of Trinity College Dublin as tutor to the son of Bishop St George Ashe, and was in Rome January-March 1717 and April-November 1718. EDWARD WRIGHT has left us nothing more than his journal, but he shows independence and is a fine stylist; he was in Rome in March 1721. JOHN BREVAL (*c.* 1680-1738), fellow of Trinity College, Cambridge, soldier and journalist, provides 'the most complete account of Italy… in English since Addison and the first to be illustrated'; he was in Rome in 1721 – and during his travels married a nun who had fled the convent! JONATHON RICHARDSON (1694-1771), the portrait painter, was in Rome in 1721, and is mainly responsible for the account of Italian art which appeared under his name and that of his homonymous father. JOHN DYER (1699-1757), poet and painter, was in Rome 1724-5, but did not publish his poem *Les ruines de Rome* until 1740. The authorship of the travels published by Charles Thompson in instalments 1730-2 has never been confirmed, but he claims to have been in Rome until October 1731. JOSEPH SPENCE (1699-1768), professor of poetry at Oxford 1728-1738 and professor of modern history from 1742, was in Rome March-June 1732 and December 1740-May 1741. THOMAS GRAY (1716-1771), the poet and later professor of history and modern languages at Cambridge, and Horace Walpole (1717-1797), novelist, art historian and politician, travelled together, and were in Rome March-June 1740. LADY MARY WORTLEY MONTAGU, née Pierrepont

Anon., Lady Mary
Wortley Montagu, in
Turkish dress, c. *1717-8*

(1689-1762), famous traveller (to Constantinople with her husband), pioneer of smallpox inoculation, object of Pope's scorn, and socialite, left England to live abroad in 1739, and visited Rome October-November 1740 and January-February 1741. JOSHUA REYNOLDS (1723-1792), later (1769) Sir Joshua, studied in Italy as a young man and was in Rome April 1750-May 1752. Nothing is known of CHRISTOPHER HERVEY, who published very anecdotal letters of travel; he was in Rome December 1760-February 1761, and again March-July 1761. TOBIAS SMOLLETT (1721-1771), surgeon, satirist and novelist, visited Rome in September 1764 after the death of his only child, for the sake of his own health. His *Travels* were wittily renamed *Quarrels through France and Italy for the cure of a pulmonic disorder.* Smollett was shortly followed by EDWARD GIBBON (1737-1794), who was there 2 October-5 December 1764, and late January-mid March 1765. Inspired by this visit, he was to write the greatest work of history in the English language. Gibbon overlapped with the lapsed Catholic JAMES BOSWELL (1740-1795), in Rome February-June 1765. SAMUEL SHARP (1709-1778), a surgeon and FRS who operated unsuccessfully on Händel for cataracts, was in Rome October 1765 and March-April 1766. DR CHARLES BURNEY (1726-1814), the musicologist, visited Rome in September and October 1770. ANN MILLER, née Riggs (1741-1781), Lady Miller from 1778, was in Rome briefly in January then March-May 1771. Horace Walpole was to claim that she could not spell a single word of French or Italian correctly in her three volume account. DR JOHN MOORE (1729-1802), surgeon and novelist, distant cousin to Smollett and father of the famous general Sir John, travelled with Douglas, eighth duke of Hamilton (1756-1799) and visited Rome November 1775-May 1776. THOMAS JONES (1742-1803), the Welsh painter, was a well established artist when he came to Rome November 1776-September 1778 and January 1779-May 1780; on the second visit he met a Danish widow whom he married in 1789. LADY PHILIPPA KNIGHT, née Deane (1726-1799), wife of Admiral Sir Joseph Knight (d. 1775) came to Rome as a widow with her daughter for financial reasons and stayed from March 1777 until May 1785. MARTIN SHERLOCK (by 1747-1797), an Irish clergyman and chaplain to Augustus Hervey, bishop of Derry, later Bishop of Bristol, visited Rome October 1778-February 1779. GEORGE HERBERT (1759-1827), eleventh earl of Pembroke, having entered on a military career which was to see him rise to the rank of general, was in Rome from September to November 1779. WILLIAM BECKFORD (1759-1846), author of *Vathek* (1782) and politician, was in Rome for a few days at the end of October 1780 and in June 1781. MARY BERRY (1763-1852) travelled various times to Italy, but was first in Rome with her father and sister Agnes December 1783-January and March-May 1784. She was later to become famous as the object of the affections of Horace Walpole. BENJAMIN HOBHOUSE (1757-1831), later Sir Benjamin, FRS, lawyer and politician, visited Rome as a young man, October-November 1784. JAMES EDWARD SMITH (1759-1828), later Sir James, botanist, FRS, to become the founding president of the Linnæan Society, was in Rome in February and then March-April 1787. ROBERT GRAY (1762-1834), later (1827) bishop of Bristol, when his palace was burned down in the 1832 riots, visited Rome December 1791-February 1792. And finally MARIANNE STARKE (*c.* 1762-1838), a talented linguist, came to Rome briefly with her aged parents in 1793, but spent longer in the city October 1796-February 1797, and October 1797-January 1798. Her *Travels in Europe* formed a prototype of Murray's Guides.

French visitors were almost as numerous. DE BLAINVILLE's first name is not known, but he left France for Holland on the Revocation and was secretary to the States-General's embassy to Spain in 1693 before crossing to England; he guided the sons of the secretary of war, William Blathwayt, in their travels and died *c.* 1733. Notable for his learning and wit, he was in Rome April-November 1707. JEAN-BAPTISTE LABAT (1663-1738) was a Dominican missionary who had served in the West Indies; he was in Rome 1709-16. The COMTE DE CAYLUS (1692-1765) is best known as a pioneer art historian and collector, author of *Recueil d'antiquités* (1752-67); he was in Rome for some time until April 1715. MICHEL GUYOT DE MERVILLE (1696-1755), dramatist, bookseller and publisher, visited Rome June-August 1719 and February-May 1721. He was to commit suicide on failing to win the approval of Voltaire. Charles de Secondat, baron de la Brède et de MONTESQUIEU (1689-1755), one of the leading figures of the French Enlightenment, famous for his *Lettres persanes* (1721) and *Esprit des lois* (1748), was in Rome from 19 January to 4 July 1729. ÉTIENNE SILHOUETTE (1709-1767) was briefly and disastrously controlleur-général of finances in 1759; from satirical portraits of him is derived the silhouette; he was also a prolific writer and translator from English. He was in Rome by June 1729. CHARLES DE BROSSES (1709-1777), most famous for his presidency of the Burgundy Parliament, wrote delightful letters of his Italian travels (although, of course, their authenticity has been contested): he was in Rome with his cousins October 1739-February 1740 and was interested in everything. Enmity with Voltaire kept him out of the French Academy. CHARLES COCHIN (1715-1790), engraver to the king (1752), was mainly interested in the north and Naples, although he was in Rome March 1750-March 1751 as companion to Mme de Pompadour's brother. His *Voyage d'Italie* became a major guide to art. Abbé JEAN-JACQUES BARTHÉLEMEY (1716-1795), royal

CH. DE BROSSES,
COMTE DE TOURNAI ET DE MONTFALCON,
Premier Président du Parlement de Dijon,
De l'Ac. R.e des Inscr. et B. Lett. né en 1709

Charles Cochin,
Charles de Brosses,
eighteenth century

numismatist, (1753) was in Rome from November 1755 until April 1757, having accompanied the ambassador, Choiseul-Stainville. PIERRE-JEAN GROSLEY (1718-1785), lawyer and military historian (he had been in northern Italy during the War of the Austrian Succession, 1745-6), visited Rome in 1758. Jean-Baptiste Richard, ABBÉ DE SAINT-NON (1727-1791), priest, lawyer and engraver, born in Paris, was in Italy with Jean-Honoré Fragonard and Hubert Robert, including Rome 1759-61. A later voyage to the south was more famous: *Voyage pittoresque* 1781-86, a vast undertaking which ruined him. To be distinguished from him is Abbé JERÔME RICHARD (?-c. 1800), born in Dijon and luminary of the academy there, who read papers on every subject, and who seems to have been in Rome 1761-2. Abbé GABRIEL COYER (1707-1782), one-time Jesuit and educational theorist, accompanying the son of the prince of Turenne, visited Rome from

December 1763 to May 1764. CHARLES DUCLOS (1704-1772), historiographer royal (1750 as successor to Voltaire) and secretary to the French Academy (1755), was in Rome January-February and March-April 1767. Another rare French Protestant was LOUIS DUTENS (1730-1812), philologist, antiquarian and diplomat, in England from his twenties, FRS, and royal historiographer. He accompanied Lord Algernon Percy, son of the duke of Northumberland, on tour, and was in Rome February, March-May 1769. Donatien, MARQUIS DE SADE (1740-1814), after a Jesuit education, had served as a cavalry officer throughout the Seven Years' War (1756-63), and had then been forced to marry to settle his father's debts. He had already been imprisoned briefly three times, twice for sexual misconduct, once for debts, including at Miolans, from where he had escaped (he was to spend a total of twenty-nine years of life in gaol, including 1777-1790). He had already visited the Low Countries in 1769. He was in Rome October-December 1775. He was very different from the generally unsympathetic French tourist, and gave strong proof of his taste in art and architecture, but was alert to pagan and sexual elements in Christian art. Stephanie, COMTESSE DE GENLIS (1746-1830), novelist, whose husband was to be beheaded in 1793, was lady-in-waiting to the duchess of Chartres, whom she accompanied on tour (and with whose husband, the later Philippe Egalité, she had an affair); she was in Rome in 1776. JEAN-MARIE DE LA PLATIÈRE (1734-1793), was to become minister of the interior in 1792; he tried to save the king, but when his wife was executed, he committed suicide. He visited Rome January-April 1777. CHARLES DUPATY (1746-1788) was a protégé of Voltaire and a prominent lawyer in Bordeaux. After a tumultuous contest in the *Parlement* there over the presidency, as a bitter anti-royalist, he was sent to Italy to study criminal law; he was in Rome in 1785. On his return he was an ardent legal reformer. ÉLISABETH VIGÉE LE BRUN (1755-1842; see ill. opposite), portraitist to royalty and the aristocracy, especially women, left France after the Revolution, and was in Rome in December 1789. She spent most of the rest of her life all over Europe as one of the most sought-after painters of her time. And finally VINCENT ARNAULD (1766-1834), monarchist and Bonapartist, author of historical tragedies, visited Rome in September 1797.

Elizabeth
Vigée-Lebrun,
Self-portrait,
after 1782

The German travellers (Protestants are asterisked) begin with *GEORG FRIEDRICH HÄNDEL (1685-1759), in Rome from early 1707 to May 1708. Baron KARL PÖLLNITZ (1692-1775), from Köln, who changed religion often, was chamberlain to Frederick I and II. He was in Rome by 1721 and 1730-33. *JOHANN GEORG KEYSLER (1693-1743), from Halle, was librarian and tutor to the Bernstorff family and accompanied the two counts on tour; in Rome *c*. February 1730. JOHANN JACOB VOLKMANN (1732-1803), from Hamburg, was a lawyer and translator; he visited Rome in 1758. The emperor JOSEPH II (1741-1790) visited Rome in 1769. WOLFGANG AMADEUS MOZART (1756-91) was in Rome April-May and June-July 1770. *JOHANN WILHELM ARCHENHOLZ (1743-1812), from Danzig, came to Rome (1778-80) after service as an officer in the Seven Years' War and later became a notable historian. ISAAK WOLFGANG

Johann Tischbein, Goethe in the campagna, *1787*

RIESCH (1749-1810), born in Vienna, was chamberlain to Stanislaus II of Poland, and in Rome *c.* 1780. *FRIEDRICH JOHANN MEYER (1760-1844), from Hamburg was a lawyer by training, later a diplomat and secretary to the Hamburg Society of Arts and Trades; he was in Rome in 1783. JOHANN HEINRICH TISCHBEIN (1751-1829), from Hainau, the famous painter, stayed in Rome 1780-81, 1783-87, and was a close friend of Goethe. KARL MARTIN PLÜMICKE (1749-1832), born on the island of Wollin in Pomerania, was a dramatist and secretary to Duke Peter Birrn von Curland, whom he guided on his travels; he was in Rome in 1785. *JOHANN WOLFGANG GOETHE (1749-1832), born in Frankfurt, was in Rome 30 October 1786-22 February 1787, 6 June 1787-22 April 1788, and wrote the outstanding travel account of the century. *JOHANN GOTTFRIED HERDER (1744-1803), the East Prussian philosopher and critic, spent much of his short-circuited Italian tour in Rome: September 1788-early January, February-May 1789. *COUNT FRIEDRICH

STOLBERG (1750-1819), born in Bramstedt (Holstein), diplomat, historian and translator, was in Rome December 1791-February 1792.[1]

There is, finally, a number of visitors from other than these three main countries. Two Spaniards need no introduction. FRANCISCO JOSÉ DE GOYA DE LUCIENTES (1746-1828), was in Rome in 1771 after making some reputation by his frescoes and etchings, but became court painter only in 1799. The other was GIACOMO CASANOVA (1725-1798), who visited in November 1743. ANGELIKA KAUFFMANN (1741-1807), the German-Swiss painter, was in Rome January-June 1763, April 1764-July 1765 and from 1782 she was in residence. From Bohemia came FRANZ, COUNT HARTIG (1758-1797), who visited c. 1775. Two Swedish visitors were JACOB BJÖRNSTADT (1731-1779), who was furiously chauvinistic, accompanying his pupil Rudbeck on the Grand Tour, Christmas 1771-May 1772, and JOHANN JACOB FERBER (1743-1790), the naturalist, in Rome March 1772. There were also two Poles: AUGUST MOSZYŃSKI (1731-1786), architect to King Stanislaus and collecting for him, who visited Rome May-August 1785, and the naturalist STANISŁAW STASZIC (1755-1826), in Rome December 1791-March 1792. It was not until the nineteenth century that Americans visited Rome in any number. An important trail-blazer was the artist BENJAMIN WEST (1738-1820), in Rome July and August 1760.

INTRODUCTION

'At length, by continually proceeding through the desert, through solitude and silence, I found myself among some houses. I could not refrain from dropping a tear: I was in Rome.' Thus Charles Dupaty in 1785. 'The arrival at Rome and the departure from it, are two moments in a journey to Italy never to be forgotten,' was the verdict of James Smith in 1787.[2]

The first hurdle was CUSTOMS, in the Hadrianeum. Johann Keysler (1730) revealed that the most searched-for contraband was tobacco, prohibited books and new linen. Charles de Brosses in 1739 was furious because he lost the second volume of Misson's Guide, which deprived him of his *cicerone*, and not even an offer of the other two volumes could effect its restoration, and de Brosses refused to lie that he had been given special permission to read it; a companion almost lost a piece of stamped velvet bought in Florence, because Rome had recently begun to manufacture such stuff. Perhaps the most vivid description of this ordeal is provided by Stanislaw Staszic in December 1791:

> We arrived at four and were stopped at the gate. There could be nothing more offensive, even just remembering it. A tired traveller, who has covered three hundred miles to visit the tomb and body of St Peter, instead of receiving hospitality from the successor of that saint, must suffer the assaults of the police, who do not allow him to go to his house, but guide him directly, rather than to a place of kindness, to a place of abuse, the customs, where for an hour without stop, they throw everything up in the air, sack it, spoil it – and if by chance they do not find the key they force the locks, declaring that such are the orders of the representative of the saint that you have come to visit.[3]

Then came the torment of finding a HOTEL or APARTMENT. By now, piazza di Spagna was the favoured location for tourists. Many travellers give their address as simply the piazza, without further details: George Berkeley (1717, 1718), de Brosses (at Mme Peti's), Joseph Spence (1740), Tobias Smollett (1765), Charles Duclos (1764), Charles Burney (1770, at Damon's), Thomas Jones (1776), Dupaty (1785), and Vigée le Brun (1789). Christopher Hervey in 1760 was nearby at Trinità dei Monti. The most often mentioned establishment in the piazza di Spagna was the Monte d'Oro. De Brosses stayed here very briefly until he could find furnished chambers: 'methinks… [it] is the best for the newly arrived traveller'. He was 'shamefully skinned', 'but how shall we regret this when we recall the puddings we ate there?'[4] Fellow lodgers here included de Blainville (1707), Baron Karl Pöllnitz (*c.* 1721) and the comte de Caylus (1715). Other famous hotels here were the Pio (Lady Ann Miller 1771, James Smith 1787, and Robert Gray 1791) and Sarmiento's, near the Immacolata (Johann Herder

1788, and Vincent Arnauld 1797). At Trinità dei Monti was the palazzo Zuccari, where Lady Mary Montagu stayed (1740) and Joshua Reynolds (1750), before he moved to the English Coffee House. George Herbert, earl of Pembroke, stayed at Marguerita's in 1779, although he wanted to be at Don Francesco's in the piazza di Spagna, and William Beckford in 1780 was nearby, 'under the villa Medici'. Via Condotti also provided accommodation: Herder was originally with a German landlord there, before Sarmiento's and finally the villa Malta on the Pincian. And Mme Trufina could be found on the via S Sebastianello (from the piazza up to the Trinità), where Mary Berry lodged (1783). The Corso attracted fewer visitors: Händel stayed (1707) at the palazzo Ruspoli (largo Goldoni); and Goethe (1786) was at nos. 18-20. In the Campo Marzio, Jean-Baptiste Labat in 1709 lodged at S Maria sopra Minerva, but he was a Dominican; and Mozart stayed with the papal courier Uslenghi, in piazza del Clementino. Michel de Merville (1719) lodged closer to the Vatican, in via Papale (presumably near Chiesa Nuova). The visitors at this time who had the most trouble with accommodation were undoubtedly Thomas Jones and Mme le Brun. The Welsh painter changed lodgings *four* times. He was first in the piazza di Spagna:

> At home I was shut up alone in a large Open Apartment, with a brick floor rougher than that of many of our English Stables – the walls hung round with dirty dismal pictures of Weeping Magdalens, bloody Ecce homos, dead-Christs and fainting Madonas – by my bedside was fixt a kind of little Altar with a Crucifix – My Curtainless bed consisted of a large bag of Straw & Mattress, placed on a few boards, which were supported by two iron benches – In this melancholy Chamber, or rather chapel, I retired to rest, and lulled to sleep by the pattering of the rain against the windows, sometimes dreamt of many Enjoyments I had left behind me in London.

He transferred thence to 'Tresham's late lodgings at the Contessina's palace in the Corso', where he was twice robbed (because he resisted the landlady's blandishments!), then to a 'little house', in the parish of S Maria del Popolo, in the keep of Thomas Jenkins' servant

Franceschino, who forced him to live beyond his means, and when he proposed to leave, accused Jones of making advances to his wife.

> – This fellow finding I wished to live in a much more parsimonious manner than what, he thought would answer his purpose – and not daring, from the Awe he stood in of his Master, to strike so bold a Stroke as the *Contessina* had done – bethought himself of a Stratagem to terrify me out of a few Sechins – so he pretended Jealousy – & trump'd up a most ridiculous Story of an Attempt I had made on his Wifes honour – which he propagated among my Acquaintance with dreadful Denunciations of Revenge – he even went so far as to fire off pistols & blunderbusses in the Middle of the Night, and play such mad Pranks, that one night what with his raving and his Wife's screaming, I was so much alarm'd, that I got out of bed, barricaded my door as well as I could, & stood centry with a drawn Cutlass till the morning when his duty call'd him off to his Master.[5]

Mme le Brun's account speaks for itself: at first she was on the piazza di Spagna at Denis's, the landscape painter, but as the piazza was the home also of the Spanish ambassador, carriages rattled by all night. Worse, there was 'an habitual concert' of singers under her window every night. After careful checking she then moved to a little house in a nearby street, where the only sound anticipated was that of a small courtyard fountain. At two in the morning, however, there erupted 'an infernal noise' precisely behind her head. It transpired that to this wall was fixed a pump used by washerwomen which they preferred to use at night. She then moved to a small palace, where the rooms were so filthy, that she had to clean them. The first night she slept there she experienced a fearful dampness, but worse, 'an army of enormous rats, which ran over my room and ate the woodwork'. Her fourth abode she would not accept without trying it for one night. 'Barely had I got into bed than I heard a most extraordinary sound above my head; it was caused by quantities of little wood insects which eat the beams.' In sum, she was convinced that 'the most difficult thing to do in Rome is to find a resting place for one's head'.[6]

Finding a satisfactory lodging was one thing; expenses were another.

The cost of living in Rome seems, however, to have been reasonable, especially for those staying long enough to rent an apartment.

Caylus had a separate apartment at Monte d'Oro for 11 écus (*scudi*) per month, and his landlord was called Duval (1715). Smollett had a 'decent first floor and two bed chambers on the second' for a *scudo* per day and the table was 'plentifully furnished' for 32 *paoli* or 16/- (1 *paolo* =10 *bajocchi*, and 100 *bajocchi* = 1 *scudo*) in 1765.[7] Duclos lodged at piazza di Spagna for 4 sequins (8 *scudi*) per month, which was extremely cheap. He seems to have been overcharged for a coach in compensation (14-15 *paoli* per day). Burney in 1770 paid 8 *paoli* per day with meals, as did Jean-Marie de la Platière in 1777 at Damon's in the piazza di Spagna. Jones' monthly rent on the Corso, where he was so outrageously robbed, was 5 *scudi*. Lady Knight first paid for an apartment overlooking the Corso in the same year £35 per annum, then for seven rooms on the Quirinal £14/10/-, then for an apartment by piazza Colonna £18, and finally for eight rooms at Campo Carleo £12. Ann Berry in 1783 had four rooms with silver and linen for 20 sequins per month. And finally Herder paid 5½ sequins per month for two rooms in via Condotti.

FOOD interested Smollett: 'The provisions at Rome are reasonable and good, the vitella mongana, however, which is the most delicate veal I ever tasted, is very dear, being sold for two pauls, or a shilling, the pound.' In the 1770s, Lady Knight recorded that beef was three halfpence (2.5 *bajocchi*) a pound, and a fine turkey less than fifteen pence (25 *bajocchi*).[8]

'A coach is what a foreigner cannot well be without at Rome,' declared Keysler in 1730, and the cost was 4 *paoli* per day at Carnival and 9 in summer. Thirty years later Smollett paid 14 *paoli* (7/-) a day, with the coachman given an allowance of 2 *paoli*. A decade later Lady Knight paid 3/6 (70 *bajocchi*) for a coach for six hours.[9]

Then there was the cost of VISITS. Here Keysler is most informative. A visit under St Peter's cost 3 *paoli*, to Castel Sant'Angelo 4-5 *paoli*, the same as most palaces. The abbé Jérôme Richard revealed that a papal audience cost 20 *livres* (4 *scudi*) in tips to staff.[10]

How much TIME was thought necessary to cover the sights? Montesquieu in 1729 suggested six months, while in the 1770s Johann

Archenholz reduced it to four, six weeks sufficed for Keysler and Dr John Moore, and in the 1790s Arnauld could manage it in two weeks, and Marianne Stark provided an itinerary for four days! Time obviously contracted as the century moved forward. Moore told the story of one impatient young Englishman who saw everything in a coach and with a guide in two days. Herder, even allowing for his characteristic unhappiness, summed up the situation: 'Everything here is so scattered, and one arrives everywhere, apart from monuments, only by waste of time and vain trouble. The foreigner must here be a bird who sees, flies about, and departs.' Anne Miller noted that one's plans are frequently upset by arriving at a palace, only to find it closed for lunch: 'the answer is frequently accompanied by a parti coloured smirk of contempt and pity for you, who alone in this creation are not at dinner'.[11]

The answer generally adopted was to employ a GUIDE or *cicerone*, and we are much better informed on these people in the eighteenth century. Those asterisked also appear below in 'Portraits'. *Francesco Ficoroni (1662-1747) guided Joseph Addison in 1706, Edward Wright in 1721, Thomas Spence in 1732[12] and Charles de Brosses in 1739. The Jesuit de Vitry did the same for Étienne Silhouette (1729); the marchese Galli also looked after de Brosses. *Colin Morison (1732-1810) was *cicerone* to James Boswell in 1765, who also met Winckelmann and the Jesuit Peter Grant (1708-1784); the last guided Charles Burney in 1770. The Scottish antiquary *James Byres (1734-1817) had the enviable task of showing Edward Gibbon around in 1764 and Dr John Moore, who was accompanying the duke of Hamilton in 1775. The historian William Beckford (d. 1799) welcomed Dr Charles Burney in 1770. John Hippisley (1747-1825) showed George Herbert, earl of Pembroke, around (1779). The painter Johannes Tischbein (1751-1829) did the honours for his friend Goethe in 1786, who also relied on *Angelika Kauffmann and *Aloys Hirt (1759-1837), who was *cicerone* also to Johannes Herder in 1788 and Friedrich Stolberg in 1792. The Portuguese abbé Correa de Serra guided James Smith in 1787; and the abbé Juan Andres guided Robert Gray (1791).

Following Goethe's reliance on books, Smollett had Ridolfo Venuti's *Roma antica e moderna*, while the comte de Sade used the volume of his predecessor the abbé Jérôme Richard, which he constantly

Pier Leone Ghezzi, Dr James Hay as a 'bear leader', *1737. Hay, a well-known guide, took at least eight grand tourists to Italy in the first quarter of the eighteenth century*

*Domenchino
(Domenico
Zampieri),*
Communion of
St Jerome, *1614
(Vatican Museums)*

criticised. Some employed no guide. Jones admitted that 'the want of a guide made me lose a great deal of time in wearysome and unsatisfactory perambulations' (once he left the Pantheon for the Forum and two hours later found himself back where he started). William Beckford declared that 'I will absolutely have no antiquary to go prating from fragment to fragment, and tell me, that were I to stay five years at Rome, I should not see half it contained.' Vincent Arnauld stated that he had no need of a *cicerone*: children could tell him the names of everything! Friedrich Meyer was most cutting of all: the *ciceroni* were a class of men 'so dangerous to the taste and purse of travellers' and were, with few exceptions, ignoramuses. They were more acquainted with courtesans than antiquities, and gorged at the table with their pupils. Many of them had begun, he claimed, as lacqueys, who had picked up information trailing around after tourists.[13]

The trouble was the embarrassment of riches. In the words of Charles Dupaty:

> What shall I first visit? They all at once invite me. Where is the Capitol? Where the museum of Clement XIV? Lead me to the Arch of Titus. Let me view the Pantheon. Show me Saint Mary Major. I would see the Transfiguration of Raphael. Where is the Apollo of Belvedere? How is it possible to fix the attention or give a preference to any aspect of Rome?[14]

There was at least a guide to the best paintings. Wright in 1721 stated that there were three paintings in Rome, besides Raphael's *Transfiguration* (see ill. Vol. I, the most celebrated of all), which were 'esteemed the most capital: Domenichino's *St Jerome* (in the church named after him; see ill. opposite), Andrea Sacchi's *St Romualdo* (see ill. below, in the church named after him), and Daniel da Volterra's *Descent from the Cross* (see ill. p. 46, in S Trinità). By 1770 Burney listed the 'four first pictures in the world' as the Raphael, Reni's *St Michael* (see ill. p. 38), Domenichino's *St Jerome*, and Guercino's *St Petronilla* (see ill. p. 29). These were his choice immediately on his arrival in September. Two weeks later he gave a different list: the Raphael, Domenichino, Volterra's *Descent from the Cross*, and Sacchi's *St Romualdo*. And in 1787 Smith listed Guercino, Raphael, Domenichino and Volterra.

Andrea Sacchi, San Romualdo, *1631 (Vatican Museums)*

It was only Vincent Arnauld who admitted that it had all been too much: 'After having seen a thousand masterpieces without really seeing one, I left museums more exhausted than satisfied. I really needed rest when I left Rome…'[15] Only in the Vatican did he find a logical arrangement – which led to the inevitable eulogy of Versailles!

It must be admitted that there were others who had more virulent criticisms. The hypersensitive Herder declared that:

> Rome enervates the spirit, as one sees with most artists, and even more so a mere scholar. It is a graveyard of antiquities, in which one becomes accustomed too soon to peaceful dreams and charming idleness… Thought and effort are completely forgotten. A thoughtless apathy is the only goddess who rules me.

Moszyński had less spiritual complaints to make:

> One discovers that there is a great difference in matters as they are spoken about and as one sees them close up. I can almost say the same about the engravings which show us superb buildings, beautiful ruins, or the most beautifully coloured paintings; seen on the spot, two thirds of these beauties vanish. One now sees only a large palace which has a semi-ruined, stale appearance, ruins which reveal only fragments of walls which Piranesi's blotting paper has been able to make something of, and paintings where only the drawing is now recognisable. The only things worth seeing at Rome are St Peter's, the Pantheon, the statues and the paintings, but not all, for greed and need in many houses have meant that copies are substituted for originals.

And the cynical Pöllnitz had his tongue firmly in cheek:

> Rome is a city which a young man must see; here he will gain a perfect idea of architecture; he will strengthen his taste in painting and sculpture, and will form a true idea of the magnificence of ancient Rome. But when he has considered everything well, I advise him always to leave, because there is nothing for him to learn, and everything to forget.

For him Rome was the saddest city in the world.[16]

There was no doubt, however, about the effect of Rome on any receptive visitor: 'I reckon my second life, a very rebirth, from the day when I entered Rome,' was Goethe's verdict. 'No one who has not been here can have any conception of what an education Rome is.

One is, so to speak reborn, and one's former ideas seem like a child's swaddling clothes. Here the most ordinary person becomes somebody, for his mind is enormously enlarged even if his character remains unchanged.' For Thomas Gray, Rome was 'a place which I shall often think of, which I shall always rejoice to have seen'. And for that supreme representative of the Enlightenment Montesquieu, it was 'a seraglio to which everyone has the key'.[17]

Not only the countryside around Rome was notorious for MALARIA (bad air), but also the city. Marianne Starke listed the remedies:

> Persons … should choose a bedroom that does not face the south, shut their doors and windows at night, burn sweet wood in all their apartments, eat light food, drink wine in moderation, put vinegar and the juice of lemons and pomegranates into their doorways, never go out fasting or before sun-rise, drink cooling liquors, avoid night air, never use violent exercise, swallow as little saliva as possible, and carry a sponge filled with Thieves' vinegar, smelling it frequently. Quicksilver, put into a quill, and fastened round the neck, so as to touch the bosom, is likewise deemed an excellent preservative against every kind of infection.[18]

Visitors also commented on unusual WEATHER during their stay. In January 1778 Jones recorded that 'the Weather [is] remarkably warm and the Beans and Almond-Trees in full bloom' and August was very hot, the thermometer for a week being at 99 degrees. The winter of 1778/9 was remarkable: 'It is said that there has not been these forty years so remarkable a dry Winter in Italy, or so keen a frost which occasioned the deaths of Numbers of Invalides – at one time the Snow was near a foot deep in the Streets of Rome.' James Byers told him rather that 'such a dry Winter and Spring as last had not been known in Italy for above a Century'. A decade later Herder in March 1789 recorded the most appalling weather: snow and unending rain. And in January 1792 Stolberg reported snow in Rome, the first for three years. That prompted him to recall Herder's winter, with five days' snow, and the horses slipping with the frost, for which the remedy was to strew the streets with horse manure – only when the snow melted, the stench was unsupportable. The Germans and English skated in the Borghese Gardens, to the amazement of the Romans, who did not understand skates![19] No one ever listed skates as essential equipment for the traveller to Rome.

It is, finally, the eighteenth century visitors who provide interesting notes on the national character of the travellers to Rome. We have, suggestively, most comments on the English. Let us hear first comments of others. Montesquieu declared that 'the English come to Rome to see St Peter's, the Pope and the Pretender'. De Brosses had some cutting observations:

> As I have already told you, the *English* swarm here, and they are the people who spend most money. The Romans like them on account of their open handedness, but at heart they prefer the *Germans*, and this is the case all over Italy. I perceive that no nation is more thoroughly detested than ours, and this comes from our foolish habit of lauding our manners to the detriment of other nationalities, and finding especial fault with everything that is not done in the French manner. The money the English spend in Rome and the custom they have of making this journey a part of their education does not seem to do them much benefit. There are a few who are intelligent and profit by their stay in Rome, but these are the exceptions. Most of them have a carriage ready harnessed stationed in the piazza di Spagna, which waits for them all day long, while they play at billiards, or pass the time in some such fashion. There are numbers of these people who leave Rome without having seen anything in it except their countrymen, and who do not know where the Coliseum stands.

Friedrich Meyer found the English especially tiresome: for the newly arrived everything was amazing and any antique was better than anything modern – but he admits that the Germans are the same. The English could be hard to please – witness Samuel Sharp:

> Give what scope you please to your fancy, you will never imagine half the disagreeableness that Italian beds, Italian

Katherine Read, English Gentlemen in Rome, c. *1750*

cooks, Italian posthorses, Italian postillions, and Italian nastiness offer to an Englishman in an autumnal journey; much
more to an English woman.

As Lady Miller put it, 'whatever an Englishman does is right'. No
one, on the other hand, was as scathing of the English as Smollett:

> The English are more than any other foreigners exposed to this
> imposition. They are supposed to have more money to throw
> away; and therefore a greater number of snares are laid for
> them. This opinion of their superior wealth they take a pride
> in confirming, by launching out into all manner of unnecessary
> expence: but, what is still more dangerous, the moment they
> set foot in Italy, they are seized with the ambition of becoming
> connoisseurs in painting, musick, statuary, and architecture;
> and the adventurers of this country do not fail to flatter this
> weakness for their own advantage. I have seen in different

parts of Italy, a number of raw boys, whom Britain seemed to have poured forth on purpose to bring her national character into contempt: ignorant, petulant, rash, and profligate, without any knowledge or experience of their own, without any director to improve their understanding or superintend their conduct. One engages in play with an infamous gamester, and is stripped perhaps in the very first partie: another is pillaged by an antiquated cantatrice: a third is bubbled [cheated] by a knavish antiquarian; and a fourth is laid under contribution by a dealer in pictures. Some turn fiddlers, and pretend to compose: but all of them talk familiarly of the arts, and return finished connoisseurs and coxcombs, to their own country. The most remarkable phenomenon of this kind, which I have seen, is a boy of seventy-two, now actually travelling through Italy, for improvement, under the auspices of another boy of twenty-two.

Even Philippina Knight admitted that 'the mode of the English is being in clusters together, cards, late hours etc. I am very apt to think that the present mode of travelling is turned rather to amusement than to improvement.'[20]

The FRENCH naturally did not fare well at the hands of the English. Walpole set the scene:

You will have a great fat French cardinal garnished with thirty abbés roll into the area of St Peter's, gape, turn short, and talk of the chapel at Versailles. I heard one of them say t'other day, he had been at the Capitale. One asked of course how he liked it – Ah! il y a assez de belles choses.

The abbé Jérôme Richard stated that the French had a bad name in Italy in contrast to the German and English. De Brosses explained why. 'The extreme vivacity of the French, joined to the bad habit we have of saying how much better we French do things compared with other people is one of the principal causes of our being more disliked by foreigners than any other nation. It makes us impossible as companions; we are blamed for wishing to dominate everywhere.' There was, of course, a tremendous influx of French following the Revolution.

Mme Vigée le Brun mentions the duc and duchesse de Fitzjames, the Polignacs, Princesse Joseph de Monaco, and the duchesse de Fleury.[21] Finally the GERMANS. Goethe obviously thought it best to avoid his compatriots:

> Almost without exception, I found German travellers very tiresome. Either they came to look for something which they should have forgotten, or they could not recognize what they had so long desired to see, even when it was before their eyes. The visitor from the north imagines that Rome will supplement his own existence and supply what he lacks: it only gradually dawns on him, to his great discomfort, that he has to alter his reactions completely and start from the very beginning.

Stolberg was probably referring to a German when he described his horror of dilettantes. Worst of all was a woman, 'who expatiates with learned rapture on a naked Apollo, argues with men concerning the feminine charms of a Venus or a Danaë, and regardless of the pain she causes to her officious husband, places her learned finger on the muscular thigh of a Hercules'! Goethe also told the hilarious story of German artists, who fell into an argument as they were crossing the Tiber on a ferry (1 *bajocco* each way) and continued crossing and recrossing until it was settled.[22]

Because guide books will not be quoted among the travellers, some impressions from them may be briefly collected here, as an indication of the expectations made of or by the eighteenth century traveller in Rome. One of the standard writers was Thomas Nugent (1700-1772), a miscellaneous writer, translator (Voltaire, Rousseau and Montesquieu) and later FSA, whose *The grand tour* in four volumes appeared in 1749. He devoted almost sixty pages to Rome.[23] He began with the vital statistics: 150,000 population, 22,000 dwellings, 41 national churches, 64 monasteries, 40 convents and 30 hospitals. The best inns were given as the Scudo d'oro, Lion d'or and La Cirena. For any lengthy stay, however, it was recommended that the travellers take an apartment, which would cost about six guineas a month (25 *scudi*). In any case, one was advised to travel with one's own sheets for the bed, and an 'iron machine' which was a device for securing a door from within.

A coach and pair could be hired for 10-12 pistoles a month (30-36 *scudi*). Aristocrats were described as generous in showing their collections to travellers. Nugent was anxious to allay fears about an infamous institution: the Inquisition was not as severe as in Spain or Portugal and did not exercise its jurisdiction over foreigners. In sum, 'There is no country in Europe where travelling is attended with so much pleasure and improvement as Italy.' A contemporary English writer, John Northall (d. 1759), captain in the royal artillery, whose *Travels through Italy* was published in 1766, had two warnings. One was against fraudulent antiquarians and guides who sold copies as originals, the other – contrary to Nugent – was against the spies of the Inquisition who frequented coffee houses: a single offensive word and one could be ordered out of the city in twenty-four or even twelve hours.[24]

And perhaps in his pocket – although not specially related to Rome – the traveller might have a copy of *The gentleman's pocket companion for travelling into foreign parts*, London 1722. It contained amongst other things 'Three dialogues in six European languages'. The first is to ask the way, with other familiar communications; the second is Common Talk in an Inn; the third is other necessary conversation. This was, then, an early form of phrase book. The first dialogue begins with 'God save you master' in French, Italian, German, Spanish and Flemish, and allows one to reply courteously when someone asks after one's health, noting a pale face. Reply: 'I have had five or six fits of the ague, which have much weakened me, and taken away my stomach.' If one has lost the way to Antwerp, ask a shepherdess, who will reply: 'Right before you, until you come to a high elm tree, then turn on the left hand.' There is much worry about reaching town by nightfall, before the drawbridge is raised. Under 'inn talk', the traveller is imagined to be indisposed and inducing the chambermaid to make him comfortable, even so far as a goodnight kiss. She replies: 'Sleep, sleep, you are not sick since you talk of kissing. I had rather die than kiss a man in his bed, or any other place.' And elegant small talk was much facilitated by the device of multiple-choice answers: 'What gentleman is that?' Answer (in six languages, so it was quite a feat to juggle those and the twelve options): he is the noblest/ bravest/

honestest/ richest/ humblest/ most courteous/ most generous/ proudest/ most covetous/ most jealous/ greatest coward/ most fearful/ poorest/ greatest flatterer in the town!

BASILICAS, CHURCHES AND CATACOMBS

Montesquieu thought it wonderful at Rome that the churches hardly resembled one another, being mostly built by great architects, while in French towns churches and other buildings were uniform. Johann Keysler described the churches as 'so many theatres, exhibiting all the beauties of architecture, painting and sculpture'. Much of that was to change with the Treaty of Tolentino. In 1730 Étienne Silhouette revealed that the most beautiful churches were considered to be that of the Collegio Romano, S Andrea della Valle, and S Luigi, but that seems to smack of French prejudice.[25]

The dome of ST PETER's was generally the first glimpse approaching travellers had of Rome (see ill. overleaf). Friedrich Meyer in 1783 had a closer revelation. He entered by the porta Angelica, and suddenly the basilica was before him: the view 'dazzled' him. He cried to the postillion to stop, but he did not hear and galloped on! The first features which usually met the eye were the colonnade and portico (see ill. Vol. I, p. 133) – and they often elicited criticism. Silhouette declared the columns of the colonnade too close to one another, which made it bulky, yet the basilica was 'the most perfect modern work', a 'précis of all the rules of art'. Charles de Brosses declared that the portico by Carlo Maderno was 'the least satisfactory portion'. After stating that the basilica needed a more impressive approach (see ill. p. 27) – a street with fine houses – the lawyer Johann Volkmann criticised the portico for being too complicated, with too many projections, the columns wrongly in niches, the entablature too heavy, the attic order too high, the columns out of proportion, and the statues clumsy, whereas the cupola was a masterpiece of proportion. There were more approving judgements. Abbé Gabriel Coyer declared that 'by this work alone (the colonnade) Bernini was marching to immortality'.

Thomas Jones,
Elegant Figures
on a Hillside,
date unknown;
the dome of
St Peter's can
be seen in the
background,
1776-1783

And Tobias Smollett, often so critical, was almost ecstatic:

> The piazza of St Peter's church is altogether sublime. The double
> colonnade on each side extending in a semi-circular sweep, the
> stupendous Ægyptian obelisk, the two fountains, the portico,
> and the admirable façade of the church, form such an assem-
> blage of magnificent objects, as cannot fail to impress the mind
> with awe and admiration: but the church would have produced
> a still greater effect, had it been detached entirely from the
> buildings of the Vatican. It would then have been a master
> piece of architecture, complete in all its parts, intire and perfect:
> whereas, at present, it is no more than a beautiful member
> attached to a vast undigested and irregular pile of building.

August Moszyński turned his vitriol on Pius VI's new sacristy:
nothing could be worse than the facade of St Peter's, disfigured by
twisted openings and balconies, but it was the ugly sacristy which
looked like a monks' dormitory and which had cost 800,000 *scudi*;
this sum would have sufficed to continue Bernini's colonnade. It is,
finally, Jean Baptiste Labat who told the story of the Pole who,
although he had been some time in Rome, had not seen the basilica.
His friends admonished him, to no avail. He finally, however, paid

his visit, fell on his knees and came away. When asked what he had seen, he replied that it was strange that St Peter was shown on horseback! A Pole who did know what he was seeing was Stanisław Staszic, who was outraged on entering the portico: 'I felt indignant, seeing these destroyers of the earth in a place of love and peace... Casting a look of contempt on these statues to greed and stupidity, I crossed the sacred threshhold.'[26] The equestrian statues of Constantine and Charlemagne stand at either end of the portico.

Montesquieu analysed the proportions of the basilica. Its beauties made one think it was smaller than in reality; it was like a painting of Raphael, which became more perfect the more one looked upon it. De Brosses on the other hand admitted that the first view of the interior was disappointing: 'a pointed roof in the Gothic style would offer a more striking effect'. The Protestant Smollett was especially disappointed with the altar: 'no more than a heap of puerile finery, better adapted to an Indian pagod... The four colossal statues that support the chair are both clumsy and disproportioned.' The many paintings and statues occasioned comment. George Berkeley especially

Giambattista Nolli's Map of Rome, *1748; the Borgo, showing the layout of streets before the clearances of the Fascist period created via della Conciliazione, essentially by demolishing the island between the Borgo Vecchio and the Borgo Nuovo*

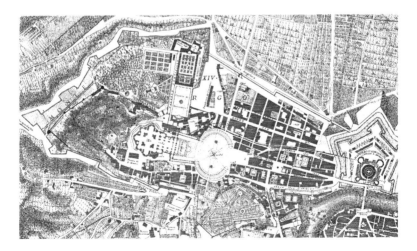

liked Domenichino's *St Sebastian*, and Guercino's *St Petronilla*, the former for the body of the saint and the expression of the bystanders, the latter for its chiaroscuro. The statues now disappointed him after he had seen some fine antique collections, but the best was Michelangelo's *Pietà*. This famous work often called forth very negative assessments in the eighteenth century. 'The figure of Christ is as much emaciated as if he had died of consumption: besides there is something indelicate, not to say indecent, in the attitude of the design of a man's body, stark naked, lying upon the knees of a woman,' declared Smollett. In 1730 Silhouette estimated that there were three sculptures in the basilica not to miss: the relief (by Algardi) of Leo and Attila, the tabernacle of the Holy Sacrament in lapis lazuli, and the *Pietà*; Volkmann in 1758 stated that Bernini's *Longinus* was one of his worst statues, while the best was Quesnoy's *St Andrew*. The bronze St Peter, whose foot was kissed by the faithful, was in a special category. Coyer was wicked: 'it is Olympian Jupiter metamorphosed, and until they gave him a hand in benediction, the ancient idolatry was obvious'.[27]

The papal tombs were surveyed by Volkmann. That of Paul III (by Giacomo della Porta) was thought to be one of the most beautiful in Rome, but the pope was not 'happily conceived' and the two statues were marred by many mistakes. That had not precluded a Spaniard having 'improper relations' with the younger. Bernini's tomb for Urban VIII Volkmann considered the best papal monument in the basilica. Alexander VII, however, did not deserve such a fine tomb. The woman nursing a child has too full a bosom and Truth was so lightly clad by Bernini that she 'excited too many lustful thoughts'; Innocent XI therefore had her clothed in bronze. The figure of the amorous but gullible Spaniard for once gains some detail with Keysler: 'he was discovered in such indecent practices as in any other popish country would have cost him his head' – but he was a relative of Cardinal Caraffa. The story could, of course, be transferred. The abbé Jérôme Richard declared that it was Truth on Alexander VII's tomb to which the Spaniard had played Prometheus.[28]

Edward Wright retold the story of Bernini's having caused the cracks in the cupola by interfering with Michelangelo's pilasters. He was jealous of Frederico Mochi's statue of St Veronica with the moving

Guercino, St Petronilla, c. *1623 (Capitoline Museums)*

drapery: 'Whence comes all this wind?' 'From the crack you made in the cupola'! Richard visited the basilica in 1761 with the 'architect', ascending even to the ball holding the cross. This was in December – in summer one would faint. That was borne out by Goethe's wonderful description:

> Then we climbed up on to the roof, where one finds a miniature copy of a well built town with houses, shops, fountains, churches (at least they looked like churches from the outside) and a large temple – everything in the open air with beautiful walks between. We went into the Cupola and looked out at the Apennines, Mount Soracte, the volcanic hills behind Tivoli, Frascati, Castel Gandolfo, the plain and the sea beyond it. Below us lay the city of Rome in all its length and breadth with its hill perched palaces, domes, etc. Not a breath of air was stirring, and it was as hot as a greenhouse inside the copper ball. After taking in everything, we descended again and asked to have the doors opened which lead to the cornices of the dome, the tambour and the nave. One can walk all the way round and look down from the height on the whole church. As we were standing on the cornice of the tambour, far below us we could see the Pope [Pius VI] walking to make his afternoon devotions. St Peter's had not failed us.[29]

The aspect of the basilica which perhaps excited most attention, however, was the mosaics. Everything in St Peter's deserves attention, declared Karl Pöllnitz in 1730, but nothing more than the superb mosaics. That of *St Petronilla* had just been finished. One of the most detailed accounts was left by Montesquieu in 1729. Each picture cost 10-12,000 *scudi*, and took two to three years; he saw work on Guercino's *Santa Cecilia*. Keysler revealed that in the finest work the pieces of stone were the size of pins, so that a surface 4' square required two million! Also detailed is Richard's account. For a painting like the *Transfiguration*, slabs of peperino were cut as wide as the work (15-16') and about 4' high, so that six were needed to cover the height; they were 18" thick. They were then covered with a thick mastic, into which were hammered the pieces of enamel. The slabs of stone were held together with metal clamps. The *Transfiguration* was costing about 14,000 *scudi*. Examples of the young mosaicists' work could be purchased cheaply: the only trouble was the weight! Samuel Sharp revealed that the *Transfiguration* took eleven men working eight to nine years to complete at a cost of 3,000 sterling (12,000 *scudi*). James Smith, finally, stated that 11,000 tints were used, kept in numbered lockers. The paste was made of Tivoli marble or rather stalactite, with lime and linseed oil. In 1787 Carlo Maratta's *Flight into Egypt* was being copied for Siena Cathedral. It must be pointed out that the main reason that the great paintings of the basilica were being copied as mosaics was the risk of their deterioration from damp. Is it possible that there could be a critical voice? Smollett knew this reason and admitted that the technique had 'been brought to a wonderful degree of improvement', yet he complained of a 'glassyness' of the surface which threw a false light on some parts of the picture; 'and when you approach it, the joinings of the pieces look like so many cracks on painted canvas'. He gave the number of tints as high as 17,000. He was offered a single head for fifty sequins (£25).[30]

Johann Archenholz provides some final general impressions. The basilica was remarkable for its cleanliness, using ingenious scaffolding. The hanging of the tapestries for St Peter's day was very dangerous work, requiring ladders placed on top of one another (the patron saint of these workers was St Venantius). Women could descend to the tomb of St Peter only on the Monday after Whitsunday, when men were forbidden, to avoid 'profane actions'! It is refreshing that Isaak von Riesch knew how to deal with the 'literalist quibblers', who claimed that the horse in Bernini's Constantine was wrong, that the drapery of his bishops on the main altar is too heavy, and that it was 'unnatural' that they supported the chair of St Peter with their fingers! It was not the French but the English who wanted to make parochial comparisons: the façade's being terminated by a straight line 'I cannot think has so good an effect as the agreeable variety, which is given by the Turrets at each end, and the Pediment rising in the middle, of the front of St Paul's', claimed Wright. The pediment was too small, and the whole west front 'far inferior in majesty to St Paul's', although St Peter's was vastly superior within, admitted Smith. Christopher

Hervey was astonished at such prejudice among his fellow country-men.[31]

In conclusion, Vincent Arnauld admitted that St Peter's was 'incomparably the most beautiful temple which exists', but 'it is less the divine power than pontifical power which this monument attests, built with the tribute of credulity rather than piety'. The last word may go to Smith. A problem for visitors to Rome was dark and cold weather. St Peter's, however, was always temperate: 'the most delightful and inexhaustible lounging place and the best recource for filling up broken days or hours that can be'.[32]

The basilica of s GIOVANNI LATERANO (see ill. Vol. I) is recorded by the comte de Caylus in 1715 as having had the same facade for about five centuries, 'that is to say, very ugly'. It was to be remodelled in 1734 by Alessandro Galilei. Strong criticisms were later expressed. The abbé de Saint-Non in 1760 asserted that the portico was full of serious mistakes which he did not then explain, but later suggested that it consisted of 'too many useless ornaments and recherché forms', while the niches of the nave were 'beneath even the Gothic'. De la Platière in 1777 blamed Bernini for ruining the church by turning the pillars into pilasters. More positively, Dr Charles Burney described it as 'the first church of the Christian world. It is amazingly rich, has three hundred and thirty five columns of the most beautiful marble.' The only criticism which he had was that, although the front was noble, it (and that of St Peter's and S Maria Maggiore) were 'more like palaces of an enormous size in front, than churches'. Most eloquent was de Sade: 'It was Clement XII who had the beautiful facade built which one sees today by the architect Galilei, a Florentine... The church is beautiful, majestic, and noble.' The best statues were considered to be those of St Bartholomew, St Andrew and St John the Evangelist. 'At the end of the nave, in front of the great altar, is the simple tomb of Martin V. The blindness, superstition and ignorance of the people are such that it is rare not to see this monument perpetually surrounded by people who want to kiss the image of this criminal, who dared keep the tiara at the cost of the life of Pierre de Lune, his rival, whom he had poisoned by the agents of his legate, the cardinal of Pisa.' The main interest of the basilica, however, continued to be its relics: the

Ark of the Covenant, the rods of Aaron and Moses, the altar of John the Baptist, a shirt of Jesus made by his mother, the table used at the Last Supper, the cloth with which He washed the disciples' feet, the gown given Him by Pilate, a phial of blood and water from His side, the column on which the cock crowed, the porphyry stone on which the soldiers cast lots, the head of Zacharias (father of John the Baptist), a tooth of St Peter, a broiled shoulder of St Lawrence, and St Stephen's clothes. The infamous 'chaises percées' were now universally dismissed as coming from a Roman bath, although the German Protestant Keysler asserted that the origin of the story was not Protestant but Catholic, in jokes on the popes' virility and begetting of children, such as against Innocent VIII Cibo (1484-92). Travellers also mentioned the porphyry sarcophagus of Helen from her mausoleum at Tor Pignttara, in the Lateran since the twelfth century, now to be moved to the Vatican by Pius VI.[33]

Almost every visitor to s PAOLO FUORI LE MURA (see ill. Vol. I) was impressed with the basilica's richness. As Keysler put it, the structure rested on 'ninety pillars of a very extraordinary largeness, many of which are of oriental granite, some of pavonazzo, and all of them antique. At the altar are thirty-six invaluable porphyry pillars, besides fourteen of a marble called saligno cippollino near the vestry.' The most detailed eighteenth-century description comes, however, in de Sade: the basilica had five naves supported on a great number of columns,

> among which especially to be admired is the superiority of those which support the principal nave, all taken from the decoration of Hadrian's tomb, today Castel Sant'Angelo. Those which support the side naves are of oriental granite. All the other columns of the double Greek cross are also very prized, especially those of porphyry at the grand altar, under the tribune, at the four side altars, and which support the canopy. The arcades of the double cross are supported by columns of Egyptian granite, red and grey, and some other precious marbles. The most admirable, however, for their size and material are doubtless those which support the great arch of the tribune.

They are of white Egyptian marble, and of such a size that four
men can scarcely encircle one. The number of all the columns
is one hundred and forty.

On the other hand, the criticisms were relentless. Caylus roundly
declared that the church 'possessed no beauty; it is big and old; after
St Peter's it is the most extensive in Rome. Its structure is ugly and
without ornament...' 'It might have been a far more magnificent
structure had it not been built in the reign of Constantine, who had
not an atom of taste in his composition,' was de Brosses' cutting
verdict. For de Saint-Non its fault was something different: it had
nothing of note architecturally, 'being entirely Gothic'! De la Platière
thought the columns superb, but the arrangement and proportions
all wrong. One might, as Hervey did, also fall back on invidious
comparisons: the Roman basilica was 'nothing like equal to its name-
sake in London' – but then, the emperors Constantine and
Valentinian were not Sir Christopher Wren! The basilica had one
weighty advantage according to Berkeley:

> I must not forget that this church is very rich in indulgences.
> We read in an inscription on the wall, that an indulgence of
> above six thousand years was got by a visit to that church on
> any ordinary day, but a plenary remission on Christmas and
> three or four other days. I asked a priest that stood by whether
> by virtue of that remission a man was sure of going straight to
> heaven without touching at purgatory, in case he should then
> die. His answer was that he certainly would.[34]

De Blainville declared s MARIA MAGGIORE, on the other hand, 'the
most beautiful of all three hundred odd churches' in Rome after St
Peter's and S Giovanni. Keysler asserted that the chapel of Paul V 'has
not its equal in all Rome' for sculpture and marble. De Brosses especially liked the external architecture by Carlo Rainaldi and the old
mosaics by Gaddo Gaddi and other Florentines. The interior he found
august, but 'somewhat old fashioned'. Richard had other complaints:
'it has nothing majestic or striking, the platform is too low and the
multitude of ornamentation too brilliant, giving it the appearance

rather of a grand meeting place than a temple'. Assessments became much more favourable in the later part of the century. To Burney, 'the inside of the church affords the most noble and majestic prospect that I have ever seen... The outside front of white stone is fresh and noble.' The most fulsome praise came from de Sade. It was 'a very noble and majestic building... The main altar combines all possible majesty and magnificence... The canopy is of a richness and magnificence unparalleled... The most admired things in this church are the two chapels of Sixtus V and Paul V.'[35]

Of the great basilicas, finally, S CROCE IN GERUSALEMME is mentioned by a few travellers, but they give only a simple description. It is de Sade again who offers comment:

> This church would be very pleasant but for the stupidity of the architect who was commissioned to restore it under Benedict XIV. To give it greater solidity, he engulfed the superb granite columns in heavy and massive pilasters which narrowed the building and made it very unbecoming in so far as it is composed of both these new pilasters and some ancient columns which remained, two styles which never go well together.

The architect in question was Domenico Gregorini. De Sade's outspoken comments on the fragments of the Cross are also interesting. They were more likely to come, he suggested, from that of a hundred thousand other rascals who were put to death in this way by the Jews. The three crosses found were without inscription, and the Cross of Jesus was identified by its curing a sick man: 'the most suspect of all miracles'.[36]

The other churches may be visited in alphabetical order. In S AGOSTINO, de Sade was principally interested in the tombs. At SANT'ANDREA AL QUIRINALE he approved Bernini's design and the precious ornaments, especially the paintings, except that a portrait of the founder (Camillo Pamphili), a 'daub', had meant the transfer to the sacristy of a sublime Crucifixion (painter unnamed). At SANT'ANDREA DELLA VALLE, de Blainville noted that exorcisms were performed twice a week, and that Domenichino's angels were 'reckoned the most beautiful in the city'. De Brosses noted that Lanfranco's fresco of Paradise was celebrated, 'a marvel of daring and vaghezza' (grace). At SANTI APOSTOLI, James Smith on 15 April 1787 saw the inauguration of Canova's tomb for Clement XIV. The figures of Humility and Temperance were 'admirable, in the true antique style; their drapery very delicate. They are altogether different from the turgid inaccurate style of Bernini,' but the pope's *right hand* 'seems clumsy and awkward. The original is said to have been so, but such a defect ought not to have been perpetuated.' The work took Canova four years and he was paid 11,000 *scudi*. 'Prodigious crowds flock to contemplate, and even to kiss, his tomb… Nobody seems to doubt his having been poisoned.'[37]

At S BIBIANA, Montesquieu was amazed at Bernini's bravura in the triple drapery of the saint's statue; de Sade recorded that it was regarded as his masterpiece. At S CARLO AI CATENARI Smith declared that Andrea Sacchi's *Death of St Anne* was 'esteemed one of the most capital pictures in Rome'. Montesquieu judged S CARLO ALLE QUATTRO FONTANE an admirable work of Borromini, in his exploitation of the small space by a façade part convex, part concave. De Sade was very moved by Carlo Maderno's sculpture of the martyred saint at SANTA CECILIA, suggesting that its effect was more powerful even than that of the girl's real body, whereas Reni's painting of the martyrdom seemed 'cold'. The same author judged the choir of S CLEMENTE 'the most beautiful and best preserved of all the monuments of Christian antiquity in Italy'. In Masaccio's frescoes of St Catherine, the 'hardness' of the drawing showing their antiquity, but there were truth and naturalness in the scene of the saint preaching. 'The head expressions of the listening doctors are truly sublime.'[38]

De Sade, again, found much to praise in S EUSEBIO: the ceiling by Raphael Mengs ('nothing fresher or more pleasing') and Rossetti's *Virgin and Child*, which called forth general observations on the delight of painters in representing Mary, 'this modern Venus of the Christians'. At S FRANCESCO A RIPA, Bernini's celebrated statue of Luisa Albertoni caught on her face the very expression of annihilation, but de Sade found the rest lacking naturalness, especially the hands. De Brosses was one of many carried away by the ostentatious riches of the GESÙ. S GIORGIO IN VELABRO was reputedly built on the site of the house of Scipio Africanus (Caylus) or the 'palace of justice of the consul Sempronius', from which the columns come (de Sade): that is, the basilica Sempronia in the Forum. This confusion is easily explained: the site of the house of Scipio was later occupied by the Basilica Sempronia (Livy 44.16), and until its replacement in turn, the Basilica Julia, was discovered in the 1780s, the southern side of the Forum was thought to extend much further towards the Tiber. In S GREGORIO de Sade praised three fine reliefs 'of an extremely delicate work' depicting the life of the pope, and Batoni's *Virgin and St Romualdo*, where the former bears the features of the painter's wife.[39]

Berkeley was particularly taken with Andrea Pozzo's ceiling *trompe l'œil* in S IGNAZIO, but de Sade found the paintings 'rough'; the mausoleum of Gregory XV (the work of Pierre le Gros), however, he thought superb. In S ISIDORO, de Sade surveyed three paintings by Carlo Maratta, where he found the figure of Mary too young, and he decried the way Italian painters depicted her head as being of the greatest beauty, 'doubtless to excite the zeal of her followers rather than approach the truth, for she is known to have been very dark, and of a rather vulgar physiognomy'! He then rather inconsistently singled out in S LUIGI DEI FRANCESI Correggio's *Virgin and Child* ('of the greatest beauty and delicacy and even more precious because it is the only work by this celebrated artist at Rome') and Jan Miel's *Saint Denis* ('the freshest colours, the most correct drawing, and the most beautiful nature in all the expressions'), but Charles Natoire's *France and St Denis* was a bad subject which would only excite Italian ridicule (Natoire's 'social virtues were infinitely superior to his qualities as a painter').[40]

S MARIA DEGLI ANGELI Montesquieu found very rich, but the tasteless monks had not provided a front, as if it were a chapel. Smith in 1787 noted an extraordinary innovation in this church: it was 'provided with spitting boxes by each of the kneeling desks, the first we have met with in Italy or France, for there everybody thinks himself at liberty to spit on any floor, sacred or profane, without ceremony or delicacy'. SANTA MARIA IN ARACŒLI reminded de Blainville of the story that it once contained a stone which the monks claimed was that on which the Archangel stood on the Mausoleum of Hadrian. Everyone

Guido Reni,
St Michael, *1635*
(S Maria della
Concezione)

knelt and kissed it, until the commissioner of antiquities, Giovanni
Bellori, saw the inscription and revealed that the stone was dedicated
to Isis! The monks denounced Bellori to the Inquisition, where he
vindicated himself. In the nearby monastery, Montesquieu climbed
up to see the whole of Rome. A monk gave him the key – and he
admitted he thought of taking it back to France! De Brosses was
shown, of all things, the tomb of Terence at the foot of the famous
stairway; he found the exterior built 'in barbarous style'. Meyer in
1783 drew attention to contrasts: the pious ascended the great stairway
on their knees, while murderers sat on them, having taken asylum
there! The Capuchin church of s MARIA DELLA CONCEZIONE (near
piazza Barberini) contained Reni's celebrated *St Michael* where Satan
resembled Innocent X. De Sade praised the combination of beauty
and strength in the Archangel's face, and Pietro da Cortona's *St Paul*
cured of blindness for its colours. What is now most remarkable about

the church, however, is the bizarre cemetery, which de Sade ascribed to a German monk (but 'worthy of an English head') and where clothed skeletons of monks were to be seen. It should have been lit by lamps, but the need to purify the air required the windows to be kept open. 'I never saw anything so striking.' The earl of Pembroke, on the other hand, saw not the slightest incongruity in the burial arrangements. At s MARIA SOPRA MINERVA, de Blainville was fascinated by Michelangelo's *Jesus on the Cross*: 'reckoned an inimitable Piece by the greatest virtuosos, who are daily seen to stare at it, with a kind of exstatic Admiration. Nay the very Vulgar are in Rapture at the sight of it... Their Zeal in kissing it is so constant and fervent that they have been obliged to cover one of its legs with a copper plate, to prevent its being quite worn out.' De Brosses declared that the church

Michelangelo,
The Risen Christ, *1519-21*
(S Maria sopra Minerva)

'has no external beauty, nor has it much within'. Smollett supported de Blainville's account of the statue: 'The right foot, covered with bronze, gilt, is much kissed by the devotees. I suppose it is looked upon as a specific for the toothache; for I saw a cavalier, in years, and an old woman successively rub their gums upon it, with the appearance of the most painful perseverance.' The only thing is that this sculpture does not represent Jesus on the Cross, but the risen Jesus, standing beside the Cross! There were many fine things in s MARIA DELLA PACE: de Sade noted the sadly damaged frescoes of Raphael, a bronze relief of Domenico Guidi of the Descent from the Cross, a fine painting by the Cavaliere d'Arpino, and a delicate and admirable *Visitation* by Carlo Maratta. Goethe had a bone to pick with his countryman Volkmann who criticised Raphael here for poor composition, caused by limitation of space. 'This is nonsense... It is one of the greatest proofs of his genius that he could fill any given space in the most exquisite manner.'[41]

A favorite church with visitors was s MARIA DEL POPOLO. Smollett told the story of its being built on the site of Nero's tomb, but it was de Sade, as usual, who singled out the masterpieces: the 'truly magnificent' Cibo chapel (second on the right) with a fresco by Carlo Maratta of the Conception (actually the Assumption) 'of the greatest beauty' and a magnificent dome, Giovanni Morandi's *St Lawrence*, and the monument to Princess Chigi ('it is difficult to see anything more light and more elegant than this monument, the execution and design of which do eternal honour to the sculptor Pena' – in reality Paolo Posi). In the Chigi chapel he especially liked Sebastiano del Piombo's *Nativity* ('it deserves all its reputation'), as well as Annibale Carracci's *Assumption* in the transept ('truly of the greatest beauty'). In that same Chigi chapel Smith (an eminent botanist) preferred Raphael's Jonah: 'I have gazed on this divine production for uncounted hours with fresh delight and astonishment', 'the first modern statue of the elegant kind, if Michelangelo's Moses be allowed the predominance in sublimity'. How bizarre that de Blainville's most noteworthy comment was that the church contained Jesus' navel![42]

s MARIA DEL PRIORATO on the Aventine had recently been decorated by Piranesi: 'the ornaments are placed so confusedly and treated with

Bernini, Ecstasy of
St Teresa, *1647-52*
*(Capella Cornaro, S Maria
della Vittoria)*

such harshness that they fatigue the eyes and will certainly be displeasing always,' stated de Sade. The current grand prior of the order was Cardinal Giovanni Battista Rezzonico. In s MARIA IN VALICELLA (the Chiesa Nuova) de Sade admired Caravaggio's *Entombment* ('one cannot over admire the truth, propriety and strength of this work'), but Algardi's statue of Filippo Neri did not please him as much as his other works. Bernini's famous statue of St Teresa was to be found in s MARIA DELLA VITTORIA; it called forth very varying responses. Berkeley found it 'wonderfully well done'; Domenichino's *Madonna and Child* he also judged 'excellent'. The abbé de Saint-Non described St Teresa as 'full of graces and the most tender expression', but the abbé Coyer was the most eloquent: 'at the moment that a cherub, in the flower of human age, handsome with a more than human beauty, lets fly at her heart a fire dart, one sees her on her back, her breast uncovered, her chest raised, her breathing interrupted, all nerves contracted, ecstasy shown in her eyes, in the confusion of her face, of her whole person, and of her clothes, which leave a leg naked'. De Sade could find fault only with an excess of drapery and the mannered way in which the angel holds his dart. Later views diverged. De Brosses had admittedly found Teresa 'a little too close to humanity'. Riesch declared that the saint's 'grimaces' indicated a physical rather than a divine ecstasy and he found the angle very mannered. Dupaty affected to experience a 'mental blush' beholding her. The harshest judgement came from an English botanist. Bernini accounted the sculpture his masterpiece. It is 'deservedly criticised for its almost lascivious expression; and indeed the most naked Venus would be much less improper ornament for a church than the luxurious saint, melting in extasy, with a little smiling cherub, or rather cupid, directing a dart to her naked bosom'.[43]

De Brosses recorded something extraordinary at s MARTINA in the Forum, site of the Academy of Painting: 'the skull of Raphael. Alas! I have held that poor relic of humanity in my hands, and verily it seems to me that that death's head is handsomer than others.' The church also contained 'some good statues and two or three good paintings'. The skull was an imposture: Raphael's head had been with the rest of his body in the Pantheon since his death. De Sade describes the lower levels of this church: *les souterrains*. The twenty-four antique columns in s MARTINO AI MONTI were said by de Blainville to have been brought from the Baths of Titus on the Esquiline; from both the Baths of Titus and the Baths of Trajan, wrote de Sade.

At the three churches of s PAOLO ALLE TRE FONTANE, Caylus was not impressed with the Bernardins, who were in charge. He noted that some people claimed that the three fountains had a different taste, but he did not find it so. Reni's *Martyrdom of Peter* was very beautiful, and the mosaics of Francesco Zuccaro were the finest he had yet seen. Wright had a sceptical note: 'The Water of these Fountains cures all Diseases. One would wonder what Occasion they have for Doctors.'[44]

One of the most famous churches in the whole city was s PIETRO IN MONTORIO, on the Janiculum, for it housed the most admired painting in Rome, Raphael's *Transfiguration* (see ill. Vol. I). Montesquieu had a criticism: in his words, 'the accessory was larger than the principal', that is, that the scene of the possessed below Christ was so large. He could not, nevertheless, 'weary of looking at it, nor weary of speaking of it'. Keysler declared it 'the most celebrated picture at present known in the whole world'; de Brosses 'the finest easel painting in existence', but badly placed and hard to see: 'were I the Pope, it would not remain there one minute longer'. It was, indeed, a Frenchman who removed it in 1798. Smollett took Montesquieu's thoughts a step further: 'if it were mine, I would cut it in two'. The major merit of the painting he described as the expression of divinity on Christ's face, and the 'surprising lightness of the figure, that hovers like a beautiful exhalation in the air'. De la Platière waxed eloquent: 'it is only by poetic élan, a divine fire, a parturition equal to that of Minerva sprung from the head of Jupiter, that Raphael has been able to conceive and create his subject, characterised above all human expression'. Goethe recorded the debate which he and friends had before the painting about the 'double action'. He was surprised at the critics. The two parts are one: the succourer and those needing succour. 'Like Nature, Raphael is always right, and most profoundly when we understand him least.' Stolberg answered the critics by describing the movements of the viewer's eye:

> Terror seizes us at the aspect of the possessed youth! We participate in the embarrassment of the disciples, the attention of the spectators, the anguish of the enquiring eyes of the father, who wishes to know if his son can be relieved, and the bitter grief of the mother and sister. Our eye wanders further: we are entranced with the disciples: with the two great prophets, we ardently aspire after heaven…[45]

Yet another church of the same saint, s PIETRO IN VINCOLI drew all travellers for another masterpiece, Michelangelo's *Moses* (see ill. overleaf). De Blainville recorded that this sculpture was 'reckoned the most beautiful of all the modern ones to be seen in Rome'. His description filled no fewer than nine pages. We hear some echo of details which were being discussed at the time. Labat declared that Michelangelo

Michelangelo, Moses,
1513-15 (S Pietro in Vincoli)

was well versed in antiquity: Moses' beard 'must have been so long and thick'! Richard described the work as 'a unique masterpiece, incomparable in antiquity and in modern times for the expression', while the muscles and veins in the neck, arm and legs are so precise that they could serve as an anatomy lesson. Boswell unexpectedly had some criticisms: 'Beard too long; horns, though sacred, yet ludicrous as like satyr; rest of the figure superb.' De Sade, on the other hand, praised the articulation of the limbs and the expression of the face; there was 'so much strength that the marble, like that of Pygmalion, was ready to come alive'. In the same church he also praised the tomb of Cardinal Lanfranco Margotti (d. 1612) and of Mariano Vecchiarelli (d. 1639), and Guercino's *St Margaret*. The earl of Pembroke may be taken to represent the Philistines. 'I think, he holds his left hand as if he had a Pain in his Stomach, and his beard is of an unpardonable length.'[46]

At S PRASSEDE, apart from being repelled by Christian superstition, de Sade singled out in the sacristy, behind a curtain of green taffeta, Giulio Romano's *Flagellation*. In S PUDENZIANA, de Blainville stated that four columns of *giallo antico* in the Caietani chapel came from the Baths of Diocletian. S ROMUALDO near piazza Venezia, long ago demolished, had an altar-piece by Andrea Sacchi, 'one of the best pictures in Rome', thought Smith. The English, he noted, were especially fond of this church. De Sade gives some impression of S SABINA before its restoration in the twentieth century. The paintings included Lavinia Fontana's *S Sabina* ('more pleasing than skilful'), Giovanni Morandi's *S Catherine receiving Christ from his Mother* ('highly esteemed', although de Sade detected faults in the drawing), but Taddeo Zuccari's frescoes over the altar were 'so ridiculous and huge' that one could only pity the artist's blindness. S STEFANO ROTONDO, built on a temple either of Janus or to the emperor Claudius, had no beauty for Caylus. For Berkeley it was originally a temple to Faunus. De Brosses added a temple of Jupiter Peregrinus as a candidate for the original building. De Sade perspicaciously rejected the idea that the church's core was a classical temple, mainly because the columns were not equal, and therefore were brought from various places. He also denounced Antonio Tempesta's martyrdoms around the walls: 'one of the most terrifying collections of horrors possible to assemble'; de la Platière dismissed them: 'nothing so singular or more ridiculous'.[47]

S TRINITÀ DEI MONTI was one of the French churches; de Blainville recalled a detail otherwise overlooked. The church contained the tomb of Marc-Antoine Muret, a criminal who praised the massacre of St Bartholomew and was condemned to death for sodomy in Toulouse in 1554, but he escaped to Venice, and from there fled to Rome. The church also contained one of the most celebrated paintings in the city, Daniel da Volterra's *Descent from the Cross* (see ill. overleaf). Montesquieu expertly summed up the main skills: 'the body of Christ seems to fall of its own weight; the upper part to collapse on the lower; the limbs of the figures seem to come out of the painting; the Virgin

Daniele da Volterra,
Descent from the
Cross, *1541 (S Trinità)*

seems to be in ultimate grief'. And the artist had not resorted to any chiaroscuro. He did not fail to draw attention also to the same artist's *Two Sibyls* ('admirable') and Giulio Romano's *The Magdalen recognizes Christ*. De Brosses admitted that he could not estimate the *Descent* as highly as Poussin had done. He had the highest praise, however, for one of the monks, François Jacquier (1711-88), a Jesuit who with a colleague Thomas Lesueur was composing a commentary on Newton, which was being published in Geneva. De Sade also had criticisms of the *Descent*: he especially found fault with the figure at the bottom of the ladder, for his forced posture and his overlong arm, and with the caryatids holding up pieces of column shaken by the earthquake at the time of the crucifixion.[48]

The CATACOMBS also attracted the travellers. The most famous was S Sebastiano. De Blainville in 1707 said of his visit that 'considering the great Danger attending this Attempt, I freely own, we ought not, in common Prudence, to have ventured upon it'. He told the recent story of eight Germans, trapped by an earthfall, unable to overlook 'such a tip top Piece of Singularity'! And he had to test Lassels' claim that heretics were converted by the experience. De Blainville emerged 'more incredulous than ever'. In order, however, not to meet the much recounted fate of visitors, he took string and pegs to stick in the wall; the labyrinth of Minos was 'little or nothing in Comparison'. He paid the guide to open three graves, but as soon as the skeletons were touched, they turned to a white paste. One thing he was sure: the Christians never lived in these 'dark, moist, nasty, filthy and stinking Holes'. The old debate was obviously continuing. Keysler in 1730 asserted that the catacombs could not have been built by so few Christians, that they could not have been kept a secret, and that they could not have served as a refuge for thousands. They were therefore pozzolana caves, first used for slave burials, and then later pagan and Christian. Pembroke in 1779 commented on the restricted passages, 3'-4' wide, sometimes as low as 5'-6', nowhere higher than 7'. 'To this day the Pope diggs [*sic*] for Saint's [*sic*] bones in these catacombes… but I believe that of late Years, the trade slackens considerably.' De Brosses visited S Agnese, 'the finest Catacombs in all Christendom. Martyrs, confessors, and virgins abound on all sides. When any relics are required outside Italy the Pope has only to come here and call out, "Who wants to go and be a saint in Poland?"' And we have a clear indication of the kind of nonsense that the guides peddled. Hobhouse in 1784 was assured by his guide that one could travel underground to St Peter's, Frascati and Tivoli![49]

The first ecclesiastical festival of the year was EPIPHANY (6 January). Goethe has left us a description of an amusing part of the celebration in 1787:

[W]e went to the Propaganda. There, in the presence of three cardinals and a numerous auditory, we first heard an address on the theme: In what place did Mary receive the three Magi? In a stable? If not, where else? Then some Latin poems on similar themes were read, and after that about thirty seminarists appeared and read, one after another, little poems, each in his native tongue: Malabarian, Epirotian, Turkish, Moldavian, Hellenic, Persian, Colchic, Hebrew, Arabic, Syrian, Coptic, Saracenic, Armenian, Iberian, Madagassic, Icelandic, Egyptian, Greek, Isaurian, Ethiopian, etc., and several others which I could not understand. Most of the poems seemed to be written in their national metres and were recited in their national styles of declamation, for some barbaric rhythms and sounds came out. The Greek sounded as if a star had risen in the night. The audience roared with laughter at all the foreign voices, and so this performance, too, ended in farce.[50]

The festival of ST ANTHONY (17 January) was notable for the blessing of the horses at his church near S Maria Maggiore. It is described by Berkeley in 1718, but much more fully by Spence in 1741:

on that day almost everyone that has a horse, mule, or ass in Rome, sends them to this church to be blessed. There is a convent belonging to the church, a court behind, two gates on each side of it, and a pretty large opening before. This you see full of the aforesaid animals, dressed out with ribbons, and some with garlands; they drive in at one of the gates, where stands a priest in his surplice and other ecclesiastical ornaments, with several tubs of holy water by him and an aspergitoire (or instrument to sprinkle it on man or beast) in his hand.

The coaches, carts, and saddle horses that are next to this gate, go in (in a sort of procession), and as they pass the priest, they give him a piece of silver, a wax candle or a wax torch, who takes care to wet them according to their present. A coach and six with a vast torch has half enough to drown the coachman, if 'twas all well placed in his face; a muleteer has but a little sprinkling and an ass-rider may come off quite dry. We drove

in our coach, and had sixpenny worth of it. After you are in the
great gate, you go on in a semicircle and come out at the other;
and there was a line of animals, always going and coming, from
sunrise to sunset. This is the chief revenue of the convent, and
they are said to make a thousand pound of what they receive
this day: the chief of which income is in wax. I have heard that
the men bring their hounds, and the ladies their lap dogs, to
partake of the blessing: what I can aver myself is that I saw a
cartload of wood blessed there among other things, and 'twas
so plentifully wetted that I believe it must have burnt the worse
for it. All the times I saw it the same priest officiated; he was
perhaps the strongest fellow in the convent, yet the last time
I was there (about 23 o'clock) he seemed very much fatigued
with blessing, and almost quite spent.

Goethe, who also described the blessing, recorded that it was forbidden to use horses on this day, 'and the people love to tell fearful stories
of unbelieving masters who forced their coachmen to drive on this
day and were punished by serious accidents'.[51]

Lent began with ASH WEDNESDAY. Hervey in 1760 was appalled:
'Never did I see people eat so in my life.' Of EASTER, Caylus was
dismissive. The ceremonies at Rome were 'prodigiously boasted over'
and attracted foreigners, but they were 'nothing special'. On Easter
Thursday, the pope excommunicated heretics, and washed the feet of
a dozen poor priests; even the *Miserere* was esteemed beyond its worth.
On Friday pilgrimage was made to St Paul's and St Sebastian's. On
Saturday at S Giovanni Laterano, the pope baptised converts (in 1715
it was only a Turk and a Jew). Holy Thursday was described in more
detail by various travellers. The washing of the priests' feet naturally
excited comment. 'The occupation of the Pope could by no means be
a very agreeable one; for I can assure you, that several of those poor
Priests' Feet smelt but very indifferently,' asserted de Blainville, and
he was at some distance. Mozart father and son were present at the
washing of feet in 1770. To manage this, they had to pass two doors
guarded by the Swiss and make their way through hundreds of people.
They relied on their 'fine clothes, the German tongue, and my

[Leopold's] usual freedom of manner which led me to make my servant order the Swiss guards in German to make way for us'. Wolfgang
was taken for a prince! He stood near the chair of Cardinal Lazzaro
Pallavicini, who asked him in confidence who he was; he was amazed
to find it was 'the famous boy'. Mary Berry was present in 1783 and
assured her readers that the feet of the priests had been made 'thoroughly clean beforehand'. At the subsequent dinner she described Pius
VI: 'His figure, standing at the top of the table in his white dress, with
a girdle round his waist, waiting till they had eaten some off their
plates, was not unlike that of a jolly cook with his apron before him.'
Smith in 1787 depicted the crowded scene: 'The number of strangers
round the table making it difficult for the servants to remove the
dishes, we set the example of assisting them, saying that "When his
Holiness served the table, anybody ought to be proud to help away
with the plates"'!

On Good Friday in 1740 Gray was present in St Peter's:

> It was something extremely novel to see that vast church, and
> the most magnificent in the world, undoubtedly, illuminated
> (for it was night) by thousands of little crystal lamps, disposed in
> the figure of a huge cross at the high altar, and seeming to hang
> alone in the air. All the light proceeded from this, and had the
> most singular effect imaginable as one entered the great door.
> Soon after came one after another, I believe, thirty processions,
> all dressed in linen frocks, and girt with a cord, their heads
> covered with a cowl all over, only two holes to see through left.
> Some of them were all black, others red, others white, others
> party coloured; these were continually coming and going with
> their tapers and crucifixes before them; and to each company,
> as they arrived and knelt before the great altar, were shown
> from a balcony at a great height, the three wonders, which are,
> you must know, the head of the spear that wounded Christ; St
> Veronica's handkerchief, with the miraculous impression of his
> face upon it; and a piece of the true cross, on the sight of which
> the people thump their breasts, and kiss the pavement with
> vast devotion. The tragical part of the ceremony is half a dozen
> wretched creatures, who with their faces covered, but naked

to the waist, are in a side chapel disciplining themselves with scourges full of iron prickles; but really in earnest, as our eyes can testify, which saw their backs and arms so raw we should have taken it for a red satin doublet torn, and shewing the skin through, had we not been convinced of the contrary by the blood which was plentifully sprinkled about them.

Smith in 1787 described the particular scene at the altar that year. The whole of the basilica was in darkness, save for the illuminated cross above the high altar. The steps of that altar were packed with foreigners as Pius VI paid his devotions. They included the duke and duchess of Gloucester, and the duke and duchess of Buccleuch. The English debated whether the pope noticed the English beauties. An 'observing lady' assured them that Pius was concerned 'to kneel gracefully and to display a very handsome leg to the best advantage'. Braschi was notorious for his vanity.

The most famous performance of this day was the *Miserere* of Gregorio Allegri. Poor de Saint-Non thought the opening was touching and pathetic, but then he found it monotonous. A young genius in 1770 thought otherwise:

> You have often heard of the famous *Miserere* in Rome, which is so greatly prized that the performers in the chapel are forbidden on pain of excommunication to take away a single part of it, to copy it or to give it to anyone. *But we have it already.* Wolfgang has written it down and we would have sent it to Salzburg in this letter, if it were not necessary for us to be there to perform it. But the manner of performance contributes more to its effect than the composition itself. So we shall bring it home with us.

One Good Friday Keysler and some of his friends inadvertently followed a crowd into a subterranean chapel. The doors were closed and everyone was given a knotted cord. A Jesuit made a long harangue about chastening the flesh and blood and 'not sparing old Adam'. The lights were then turned out, and the doors were not reopened for some time.

Elisabeth Vigée le Brun described the scene on Easter Day in 1790 (see illustration overleaf for the same scene twenty years earlier):

Louis Desprez, Papal benediction, *1770s*

This immense Piazza was crowded from early morn by peasants and people from the neighbouring towns, all in divers and many hued costumes, along with several pilgrims. The galleries each side were filled with Romans and strangers, and in front of them were the Papal Guard and Swiss soldiers, with their ensigns and banners unfurled.

A most devout silence reigned over all; this crowd was as immoveable as the superb obelisk of oriental granite which adorns the Piazza, one only heard the sound of the water falling from the two beautiful fountains.

At ten o'clock the Pope arrived dressed in white with his mitre on his head. He sat on a splendid crimson throne in the middle, outside the church. All the Cardinals surrounded him in their fine robes. I must say that Pope Pius VI. was superb. His healthy face bore no traces of age. His hands were white and plump. He knelt to read his prayer; after which he arose and gave three benedictions, pronouncing these words, '*urbi et orbi*' (to the city and to the world).

Then as if struck by a flash of lightning, the people, strangers, soldiers, everybody knelt, whilst the cannon resounded all around, a sight to believe none can behold without being affected thereby.

The benediction given, the Cardinals threw from the tribune a great number of papers, which I was informed were indulgences. It was only then that the crowd all dispersed, and thousands of arms were raised to seize one of these papers. The movement and eagerness of this crowd was beyond all description. When the Pope left, the military bands played, and the troops departed to the sound of the drums.[52]

ST PETER'S AND ST PAUL'S day (29 June) was described by Dupaty in 1785:

What noise! What confusion! Occasioned by the floods of people who are perpetually pouring in, and the floods perpetually rushing out; by devotees, who pressing around the feet of St Peter, are contending for the happiness of kissing them; by persons, of every sex and age, kneeling before confessionals filled with monks, and receiving absolution for venial sins, dispensed at the end of a long switch which the monks shake over their heads; by young men and girls, wandering from tomb to tomb, wantoning with each other, and talking of love. Here I see Englishmen, gravely taking the dimensions of the pillars; Frenchmen skipping about and jesting; Germans astonished to find on the bronze gates of the first church in the world the most lascivious pictures. On the other side of the church I perceive a row of abbés bending their bodies to the earth and flattering the cardinals who, as they pass, assume state and act the patron; and a number of mendicants, who to impose on pity, or fatigue delicacy, are shocking every eye with nudities and sores. In the interim the signal for the march is given. Behold now a numerous train of dirty penitents, who file off and make room for dirty monks, dirty curates and a thousand dirty wretches of the populace, clad in dirty surplices, bearing each of them a flambeau, and exciting everywhere as they pass, by their grotesque accoutrements, a universal laugh. At length behold the prelates, cardinals, and the pope. At the bottom of the staircase of one of the galleries, the pope finds his military attendants, who receive him and the holy sacrament that is waiting for him. The union of the two powers now immediately takes place, to the sound of trumpets; the pope and the sovereign are intermingled; and the crown and the tiara unite on the same head; the pontiff king then mounts on a throne, and seats himself with the host before him; yet by his position, and the manner in which his ornaments are arranged, appears to be on his knees; while a dozen robust men concealed under the estrade bear him along. The pope advances, truly magnificent and venerable, holding the sacrament in his hands, his eyes lifted towards heaven, overflowing with pious tears: whilst a general murmur runs amongst the people who whisper – How handsome the pope is! All his military attendants follow on foot or on horseback – the procession has returned into the church – A thousand torches are ranged along the whole extent of the nave and round the high altar; the pope descends, crosses the church, mounts and depositing the host, falls upon his knees, rises up, gives his benediction – and all is ended.

Goethe described another notable aspect of the day, the illuminations: 'like a scene from fairyland... To see the colonnade, the church, and, above all, the dome, first outlined in fire, and after an hour, become one glowing mass, is a unique and glorious experience. When one thinks that, at this moment, the whole enormous building is a mere scaffolding for the lights, one realises that nothing like it could be seen anywhere else in the world.' Meyer explained the mechanics. The cupola of the basilica burst into fire on the sounding of a bell; one hundred workers hidden behind the windows ignited torches and vases of powder. Then everyone surged towards ponte Sant'Angelo to see the girandola, set off by five thousand fuses (see ill. opposite).[53]

November 2 was ALL SOULS' DAY. This was described by Grosley in 1758:

In the very spacious hall under their chapel [the Fraternità della Morte] one first comes to a kind of hall hung with red paper,

Joseph Wright (of Derby), The Annual Girandola at Castel Sant'Angelo, c. *1776*

and having pilasters or niches, the bases and chapiters of which are made of real death's heads with lights so disposed within them, and bits of paper laid over eyes and jaws, as to shed a dim and reddish glimmer, the only illumination in this lugubrious place. In the niches are large dessicated skeletons, among which I was shown that of the beautiful Paula, whom her red tresses still covered down to her middle… Further on in another vault, resembling a large burial place lighted with torches, are laid seven or eight dead bodies, as natural representations of the progressive degrees of putrefaction. In this mansion of death, in the midst of the spectacle, the sadness of which is increased by the strong *faetor* of the bodies, amidst the loud thumps with which a crowd of well-meaning souls were bruising their breasts, I observed signs made to the *zitelle*, or girls, to keep them in heart…[54]

SANTA CECILIA has always been a favourite Roman saint. Her day was 22 November. Goethe attended in 1786:

> It would take pages to describe the decorations of this church, which was packed with people. One could not see a stone of the structure. The columns were covered with red velvet wound around with ribbons of gold lace, the capitals with embroidered velvet conforming more or less to their shape – so, too, with the cornices and pillars. All the intervening wall space was clothed in brightly coloured hangings, so that the whole church seemed to be one enormous mosaic. More than two hundred candles were burning behind and at the sides of the high altar, so that one whole wall was lined with candles, and the nave was fully illuminated. Facing the high altar, two stands, also covered with velvet, had been erected under the organ loft. The singers stood on one; the orchestra, which never stopped playing, on the other.
>
> Just as there are concertos for violins or other instruments, here they perform concertos for voices: one voice – the soprano, for instance – predominates and sings a solo while, from time to time, the choir joins in and accompanies it, always supported, of course, by the full orchestra. The effect is wonderful.[55]

It is, naturally, a Frenchman who leaves us a most memorable account of 18 December, ST LOUIS' DAY, in this case de Brosses in 1739:

> Every year, on the festival of St Louis, December 18, the French Ambassador celebrates the anniversary of that conversion by a very expensive banquet. The Duke of St Aignan [Paul Hippolyte Beauvilliers, French ambassador] had wished to dispense with holding it this year, and had suggested to our Court the advisability of giving the money it would cost in charity, but the Court refused his petition. This dinner is not one of the least curious of the sights to be seen here. We sat down to dinner to the number of five hundred and fifty, at a table shaped like a horseshoe. There were seven or eight cardinals present, as well as all the principal Frenchmen and foreigners of distinction in

Rome, and a great number of Roman nobles, especially those favourable to France. The Duke said this dinner cost him eight hundred pounds. We were requested not to give up our plates and dishes to any but those in the Duke's livery. The pillage that takes place is incredible. The soup had scarcely been removed before we were importuned by a horde of strange waiters to give them provisions for their masters. One especially singled me out, probably thinking I looked the greatest idiot in the company. I made him a present of a turkey, a chicken, a slice of sturgeon, a partridge, some roedeer, some tongues, and ham; but he always returned. 'But', I said to him, 'the table is equally well garnished elsewhere; wherefore do you always come back to me? Besides, your master is able to get all he can require. Neither have I ever seen any one eat so much as he is doing.' Detroy, who was sitting near, said, 'You must be very simple to think he asks all this for his master; it is for himself,' and looking round I saw on all sides things being carried off in the pockets or napkins of these gentlemen. The Ambassador told me that he was annually pillaged on these occasions to the tune of twenty-five to thirty pieces of silver plate. At dessert there was a general scramble, and nothing was left.[56]

Of CHRISTMAS, only Gray in 1791 offers a memory. He recalled that Pius frequently changed dress during the Mass on Christmas day in St Peter's, 'sometimes stripped to his flannels'![57]

PALACES

We may begin with some general remarks. The most important were the criticisms of the design of such dwellings, most eloquently expressed by Charles Thompson in 1731. Italians had 'no notion' of the arrangements of apartments:

Most of these consist of a long Series of Rooms one within another, but when you are got to the End, you must return the same way you came; for they have no Back Stairs, nor have they any Dressing Rooms, Closets, Rooms for Servants or other Accommodations fit for grand Apartments. Their floors are of Brick, Wainscotting they know little of, and their Glazing is intolerable. Their Hangings are almost everywhere the same, consisting of red Damask, with an upper Border of Velvet of the same Colour, adorned with a gold Fringe at Top and Bottom, for Tapestry is rarely met with in Italy. Those Rooms that are not lin'd after this Manner are cover'd with Pictures, which though the most perfect in their Kind, are disgraced by their sorry old fashioned Frames, that make a very mean Appearance. The Furniture is generally antique, having been bought by Popes perhaps a Century ago...[58]

The palaces will be visited in alphabetical order. Those items still in the collections where they were seen in this century will be noted by an asterisk; the present whereabouts of those items which have moved, when known, will be indicated. It is obvious that so many attributions were fanciful, which makes the paintings now particularly hard to trace.

We are introduced to the PALAZZO ALTEMPS by Charles de Brosses, who pays Cardinal Rezzonico (later Clement XIII) a visit 'not for love of him, but for the Sake of some antiquities which he has in the Palace Altemps, *and* especially for the sake of a celebrated Bacchante in bas relief'. Johann Keysler gave a list of the antiquities: statues of Flora, Faustina, Hercules, Æsculapius, Mercury, Bacchus, the celebrated gladiator, reliefs of Bacchus and Ariadne from the palace of Nero, and of a Bacchanalia, and a pillar of porphyry with heads of Drusus and Nero.[59]

The PALAZZO ALTIERI was preferred by de Brosses to any other in Rome. 'It opens out on two streets, and contains very fine rooms full of paintings, and is richly furnished.' Keysler again gave a list of antiquities: on the staircase statues of Hercules, Pomona, and Bacchus, and Brussels tapestries; statues of Venus, a bust of Pescennius Niger. And Tobias Smollett admired the paintings: Maratta's *Saint destroying blasphemers*, Correggio's *Holy Family*, and Titian's *Judgement of Paris*.[60]

Giudo Reni,
The Penitent Magdalen, *1633*
(Barberini Corsini
National Galleries)

Of the PALAZZO BARBERINI, de Blainville reveals that it had a sobriquet: *Mons Martyrum*, because of the many families which the Barberini had ruined! Of its many antiquities the marble Faun was 'as highly esteemed as any in the whole palace'. Caylus most admired a life-size statue in bronze of Septimius Severus. George Berkeley thought the Barberini the noblest palace in Rome; it was divided into two apartments, one for the prince, one for the cardinal. He singled out Reni's *Magdalen* (Corsini Gallery), 'the best piece he ever did' and frescoes from Tivoli, including one of Venus and two cupids. Of the Faun, John Breval declared that there was 'not a part of him but sleeps', and Poussin's *Death of Germanicus* (Minneapolis) was his masterpiece in the antique genre. In one of the most detailed catalogues of the collection, room by room, Keysler comments on only a bust of Alexander ('exceedingly admired'), the life-size bronze of Severus ('highly esteemed'), the 'celebrated' *Judith* by Leonardo (in reality, by Jan Massys), and the Faun ('esteemed one of the greatest curiosities in Rome'), but he also mentioned the library of 60,000 volumes. De Brosses also gave the palm to this palace, but 'it is a pity that the owner, the Prince of Palestrina, is ruined. It is said that he sells as much as he can get rid of out of this palace without its showing.' De Brosses accounted him a good bargainer; for when he wanted to buy a neglected copy of Raphael's *Transfiguration*, which he thought worth 7-800 francs (*c.* 150 *scudi*), Palestrina could not be budged from 7,000 sequins (14,000 *scudi*). Perhaps for that reason, de Brosses paid most attention among the paintings to the *Fornarina*. It was shuttered, and he described it as 'admirable in tone and finish', evidence of Raphael's skill as a colourist; Titian and Reni could not paint anything 'softer or more refined than this head; the silk of the dress is of marvellous quality'. The abbé de Saint-Non in 1760 noted the barbarous state of order and maintenance, with the owners living above and caring nothing for the collection. Smollett also singled out as the two masterpieces Reni's *Magdalen* and Poussin's *Germanicus*. Dr Charles Burney in 1770 again found 'an immense collection of pictures and statues, but all miserably dirty and disordered'. We now understand why de Brosses could not buy cheaply the copy of Raphael: it was by Giulio Romano and great sums had been offered for it 'by most of the princes of Europe'. Burney gave a comprehensive catalogue, and he singled out the *Fornarina*: 'left hand clumsy, but all the rest divine'. The most complete catalogue is given by de Sade, and he commended Reni's *Magdalen*: 'one sees, feels and is silent'. Such catalogues become increasingly valuable, because in 1776 Jean Marie de la Platière lamented, 'how many beautiful things from it have been withdrawn or sold'. James Smith in 1787 judged the ceiling of the great hall by Pietro da Cortona 'the most magnificent fresco in the world' and Caravaggio's *Gamesters* (Fort Worth) 'perhaps the best picture in the house'.[61]

Blainville at the beginning of the century gave a detailed catalogue of the art collection of the PALAZZO BORGHESE: 1700 pictures in, incredible to say, twelve rooms, but with little comment – save on the 'lascivious' ones (such as Titian's *Venus* and da Vinci's *Leda and the Swan*) in the prince's own room. Berkeley singled out *Titian's *Venus binding Cupid's eyes*. Keysler in 1730 gave another detailed catalogue, declaring the palace the best collection of paintings in Rome. Of *Michelangelo's *Crucifixion* he told the old story about the artist using a live model. Asserting that neatness was not an Italian virtue, Thompson found the house and gardens of the Borghese 'kept in better order than those of the other Roman nobility'. The arrangement of the picture gallery on the ground floor was often commented on, opening out onto the garden with its fountains facing the Tiber. De Brosses recommended some discrimination: 'The frames are old and unworthy of their contents, and in so vast a collection there is naturally a good deal of rubbish among much that is good.' Smollett particularly admired 'a Venus with two nymphs, and the other with Cupid, both by Titian; an excellent *Roman Piety*, by Leonardo da Vinci; and the celebrated *Muse* [now rather identified as a Sibyl] by Domenichino, which is a fine, jolly buxom figure' (see ill. overleaf). De Sade also gave a very detailed catalogue, singling out, however, *Pier Francesco

Giuseppe Vasi, Palazzo Borghese, *1754*

Domenichino,
Sibyl, *1616-17*
(Borghese Gallery)

Mola's *St Peter in prison awakened by an angel* ('one cannot sufficiently praise this sublime piece'), two women by Titian ('worthy of his whole reputation'), *Domenichino's *Diana and the hunt* (see ill. opposite) ('divine, full of nature and truth'). He also criticised the disorder and damp, the ostentation rather than taste, and told of the grasping concierge, egged on by the prince, Marc Antonio IV ('un petit personnage tout rond, bien bouffi d'orgueil et de bêtise': 'a little round person, all swollen up with pride and stupidity') with whom he had to share his takings![62]

De Blainville described the PALAZZO DELLA CANCELLERIA, beginning with the wonderful library built by Alexander VIII, including 7000 books formerly belonging to Queen Christina (1900 manuscripts had gone to the Vatican) and which was open to the public. In the gallery he mentioned 'an Ebony Cabinet, inlaid with silver, containing all the Vases, Pots and other Utensils, fit for an Apothecary's Shop, the whole made of silver; a Castle of the same Metal, representing that of

Sant'Angelo, with all the Bulwarks, Bastions and other Fortifications belonging to it..., a statue of the Virgin Mary by Michelangelo, a magnificent Fountain of Verd Antique, and a Silver Figure representing Europa carried off by Jupiter under the shape of a Bull'. A Canopy and chairs had previously been in Christina's audience hall. By 1730 Keysler asserted that Cardinal Pietro Ottoboni was selling the collection piece by piece to pay his debts.[63]

Of the PALAZZO CHIGI, de Blainville recorded only the most remarkable items: statues of Jupiter, Apollo, Vertumnus, Pomona, Silenus, the Vestal with the sieve, Cleopatra, Tullia, Tiberius, Germanicus and Agrippina. The gallery was full of masters. Edward Wright described the palace as 'a world of pictures and very rich furniture of all sorts'. Jonathon Richardson, the famous painter, gave a different list of antiquities: a small Caracalla, a Bacchant and Faun, Diana taking an arrow from her quiver, Leda and the swan, Caligula's head in porphyry, a gladiator, Bacchus, Silenus lying on a wineskin, four fauns, and Apollo and Marsyas. By 1730 Keysler reported the last sold to the king of Poland, but de Brosses in 1739 noted it without comment.[64]

Domenichino, Diana and the hunt, *1616-17 (Borghese Gallery)*

Giuseppe Vasi, Palazzo Colonna, *1754*

The PALAZZO COLONNA was famous for the relief of Homer (see ill. opposite), of which the most detailed description was given by Joseph Addison, noting that it was shown only on request. De Blainville described it as 'the most curious Bas-Relief in all Italy'. The antiquities collection included busts of Annius Verus, Titus, Julia Mammæa, Macrinus, Gordian, Gallienus, and Commodus, a bronze head of Nero, a relief of the deification of Claudius, a 'columna bellica' of red marble (supposedly from the temple of Bellona), a statue of Pyrrhus, and a porphyry head of Medusa. The picture gallery contained 8000 pictures. He singled out a Raphael depicting Jesus, Mary, various saints, God, angels and cherubim; Domenichino's (*Salviati's ?) *Adam and Eve*; and Reni's (*Albani's?) *Rape of Europa*, and *Ecce Homo* (Corsini Gallery). The *Hermitage*, by Lorrain, was described as 'mostly nudities capable of tempting the most rusted anchorite of the ancient Thebais'![65] The present head of the house he declared was 'a very different character'. This was presumably Filippo (1663-1714). Breval described the gallery, with the ceiling fresco of Lepanto, the four columns of *giallo antico*, the floor of finest stone and the walls covered

The Apotheosis of Homer *(in the lower left-hand corner): previously Colonna collection, now British Museum. This Hellenistic relief (c. 150 bc) was one of the most desired of Roman antiquities: the Colonna sold it to Ludovico Mirri during the Jacobin Republic (1798-9) for 700 scudi, and then it was sold on to an English collector for £4,000!*

with paintings by the masters, as 'one of the noblest Rooms in Europe'. Wright agreed: 'of all I saw the finest in all respects'. De Brosses judged the gallery 'preferable on the whole to that of Versailles' because it was 'more august'. He singled out Reni's *St Francis*, Guercino's *Mater Dolorosa* for its brilliant colours, and thought that he would 'go wild' over a little Corregio of girls bathing in a river – which he could have pocketed![66] De Saint-Non remarked on Lorrain's landscapes, and those of Duphet, Titian's *Ganymede*, Veronese's (*Bronzino's ?) *Venus*, Poussin's *Plague* (London), Rosa's *Carthaginians torturing Regulus* (Richmond, Virginia), and a *Bacchanal* by Rubens. Smollett particularly liked Reni's *Herodias*, a *Young Christ*, and a *Madonna* by Raphael, and landscapes by Lorrain and Rosa. Burney agreed that the gallery was 'the largest and most beautiful I had seen and filled with pictures by the very first rate painters', but he was naturally attracted to musical themes: a statue of a faun playing the cymbalum, and Tintoretto's *Old man playing a harpsichord*. De Sade gave a very comprehensive catalogue, according special mention to Correggio's *Magdalen* ('with all that painter's grace'), Espagnolet's *Notaries*, del Sarto's *Holy Family* ('in his most beautiful style') and Guercino's *Pietà* ('above all praise').[67] Isaak Riesch struck a dissenting note about the famed relief of Homer, found, he stated, at Frattochie: it was not fine or careful in style. Friedrich Stolberg, finally, declared in connection with this building that 'the palaces and apartments of our princes and kings are tinsel compared to the grandeur of the principal Romans'. Of the paintings he singled out two Raphaels: *Mother and Child*, and *Jesus blessing John, with Peter and Paul*.[68]

The PALAZZO DORIA, despite its fine gallery, was more rarely visited. Burney's list makes most of *Rosa's *Cain and Abel*, Albani's *Mother and Child*, Titian's *Magdalen*, and a *Nocturnal Concert* by Lanfranco.[69] De Sade's extensive catalogue, listing only the best, comments on Guercino's *Prodigal Son*, and his *Bathsheba*, and Titian's *Sacrifice of Isaac*; he also singled out as a piece of ineptitude *Garofalo's *Jesus and saints*, because the latter lived three or four centuries later![70] At the end of the century, Smith singled out *Velázquez's *Innocent X* ('brilliant'), *Rosa's *Cain and Abel* ('extremely celebrated') and *Reni's *Madonna and sleeping Child* ('far-famed').[71]

Giuseppe Vasi, Palazzo Farnese, *1754*

Amongst the most celebrated palaces remained the FARNESE. Its famous classical collection was to be exported to Naples at the end of this century. De Blainville illustrated age-old tricks: 'nothing is more admired by the Connoisseurs than the Rope which binds the unfortunate Dirce to the Bull's Horns' (see ill. Vol. I, p. 161). With the praises of the Colonna Gallery still in our ears, we now find that 'the best judges are of the opinion that no Gallery in Rome, not even in the whole Universe, can compare to this'. He told the story that Paul III asked Carracci's rival, Giuseppe d'Arpino, how much he should pay for the fresco (see ill. Vol. I, p. 162), and he replied 2,000 *scudi* (not 100,000). Carracci left for Naples, and staying at Piperno paid for his stay by inventing a new inn sign, showing an ass with its driver, in which everyone recognised the pope and d'Arpino. Wright reflected about the palace that 'noble and fine as it is, one cannot see without some Regret, when one considers the Havock which was made in the Amphitheatre for the building of it'. The palace in 1721 he described as 'uninhabited, and in a manner desolate'. For Étienne Silhouette, it was the most beautiful in Rome, but de Brosses judged it to have 'more majesty and solidity than general elegance'; he also mentioned the plundering of the Colosseum, which he would have preferred to have seen restored. As for the sculptures, the Flora was 'the most perfect of ancient statues as regards its drapery'. Of Dirce and the Bull, 'the details are poor enough, as is often the case with the best antique sculptors, where one finds a principal figure of exquisite workmanship, with many inferior accessories'. Smollett also recorded the tricks of the 'connoisseurs': the rope binding Dirce 'is so surprizingly chiselled, that one can hardly believe it is of stone' and the dog, similarly, was much admired. Burney complained that the head, arms and feet of the Flora had been 'but ill restored' by Giacomo della Porta. In the gallery, the statues and busts of 'lower class' were innumerable, but the Caracalla stood out. As for Carracci's fresco, he found it 'full of taste, poetry, learning, fine design, and fine colouring – I was never more pleased'. Anne Miller declared the Hercules (see ill. Vol. I) to be 'disagreeable and odious'. How interesting that John Moore at the same time noted this. 'I am told that women in particular find something unsatisfactory and even odious in this figure.' A woman explained that she hated the 'stern countenance', the 'large brawny limbs' and the club, and that 'it was not in the nature of things that a man so formed could ever have been the reliever of distressed damsels'! Charles Dupaty returned to male sentiments: 'there is not, in fine, in the whole marble, a single stroke of the chisel that does not bear the stamp of genius'. Goethe in 1787 announced the imminent departure of the collection for Naples – 'all the artists are in mourning' – but there was to be a compensation. The statue had been discovered without the lower legs, and Giacomo della Porta had restored them; then the legs were discovered by the Borghese and were now being given to the king of Naples, so that for the first time the whole statue would be authentic.[72]

The PALAZZO GIUSTINIANI at this time still housed one of the most famous collections in Rome. 'No house in Rome contains such a multitude and vast Variety of Statues, Busts and Paintings': de Blainville counted almost nine hundred statues and six hundred pictures. Of the former the most esteemed were the dying Cleopatra, Apollo, Leda (Torlonia), Harpocrates, Ephesian Diana (Torlonia), Venus

Hermaphrodite, Roma Triumphant, Scipio Africanus, the seated Marcellus (Capitoline), C. Cestius (of pyramid fame), heads of Jupiter Ammon, Homer, Alexander, Vitellius, Nero, and the Tiburtine Sibyl – 'but nothing comes up with the statue of Minerva', 'beyond Expression beautiful. All Virtuosos are perfectly in love with this Statue.' Richardson singled out different items in part, adding a relief of the worship of Terminus, Apollo and Marsyas, Silenus and the wine skin, the head of a Faun, a small bronze Hercules, a bronze Mercury, and an Apollo with crossed legs, but he gave the palm to a Meleager. He quoted the cost of the Minerva as 67,000 *scudi*. Keysler in 1730 gave a detailed catalogue, but a mere fraction of the

The Giustiniani Minerva
(Vatican Museums)

nineteen hundred antiquities and seven hundred paintings. He thought the bust of Nero the best in Rome. De Brosses revealed the Giustiniani's secret: their palace was built over Nero's Baths. He paid special attention to Poussin's *Judgement of Solomon*, but a whole room of Raphaels was too much: 'here for one good original there are thirty poor copies'. He noticed, of course, the Diana, as well as Dea Salus, Meleager, Jupiter Imbraticus (*sic*: Imbricitor, the Bringer of Showers), Capronia, Cleopatra, Isis, Apollo and Marsyas (he holds the skin the way 'a waiter holds a napkin') and Michelangelo's *Joseph of Arimathea holding Christ*. 'I met Prince [Vincenzo] Giustiniani at dinner yesterday at the King of England's [James Edward, the "Old Pretender", father of Henry and Charles Edward], and from his appearance and the way he was received I should not have given him credit of possessing either a Principality or a Raphael'.[73] De Saint-Non in 1761 declared

69

that the collection was in the same condition as the Barberini: the gallery was like 'a merchant's storeroom'. He singled out Caravaggio's *Evangelists* (destroyed in Berlin in 1945), Domenichino's *Evangelists* (Glyndebourne), Correggio's (in reality, Cambiaso's) *Charity*, and Poussin's *Massacre of the Innocents* (Chantilly). De Sade gave one of the most extensive catalogues, commenting especially on the Venus naked to the thighs and a superb Bacchus, and Domenichino's *Evangelists*, Caravaggio's *Crowning with Thorns*, and *Deposition* (Vatican), and especially Gérard des Nuits' *Jesus before Pilate*.[74] Goethe preserves an amusing tale about the Minerva. The custodian's wife told him that the English worshipped it, being of the same religion (!) and came to kiss its hand (one was white). By the end of the century, complaints, however, were multiplying: 'one of the dirtiest, darkest houses in Rome', declared Smith. Honthorst's *Christ before Pilate* was thought the best painting, but Smith preferred Poussin's *Massacre of the Innocents*. The antiquities were 'kept in very dirty condition, under pretence that washing might damage them': the Minerva, Faun, Marcellus, the little naked boys asleep in a dish, Jupiter nursed by a goat, and Jupiter drinking out of a horn.[75] It was, in fact, at the beginning of this century (1710s) that the dispersal of the collection began, notably purchases of busts by both Cardinal Alessandro Albani and Lord Pembroke, and the prince of Anhalt-Dessau bought the Faun in 1766.

A much smaller and more miscellaneous collection was in the PALAZZO GUALTIERI, which seems to have been formed by Cardinal Filippo Gualtieri (1660-1728). Wright in 1721 listed eighteen rooms of 'curious things', and Keysler noted a beautiful marble Vesta, Caravaggio's *Scourging*, Pietro da Cortona's *David*, Dürer's *Mary and Christ*, and Reni's *Rape of Europa*, as well as a fine collection of eastern porcelain.[76]

Of the PALAZZO MASSIMO (see ill. opposite) Breval noted the statue of Pyrrhus in the great court, while Wright drew attention also to the mosaics of gladiators, a relief showing a sacrifice, paintings from the tomb of the Nasones (Ovid's family), and the funerary inscription of C. Seius Calpurnius (CIL 14.2831) found on the via Latina by Francesco Ficorini, the famous *cicerone*. Keysler, finally, alerted the visitor to the fact that the Pyrrhus was the only one in Rome, and singled

Giuseppe Vasi, Palazzo Massimo, *1754*

out statues of Æsculapius, Apollo, the gladiator, Bacchus, and busts of Claudius, Commodus, Gordian, Antoninus Pius and Macrinus. The Pyrrhus was bought by Clement XII for 8,000 *scudi.*[77]

The PALAZZO MATTEI contained both antiquities and paintings. Keysler singled out a Jupiter, Flora, a relief of a sacrifice in front of the Pantheon, and a marble chair, and of paintings *Domenichino's *Rachel,* Caravaggio's *Christ on the Mount of Olives* (Berlin, destroyed) and Reni's *St Peter.*[78]

We rely on de Blainville for a detailed description of the PALAZZO ODESCALCHI at Santi Apostoli (see ill. p. 73) at the beginning of the century. After a portico containing statues of Jupiter, Apollo, Ceres, Claudius and Maximian, there followed five rooms, where he specially mentioned in the first room a reclining Cleopatra, Cæsar with his head covered, Augustus, a Faun, and Adonis; in the second room Apollo and the Muses, busts of the twelve Cæsars, and twelve columns of *giallo antico*; in the third room 'Clytie' on a sunflower (in reality, Antonia, British Museum; see ill. overleaf); in the fourth room Castor and Pollux and Leda in one piece, a Venus rivalling that of the

Medici collection, busts of Alexander, Pyrrhus and Antinoüs, and two alabaster columns; in the fifth room Cæsar and Augustus in alabaster with gilt bronze feet (Don Livio was having the other ten emperors done in the same style!), Ptolemy, Seneca, Venus leaving her bath, a faun carrying a lamb on his shoulder, and Bernini's portrait of Queen Christina. To the paintings he paid little attention, but in the queen of Poland's apartment were thirty-six tapestries of the deeds of Antony, Cleopatra and Augustus (they had belonged to the duke of Mantua, were carried to Prague, and then to Stockholm, before Christina brought them to Rome). Breval noted that Queen Christina's paintings had now been sold to the duke of Orleans for 90,000 *scudi*, but Berkeley particularly admired Raphael's small *Virgin, Christ and John with two putti*. De Brosses in 1740 could only lament that the former 'superb gallery of paintings by Raphael, Titian, Veronese, all in perfect

'Clytie', *now identified as* Antonia

Giuseppe Vasi, Palazzo Odescalchi, *1754*

condition, cartoons by Giulio Romano, and some Correggios *del primo grido*' were now all in Paris.[79]

The same French visitor, de Brosses, gives us an amusing description of the PALAZZO QUIRINALE (see ill. overleaf). Benedict XIV

has always inhabited this place since the commencement of his reign, and the Vatican has been deserted. It is certainly better, as regards situation and comfort, than the latter; the mass of buildings serve to house his dependants, and, although not so large as the Vatican, it is very spacious. The courtyard is vast, surrounded by porticos: the staircase handsome. The building has little ornament about it, and the interior is plain, the rooms being simply furnished with not over new damask furniture. Although the rooms contain many paintings, they appear but few on account of the size and number of the apartments; besides, those worth looking at are rare. A visit to the Holy Father, who, in bed, will receive you with the greatest courtesy, is really the main object of going over this palace. The gardens are large and handsome, but I prefer those of the Belvedere.

Giuseppe Vasi, Palazzo Quirinale, *1754. The main palace is in the centre, the 'Coffee House', by Fuga, sits at the extreme right, and stretching off the extreme left is the Manica Lunga. The Pope, taking the air, is shielded from the sun by a servant with a parasol*

There are numerous fountains, and a summer-house containing a Mount Parnassus, where Apollo and the Muses give, if you wish to hear them, a concert by the aid of water pipes. Before the palace the level of the ground slopes very abruptly, which, combined with a large tower, guarded by the Swiss Guard, gives quite a fortified look to the place. These soldiers are well equipped and have a martial air, but they would find it difficult to tell you what fire they had seen except that on the Feast of St John. The sun and rain are their enemies, and before these they take flight. When either appears they leave their posts, and take refuge under a covered *corps de garde.* Their duties consist of mounting guard at the door of the Opera. The officers have excellent pay, and they are better off than canons; nor are they, like those, obliged to read the breviary.

On All Soul's day, the palace was open to the public, and Goethe took the chance to admire Guercino's *St Petronilla* (see ill. p. 29:

Capitoline), formerly in St Peter's and then (1786) replaced by a mosaic copy, and Titian's *Bishop in rapture* (Vatican). 'There must be some ancient tradition which made it possible to combine all these various and seemingly incongruous figures into a significant whole. We do not ask how or why: we take it as it is and marvel at its inestimable art.' Smith at the same time described some 'very capital paintings': the Guercino, of course, Andrea Sacchi's *Gregory the Great*, Jean Valentin's *Martyrdom of Sts Processus and Martinianus*, Poussin's *Death of St Erasmus* (Vatican), Carlo Maratta's *Virgin and Child*, Reni's *Virgin with sleeping Christ* (Galleria Doria Pamphili), and *Virgin sewing, watched by angels* (now lost) ('with all the grimaces of boarding school misses flattering and fawning upon their governess')![80]

Goethe visited the PALAZZO RONDANINI in the Corso, where he particularly admired the Medusa, and even had a cast made of it. Stolberg agreed: 'one of the most excellent works of ancient art', and also mentioned a sarcophagus with husband and wife portrayed on the lid, a head of Brutus, and a colossal Hygeia.[81]

The PALAZZO ROSPIGLIOSI in via Ventiquattro Maggio was built over

Giuseppe Vasi, Palazzo Rospigliosi, *1754*

Guido Reni, Aurora before Apollo's chariot, *in the Casino, 1614 (Pallavicini-Rospigliosi Palace)*

the ruins of the Baths of Constantine on the Quirinal. It had been founded by Scipione Borghese, passed through many hands, including Cardinal Mazarin, and finally in the early eighteenth century to the Rospigliosi and Pallavicini. De Blainville noted that it contained six of the largest paintings in Rome: Albani's *Armeda and Rinaldo*, and his *Diana in her bath*, Domenichino's *Adam and Eve*, Reni's *Andromeda*, and Poussin's *Samson crushing the Philistines*, and his *David with Goliath's head.* Keysler drew attention to Reni's masterpiece, the *Aurora* in the casino, as well as some antiquities: statues of Minerva, a Faun, Hercules and a bust of Nero, and a relief by Michelangelo. De Brosses here noted only the *Aurora*, but admitted that he was not sure whether he admired it as much as Guercino's *Aurora* at the villa Ludovisi.[82]

In the PALAZZO SACCHETTI Keysler noted two paintings by da Cortona: the *Rape of the Sabines*, and *the Battle of Arbela*, while in the PALAZZO SAVELLI-ORSINI all the famous paintings had by now (1730) gone.[83]

The PALAZZO SPADA was known for statues of Flora and Seneca, according to Keysler, and Guercino's *Death of Adonis*, Reni's *Rape of Helen*, and his *Cardinal Spada, Tedescho's *Death of Lucretia*, and del Sarto's *Mary and Elizabeth*.[84] Here were strange gaps. Anne Miller mentioned, of course, the most famous statue of all, the Pompey, and a Venus, a gladiator, a Greek philosopher, and Ceres. And as well as Reni's *Helen*, there was Caravaggio's *Flight into Egypt* (Galleria Doria

Pamphili). Not to be overlooked was the renowned *trompe l'œil*. Breval told the famous story of the contest over the ownership of the Pompey between a blacksmith and a cobbler ('I have been reliably informed'!) when the statue was found straddling the two properties – hence the break in the neck.[85] In 1812 Carlo Fea was to prove that the head did not belong to the body at all – but the credulous can still be found despite his immaculate logic.

The PALAZZO STROZZI had a miscellaneous collection, which was visited by Montesquieu: many cameos, including a Medusa and an Augustus, a book of all sorts of marble, and a coin collection, as well as shells and butterflies. Another visitor, de Brosses, was also enthusiastic about the cameos: the 'celebrated' ones of Livia and Septimius Severus, and the Medusa, made of agate onyx, 'considered the finest cameo in existence'. The marble book caught his eye also: 'a small book, in which, painted on vellum, are all the ancient and modern marbles, done with marvellous skill, so that each sheet looks like a solid piece of marble'. De Brosses rather scandalously regretted not having asked for it, because he did not think it appreciated, and thought it would probably have been given to him![86]

By way of introduction to the VATICAN PALACE, it is noteworthy that several visitors had very negative reactions. Karl Pöllnitz thought the palace detracted seriously from St Peter's, and Samuel Sharp in 1765, recording talk about the demolition of the streets leading to the basilica, thought rather that the Vatican with its 11,000 chambers should also be removed: it was an 'ugly excrescence'. The original core of the museum was the BELVEDERE. In some matters of taste things never changed: Berkeley declared that the Apollo (see ill. p. 79) and Laocoön (see ill. overleaf) 'can never be enough admired'. Montesquieu added the Antinoüs (see ill. p. 80) and stated that these three along with the Farnese Hercules were the most beautiful (or fine) in Rome. Breval had noted that preference for the Apollo or the Antinoüs was much argued over, but whereas the latter was only 'a most lovely and delicate Youth', the former 'will always be known for the god... by the lightness of his whole Attitude'. Silhouette singled out the Laocoön for its combination of strength and gentleness ('force et douceur') and noted that even the toes of the figures were contracted with pain.

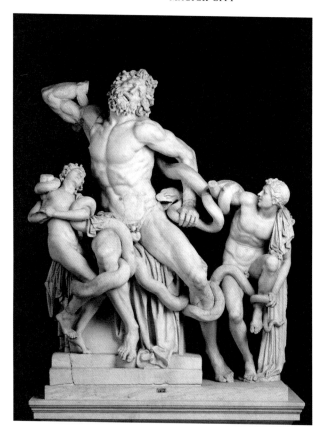

The Laocoön
*(Vatican
Museums)*

De Brosses described the court: dark and small, surrounded by arcades which were closed with large wooden doors painted red (these were to protect the sculptures). 'The Laocoön is the monarch and head of all the world of sculpture,' he stated. De Saint-Non judged the Apollo 'the first of all ancient statues', followed by the Laocoön. Benjamin West was more American than artist: when the doors of the Apollo were thrown open he could only exclaim: 'My God, how like it is to a young Mohawk warrior' – because of their skill with the bow! The abbé Gabriel Coyer, usually devoted to comparisons of things Italian with things French, to the latter's advantage, asked how one could look at the Laocoön without having one's entrails rent ('les entrailles déchirées'). James Boswell visited the court twice, once after praying to 'keep the clouds of Presbyterian Sundays from rendering the mind gloomy', when he found '"Meleager" [the alternative then current for Antinoüs] well enough. Laocoön supreme; equal to all ideas. Nerves contracted by it, so that beautiful Apollo could not be felt', and again after attending a burial in the Protestant cemetery: 'Apollo, baddish

The Apollo
Belvedere
(Vatican
Museums)

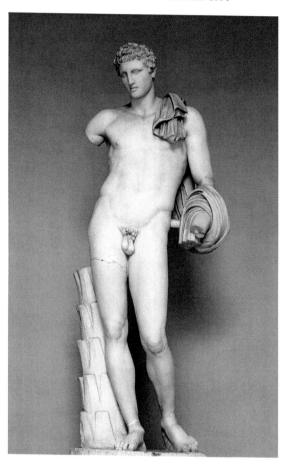

The Belvedere
Antinoüs
(Vatican Museums)

knees; Laocoön's sons too much formed: men in miniature.' Smollett took the Apollo to be 'the most beautiful statue that ever was formed', while he agreed with Pliny that the Laocoön was 'the most excellent piece that ever was cut in marble'. Poor Moore went with a callous companion who, on seeing the Laocoön, exclaimed: 'Egad, I was afraid those d—d serpents would have left the fellow they are devouring, and made a snap at me!' He records his own reaction to the Apollo: 'endowed with the finest expression of grace, dignity, and understanding than ever were seen in living features'. And the

Antinoüs was 'an exquisite representation of the most beautiful youth that ever lived'. Riesch examined the Antinoüs with a torch to see the musculature, and declared the legs not equal to the torso, and that in fact it was a Meleager. He was struck by the Apollo's 'majestic calm' and the beautiful hair, and noted that the left leg was larger than the right in order not to appear too short. Dupaty came continually to see the Apollo: 'marble made a god by one of those creative chisels, which, by selecting, combining or imitating Nature, have surpassed Nature'. Goethe's preference, however, was for the Torso, which he thought met Mengs' demands for the combination of high style and realism: 'I am inclined to believe that this fragment is the most

*Belvedere Torso
(Vatican
Museums)*

beautiful work I have ever seen.' And at the end of the century, Friedrich Stolberg fantasised that the sculptor himself destroyed the rest of the figure in order to enhance the torso.[87]

By 1771 a new museum had been formed, what was to become the PIO CLEMENTINO. Riesch was enthusiastic over the draped Juno, Livia with her head leaning on her right hand, the seated consul, Narcissus, busts of Niger, Septimius Severus and Verus, Antinoüs, the Diskoboulos, the reclining Cleopatra (but she was rather a nymph, because he noted that there was no snake), and the gallery of the animals (all masterpieces). Friedrich Meyer complained of the ubiquitous boastful inscription 'ex munificentia Pii VI'. August Moszyński found it only a pale reflection of the Belvedere; Goethe, on the other hand, thought this museum more remarkable, on the whole, than the Capitoline. The highest praise was conferred by Johann Archenholz, who declared that 'the greatest ornament of the Vatican is the Clementine Museum, which surpasses all other collections of its kind in the world'; perhaps the key is in 'of its kind'.[88]

Marianne Starke, finally, had some advice for would-be visitors:

> many parts of this immense building are extremely damp and cold; the museum is especially so; and Persons who go there previous to seeing other parts of the palace should send a servant and get the door opened before they quit their carriage; otherwise they may be standing a considerable time in an eddy of cold damp air.[89]

Joshua Reynolds did, in fact, catch cold there and was rendered permanently deaf.

After the museum came the frescoes. Michelangelo's LAST JUDGEMENT called forth very differing responses. Montesquieu was concise: 'nothing gives a better idea of Michelangelo's genius'. De Brosses declared the *Judgement* 'one of the greatest frescoes in the world', 'a veritable anatomical fury' with a 'tone of colour without harmonious tones'; in sum, 'it astonishes one more than it gives pleasure, so full is it of terror and confusion'. We have no clear statement by Joshua Reynolds at his first sight, but to a student in Rome in 1769 he averred:

'The Capella Sistina is the production of the greatest genius that ever was employed in the arts.' Others found great fault, often when comparing it with the ceiling. Breval stated:

> A Man must be perfectly insensible to outward Objects, that can behold this vast Composition, and not be touch'd with a secret Dread and Horrour, as if he fancy'd he heard the Sound of the Last Trump.

At the same time he found some 'improprieties': 'every Man is a Hercules and every Woman an Amazon'. Wright also found the female musculature excessive. The German lawyer Johann Volkmann objected to the composition (the groups were not linked), and that the figures were 'too natural' (Michelangelo was primarily interested in anatomy). He did deign to look up, and criticised the drapery of the Sibyls, but nothing was more noble than God the Father. Abbé Jean-Baptiste Richard thought that the ceiling was superior to the *Judgement* 'for beauty of expression and regularity of design'. He also claimed to have seen (in 1762) 'very mediocre artists' covering naked figures with clothes, but this was primarily the work of Daniele da Volterra *c.* 1560. Smollett also objected to the disunity of the composition. De la Platière was besotted with Raphael, and so his heart rebelled at the 'Etruscan nature' of the *Judgement*; God the Father on the ceiling, however, was 'divine majesty in action'. Moszyński's reactions were contradictory: the colours and composition were horrible, the figures too alike and too massive; on the other hand, the chaos was right, and it was a masterpiece because every figure was an academic study; in short, no picture was more courageous! Goethe was lucky enough to be able to go up into the gallery to see the ceiling more closely. Michelangelo had made him lose all taste for nature, because he lacked his eye of genius. 'Until you have seen the Sistine Chapel, you can have no adequate conception of what man is capable of accomplishing.' Goethe later recorded that it was at this time that artists 'rediscovered' Michelangelo, especially for his sense of colour, and Count Joseph Fries commissioned Fritz Bury and Johann Lips to make watercolour copies of the Sistine frescoes. 'The custodian was handsomely tipped and let us enter by the back door next to the altar and settle down there whenever we liked. We even used to have meals there, and I remember that one day I was overcome by the heat and snatched a noon nap on the papal throne.' The English botanist Smith declared, on the other hand, that the *Judgement* was a 'dark uncouth picture. The Saviour has great wrath, but little dignity, and the anatomy and attitudes are caricatured.' Stolberg, finally, liked best the *Creation* in the ceiling. Such personifications 'would have been insufferable from any other hand than that of Michelangelo'.[90]

We turn naturally to the RAPHAEL STANZE. Montesquieu was most praising of the naturalness of Raphael's lighting. It was to be expected, therefore, that he should focus on the *Deliverance of St Peter*, where there are four sources of light (two angels, the moon and a torch). De Brosses lamented the damp and the damage done by the German soldiers in 1527, especially to the *School of Athens*, which was nevertheless 'remarkable for the science, the invention, the splendid grouping and perspective with which it abounds'. His favourite, however, was *Heliodorus driven out of the temple*, despite the anachronism of Julius II: 'Raphael never equalled this horse and his rider dashing on Heliodorus, or excelled the vigour of these flying, wingless angels, who speed across the scene without touching the ground.' It is unfortunate that we do not have clearer judgements by Joshua Reynolds on Roman art; there is only his admission that on first viewing Raphael's paintings in the Vatican he did not appreciate their greatness, and the fact that he made a caricature of the School of Athens to include contemporary artists. De Saint-Non especially liked the *Fire in the Borgo*, while his countryman the abbé Richard gave the palm to *The deliverance of St Peter*: 'the art of painting carried to the highest level', the 'most beautiful composition, the most daring and the most skilful that any painter has ever imagined'. Smollett mentioned only the *School of Athens*, and used it to support the art critic Daniel Webb's view that Raphael was a master at expressing sentiment, but could not 'strike off the grand passions'. Burney knew that the *Battle of the Milvian Bridge* was painted by Giulio Romano from Raphael's designs, and judged it 'perhaps the greatest of all', but then, despite its damaged state, declared that in the *School of Athens* 'there is so much learning, clearness and propriety and the subject moreover so agreeable that in giving way to my own feelings I don't hesitate in pronouncing it the greatest or at least the most agreeable work of this divine master'. Wright was rhapsodic:

> Every face is a page of history; every attitude and gesture so true and so intelligent; every part of the composition so well judged and ingeniously contrived, that it is no wonder these pictures have obtained the rank they hold in the estimation of conoisseurs.

The most remarkable in his view for composition and effect was the *Fire in the Borgo*, for ingenuity of composition the *School of Athens*, and for lighting the *Deliverance of Peter*.[91]

Johannes Tischbein on his first visit in 1780-81 gives a disconcerting impression of the Stanze, which he himself haunted for months as a copyist. He found it 'entertaining' to work there, where 'there were so many different artists at the same time copying in so many different ways'. Some were copying whole frescoes on a grand scale, others in miniature, some were copying only certain figures, others groups, some merely heads; many were making only light sketches. Such copying was, however, having disastrous effects. The Polish visitor, Moszyński in 1785 provides appalling evidence for more recent damage to the frescoes. He mentions scaffolding erected by copyists working for the English and the use of waxed paper, attached to the wall with wax and pins, and which pulled away the paint when it was removed. Elisabeth Vigée le Brun lamented that young artists were allowed to trace over the heads in chalk.

Alongside the Stanze were the LOGGIE, although much less frequently the subject of comment. Montesquieu gave these much more attention than the Stanze: 'divine' for drawing and colour. De Brosses declared that these paintings could not be studied too much, but those by Raphael were the best: especially the *Creation, Adam and Eve* (see ill. Vol. III), and *Jacob's ladder*. Richard, similarly, thought *Eve in the Garden* the highlight: 'she is of the greatest beauty, of an eloquence and a purity of design so perfect that one would believe she was the work of Raphael' (it is probably by Giulio Romano). Goethe, finally, records a remarkable project. Using Johannes Reiffenstein's promotion of encaustic painting, a copy was made of the whole loggia for Catherine of Russia: 'exact copies of the panels, walls, socles, pilasters, capitals and cornices were manufactured from very thick boards and solid blocks of wood; everything was then covered with canvas and painted so as to provide a firm foundation for the encaustics. Under Reiffenstein's direction a number of artists, (Christoph) Unterberger in particular, were busy on it for several years.'[92]

After the art galleries in the Vatican, a visit to the LIBRARY was mandatory. The same books were being shown to visitors, Berkeley reveals, as in the previous century: manuscripts of Virgil, Terence, a Septuagint, Henry's love letters to Anne Bolyn, and his book against Luther. Thompson asserted that 'the library engages our attention beyond all the other beauties of the Vatican', being the richest in the world in manuscripts and printed books. De Brosses was not the usual cut of visitor. The library, he observed, is not open to the public, being the pope's private library, 'but if one is at all known one is civilly received, and one is allowed to work several days of the week in a large ante-salon, where the librarians have the MSS which you wish to consult brought to you'. Cardinal (Angelo) Quirini was the librarian, assisted by (Giuseppe) Assemani. In the centre of the manuscript library was a column of transparent alabaster, from the Gardens of Sallust. De Brosses also most presciently noted a gallery nearby, which he thought would make an excellent museum for antiquities: it was to become the Museo Pio-Clementino. Smollett seems to have been disappointed: the library did not contain more than 40,000 volumes, and they were all locked away in presses. What could be done by a serious scholar is shown by Burney: he had obtained a letter of permission from an archbishop, and was helped by Abate Elie, and they spent four hours alone, it being holidays, looking for some of the oldest music books, especially Provençal songs. Jacob Björnstahl mentioned the great fire in the library on 30 August, 1768, which destroyed many manuscripts and the first three volumes of the catalogue. He also claimed that the cupboards of books were opened on payment for an indulgence (in the usual Roman way), and that many volumes had been lost, and some of them had been seen in Albani's collection.

Johann Herder was also most distressed: he could not get 'free use of the catalogue or free view of the shelves': hours and days slipped by.[93]

Few mentioned the PALAZZO VENEZIA. Perhaps de Brosses explains why. 'We will not enter the Palace of St Mark, for it is an ugly old lodging, and quite unworthy of housing a Procurator-General of the King; although a king himself has lived there, for this was the lodging of Charles VIII, on the occasion of his triumphal entry' (1495).[94]

The PALAZZO VEROSPI on the Corso (no. 374) had a collection of antiquities described by de Blainville: statues of Hercules, Apollo, Ceres, Hadrian, Antoninus Pius, Marcus Aurelius, Jupiter Ammon, Alexander, Cleopatra, Trajan, Gordian, and busts of Cæsar, Augustus and the two Agrippinas.[95]

In the same main thoroughfare (no. 300) was the PALAZZO VITEL-LESCHI – which was by chance to pass to the Verospi in 1744 – where de Blainville listed a Jupiter, two Apollos, Minerva, Diana, Ceres, Terminus in black marble, a sleeping Cupid, Silenus, Germanicus, Diogenes, Pertinax, busts of Plotina, Marciana, Matidia, Scipio Africanus, Augustus, Livia, a colossal Antonia, a porphyry Vespasian, a sarcophagus of the same, two Egyptian idols, tables, coins and columns.[96] The manner of listing leaves us with a final indelible impression of both the unscientific presentation of such eighteenth century collections and the fanciful identifications of so many of the portraits.

We may conclude our visit to the art collections of the palaces with the words of Joshua Reynolds, which bring his contemporary travellers before our very eyes:

> The manner of the English travellers in general, and of those who most pique themselves on studying Vertu, is, that instead of examining the beauties of those works of fame, and why they are esteemed, they only enquire the subject of the picture and the name of the painter, the history of a statue, and where it was found, and write that down. Some Englishmen, while I was in the Vatican, came there, and spent above six hours in writing down whatever the antiquary dictated to them; they scarcely ever looked at the paintings the whole time.[97]

VILLAS

There were six or seven villas which were the focus of visitors' attention in the eighteenth century: the Albani, Aldobrandini, Borghese, Ludovisi, Mattei, Medici and Pamphili.

The VILLA ALBANI (see ill. opposite) was initiated in 1747 outside the porta Salaria by Cardinal Alessandro Albani (1692-1779), nephew of Clement XI, assisted by his secretary and librarian Johannes Winckelmann (1717-1768), the son of humble parents, who became the most famous art historian of his age. He was Commissario di Antichita' from 1763 until his murder in Trieste, and was the author of the monumental *Geschichte der Kunst des Altherthums* (1764). Dr Charles Burney in 1770 found it 'new and fitted up with infinite taste', the house 'cleaner than any one I have seen in Italy'. He was overwhelmed with the riches: 'The statues which struck me most in the villa are the Antinoüs (see ill. Vol. III) in alabaster – Lucothea and Child and Minerva in the gallery – Jupiter Sarapis – Etruscan bassi rilievi, vases, etc. etc.' Anne Miller declared it 'the most esteemed', with the garden 'laid out in the old taste of parterres, terraces, and formal walks'. Jean-Marie de la Platière was more sceptical: 'no where else has one so restored and baptised statues and busts'! In the late 1770s, Johann Archenholz, although he found the gardens indifferent, described the villa as second only to the Borghese:

> Its situation, the judicious position of the statues, busts, urns, tombs, altars, ruins, grottoes, fountains, and the numberless bas-reliefs, the Egyptian obelisk, which stands in the middle of the garden, and the building of royal magnificence make this villa a real fairy seat.

It is, therefore, remarkable that Goethe visited the villa most cursorily, at the very end of his stay. Isaak Riesch gave one of the more extensive catalogues: busts of emperors, a bust and a head of a faun, the relief of Antinoüs, Minerva (perhaps the best in Rome), Apollo Sauroctonos, a very rare bust of Gallienus, a young comedian, Anubis, Isis in alabaster, a sleeping hermaphrodite, Bacchus, Æsculapius, a

Antonio Capellani-Francesco Piranesi, The hemicycle of the Villa Albani, *1780*

Bacchant, an athlete holding a flask of oil, a sleeping cupid, Caligula as pontifex maximus, Domitian, Thetis draped perfectly to show her thighs (from Lanuvium), a dancing satyr, a colossal head of Livia, a bust of Antinoüs, the head of a satyr, a head of Jupiter, a basalt Serapis, Berenice, Apollo, a sarcophagus with marriage of Peleus and Thetis, a drinking satyr, Achilles as a woman with the daughters of Lykomides, a water basin held by four caryatids, and an Egyptian pyramid.[98] These collections had been housed first at the palazzo Albani at Quattro Fontane, and had been sold to Saxony in 1728 and to Clement XII in 1733 for the Capitoline; this second collection in the villa was bought mostly by the French and Ludwig of Bavaria in 1815.

The VILLA ALDOBRANDINI on the Quirinal had been established by Cardinal Vitellozzo Vitelli in the 1560s, but by *c.* 1600 had passed to the Aldobrandini (Clement VIII, 1592-1605). George Berkeley in 1717 saw 'a vast number of ancient statues, the greatest part of which had nothing extraordinary, many of them but indifferent', but there was a relief on the outside which he thought showed the combat between

The Aldobrandini Wedding *(now Vatican Library)*

Dares and Entellus. The 'greatest curiosity of the house' was, of course, the painting of the *Wedding*, from the Baths of Titus. Jonathon Richardson was rude enough to dismiss it as conveying 'a sort of worminess disagreeable enough'. Montesquieu gave qualified admiration: 'the drawing is good, the attitudes fine – but we paint better'! By the time of de Brosses' visit in 1740, the villa had passed to the Pamphili. He found the painting above a door in an uninhabited room, and the villa 'very shabby'. He mentioned a few antiquities, notably a Faun, and some paintings: Leonardo's *Queen Joanna* (now Luini, *Portrait of a Lady*, Washington), Raphael's *Two lawyers* (Galleria Doria Pamphili), Titian's *Bacchante* (i.e. Bacchanal, London), and Carracci's *Psyche*. Anne Miller was wicked about the *Wedding*: 'The bridegroom seems not very far from his grand climacterick, the bride is too young, and looks sorrowful.' By de Sade's time, the villa had passed to the Borghese, who had left little, but he was still able to list 'a few fairly good' pieces (a Satyr pursuing a Hermaphrodite, Leda and the swan, busts of Cæsar, Bacchus, Seneca, an old Vestal, Vespasian, Trajan, a gladiator, an alabaster relief of Nero, and statues of two children looking down; a *Beheading of St John*, Baroccio's *Flight into Egypt*, Carracci's *Concert*, Vaga's *Holy Family*, Titian's *Bacchanal*, and a *Virgin* by Raphael). Now the *Wedding* was in a garden pavilion, and was claimed as having been found near S Maria Maggiore. He judged it quite lacking in perspective and expression: its only merit was its age! In the 1770s Henry, tenth earl of Pembroke, visited the villa with the painter Henry

Tresham. Some of the attributions had changed: the *Concert* was now by Caravaggio; there was also a *Feast of the Gods* by Belleri (Bellini ?), and a Leonardo, *Smiling Woman*. Reliefs in the front included two boxers. Of the *Wedding* they liked the colouring, but found the perspective bad. In 1792 Friedrich Stolberg singled out Leonardo's *Christ among the Pharisees* (now attributed to Luini, in Washington): 'no painter, I will not except Raphael himself, has presented us with a more noble and beautiful figure of Christ than this'.[99]

Perhaps the most famous villa in the eighteenth century was the BORGHESE. De Blainville described it whimsically as 'not above a musket shot from the town'. 'Having thoroughly viewed all the Country Seats in and about Rome, I cannot but acknowledge that this outdoes all others in almost every Respect.' Of all the antiquities he noted the Gladiator (see ill. overleaf) as 'reckoned the most perfect in Rome, and therefore called, by way of Eminence, the Statue without Defects'; it had been found in the harbour at Antium. Otherwise de Blainville described the trick chair which imprisoned careless sitters, and which rumour claimed had been devised by 'one of the

Alessandro Specchi, Villa Borghese, *1699*

PRIMO PROSPETTO DEL PALAZZO DELL'ECC™ SIG™ PRENCIPE BORGHESE FVORI DI PORTA PINCIANA
Architettura di Giovanni van Sanzio Fiammengo.

The Borghese
Gladiator

Borghese family who was fonder of the He's than the She's! – a version
de Blainville himself did not believe. The comte de Caylus paid attention to the the Silenus, the Gladiator, the Centaur, a porphyry Juno,
and the Seneca in black marble (see ill. opposite), and he revealed that
the French royal collections contained copies of Bernini's *Apollo and
Daphne* and *David* (see ills pp. 95 and 94). The villa had 'the
richest outside' that Berkeley had ever seen anywhere. Of antiquities

he noticed the Hermaphrodite, the Gladiator, and the relief of Curtius. And Bernini's statues raised his estimate of the modern art 'almost to an equality with the famous ancients' for their 'graces, softness and expression'. John Breval liked the begging Belisarius, the dying Seneca, Somnus, the sleeping Hermaphrodite, and the Gladiator (for the sculptor's consummate knowledge of the laws of gravitation), but considered the reliefs on the outside of the villa a mistake: 'an ill-judged Extravagance', and they were not visible, but were exposed to the weather (comments unusual but accurate). John Dyer bought

The so-called Dying Seneca, *an old man standing in a footbath*

Bernini, David, *1623-4*
(Borghese Gallery)

a cast of the dancing nymphs from the villa, but could not afford to take it home. Montesquieu here was unusually critical, especially of Bernini: David's muscles were too heavy, his physiognomy even evil, while Daphne's limbs were too thin, too perfectly round – but it was a masterpiece for the hair and laurel. De Brosses described the villa as 'simply overrun[ning] with antique statues'. The Gladiator was considered by the learned as the most perfect statue in Rome, but de Brosses preferred the Laocoön. Bernini's *Apollo and Daphne* he judged 'amongst the finest creations of modern sculpture'. Among the antiquities, Smollett particularly liked the relief of Curtius, a Bacchus, the Meleager sarcophagus, Silenus and Bacchus, the Gladiator, a Moor in black marble and white alabaster, a bull in black marble, a 'gipsey' with extremities in brass, Bernini's *David* and *Apollo and Daphne*, two statues of Venus, a weeping slave, and the youth extracting a thorn.

Bernini, Apollo and Daphne, *1622-5 (Borghese Gallery)*

Anne Miller incredibly singled out the Seneca and the Hermaphrodite as masterpieces. By the time of the earl of Pembroke's visit in 1779 it was necessary to have permission signed by the prince to be admitted to the collection. He found the interior much like the English Coffee House in the piazza di Spagna, and therefore unsuited to such a fine collection, and the pieces arranged without taste. 'The Prince says he has none, but he might at least apply to someone that had...' Full marks go to Pembroke for realising that the 'dying Seneca' was no such person: he suggested an attendant at the baths. The Gladiator was the finest statue, but its position was unnatural: 'if you try to putt yourself in the same, you will most likely have the satisfaction of measuring your length on the Floor'. This and the bust of Verus and the Hermaphrodite, in his view, constituted the cream of the collection. Isaak Riesch described the Gladiator as 'unique for the truth of the design, the expression, and the grandeur of style', while Bernini's *Apollo and Daphne* was most beautiful for its lightness, elegance, and flowing contours, and the beauty of the foliage. Meyer in 1783 had noted that Prince Marc Antonio was employing Germans to redecorate the villa. Mary Berry identified some of the artists then employed: Gavin Hamilton, Jacob More and Philip Hackert; the gladiator's room cost 36,000 *scudi*, the gallery 52,000.

Then there were the gardens: Blainville described one with flowers, orange trees and an aviary, another which was a large square with statuary and a fountain in the middle, and a third an enclosure with stags, deer, and roebuck, a bird thicket, the Casino della Principessa, and a pond with fish, swans, geese and ducks, and a menagery. Berkeley admitted that the gardens, 'if they are not so spruce and trim as those in France and England, are nobler and, I think, much more agreeable'. Tobias Smollett gave a detailed description, concluding that it was in his opinion, 'a very contemptible garden, when compared to that of Stowe in Buckinghamshire, or even to those of Kensington and Richmond. The Italians understand, because they study, the excellencies of art; but they have no idea of the beauties of nature.' The earl of Pembroke also found the gardens wanting: 'the principal beauty in our Gardens, Parks etc, is here much wanted, verdure, of which I did not see a suspicion'. Friedrich Meyer declared the

Borghese his favourite villa, because of the rise and fall of the ground levels, the trees which were allowed to grow with strength and pride, and the emotion of walking here alone, 'devoted to delightful dreams on the edge of the lake' at the start or end of the day. Prince Marco Antonio extended unlimited freedom to strangers in his park. A notice proclaimed: 'Walk where you wish, pick what you want, leave when you like' as long as you do not violate the 'laws of urbanity'. Stolberg, finally, described the park in some detail:

> There are very pleasant walks in this garden, which lead partly among laurel and evergreen prickly oaks, and partly among oak trees… There is more of the artless beauty of nature in this garden than I have met with in any other garden of Italy

Miller recorded that the English were allowed by the Borghese to go to the park twice a week to play cricket and football! Thomas Jones recorded one such English cricket match in March 1780, but also the fair for the whole people in the second half of October 1779:

> The English Cavaliers with as many of their Country men among the Artists as they could muster, play'd at the game of Cricket in the Borghese Park –

> *Thursday 14th* This day the Prince of Borghese threw open his Park & Gardens where all the idle people of Rome might be amused in the true stile of Bartholomew fair in Smithfield – The principal Machine & which was intended for the gentealer sort, was an immense large horizontal Wheel – put in Motion by a number of People placed in the Center for that purpose – On the Circumference were alternately fixed large wooden horses & chairs – the one for the Ladies, the other for the Gentle-men – just without the Circumference of the Wheel was fixed a Post, on the top of which was a small brass ring, for those who entered the Lists, to carry off on the point their Lance or javelin – It was so contrived that when one Ring was taken off, another immediately dropp'd in its place & those who bore off the greatest number were the Conquerors of course – It must be owned that the Officers of his Holiness's Guards exerting

themselves with a becoming Emulation, & great adroitness on the Occasion nor could their becoming gravity & self complacency be exceeded by the heroic knight of La Manca –

The other Machine was a Wheel of almost the same dimensions, but moved vertically, & was turned by large Winch handles placed on each side – Round the Circumference were placed at equal Distances a number of small armed chairs each Chair moving on an axis of its own, so that the person sitting in it, always whether ascending or descending, preserved a perpendicular Situation – The Whole had a most ludicrous Effect – Besides these two Wheels there were Swings and other Contrivances for the Amusement of the Rabble, and which, besides Consorts & Balls on Thursdays & Sundays, were continued every day to the End of the Month –.[100]

The VILLA FARNESINA attracted more attention now than it had in the last century. Montesquieu, in particular, devoted a long discussion to the brilliance of Raphael's frescoes in distinguishing foreground from background without weakening the colours of the latter, in the way he has rendered every face individual, perfectly representeing the character and the emotions, and also made every female body individual, although with time the flesh colours have become too red. De Brosses in 1740 recorded that the villa was occupied by Celestino Galiani, the Neapolitan envoy, and told the famous story of Michelangelo's visit to the villa while Raphael was away, and his drawing a head, which the latter understood as a recommendation to make his figures larger. Goethe had the enormous good fortune to visit the villa with Angelika Kauffmann. He declared the paintings the 'most beautiful decorations I ever saw', but stated that they had been ruined by restoration.[101] Carlo Maratta repainted the background a deep blue, which made the colouring of the figures harsher. It is interesting that none of these visitors saw Sodoma's painting on the upper floor.

De Sade was particularly enchanted by the VILLA GIULIA beyond the Borghese. The architecture of the court 'could not be more pleasing', but what he thought most beautiful were the four caryatids. The villa itself, however, was damp and neglected. The only use made of it at this time (1775) was as a residence for foreign ambassadors before they

Giuseppe Vasi, Villa Ludovisi, *1761*

made their formal entrance into the city. James Smith in 1787 noted
that it was seldom visited by strangers. Apart from objections to the
arcade decorated with naked boys and girls, one group of whom was
'too abominable to be described', the sunken grotto delighted him:

> Never did I see anything which conveyed so strongly the idea
> of an enchanted palace, more especially as we entered the villa
> at a door that happened to be unbarred, and rambled about at
> our leisure without meeting a living creature.[102]

The VILLA LUDOVISI between the porta Pinciana and the porta Salaria housed a celebrated collection of antiquities. At the beginning of
the century de Blainville described an avenue along the walls where
one could see a colossal Messalina, Jupiter, Macrinus, a satyr, and the
sarcophagus of the consul M. Aurelius and his wife Theodora. There
was also a 'labyrinth' which contained a sleeping Silenus, a Satyr and
faun, Leda and the Swan, Venus, Mars, Diana, Victory, Nero sacri-
ficing, two captive barbarians, and twenty busts of emperors. An
obelisk lay on the ground (this was given by the Ludovisi to Clement

Francesco Piranesi,
Orestes and Electra
(Museum of Rome),
engraving dated 1783

XII in 1733 and raised by Giovanni Antinori at Trinità dei Monti in 1789). The most esteemed pieces were in the villa itself: two Apollos, Meleager, Antoninus Pius, a Faun and Venus, 'Papirius and his mother' (now Orestes and Electra), Fulvius committing suicide, Pluto carrying off Persephone, Pætus and Arria (or the Gallic couple; see ill. opposite). The Dying Gladiator had recently been sold for 15,000 *scudi* (it had, in fact, been ceded to the Odescalchi in payment of debts, was returned in 1715 and was acquired by the Capitoline in 1737). De Brosses announced that he went to this villa every evening. The gardens were 'the largest in the town, the best kept, and being near the most populous part of the city, are much frequented' – although they might be *better* kept, and came nowhere near the Palais Royal, not to mention the Tuileries. Of the antiquities, de Brosses gave the palm to 'Papiria questioning her son' (*sic*) 'the expression of curiosity on her face is inconceivable'. Guercino's *Aurora* he preferred to Reni's: 'it has more spirit and is richer in colour'. De Sade also gave a detailed catalogue, but nominated as his favourites the 'Papiria' because of its realism, and Pætus and Arria for its emotion and warmth. By this time (1776) ownership had passed to Prince Antonio Piombino (d. 1805), and his mother, a 'ficklesome old lady', kept the key, so that the earl of Pembroke, in 1779 could not see the house, but only the garden and casino. By the end of the century, some attributions were beginning to be questiond: Papiria and son might be Phædra and Hippolytus, or Electra and Orestes, because of her short hair and the fact that she places her hand on his shoulder; Arria and Pætus should not be naked: perhaps the man is a herald. In 1787 Smith reported that the garden was open to the public on Saturdays. 'The most admired statue in the garden is an animated satyr by Michel Angelo,'

The dying Gallic couple
(Museum of Rome)

whereas inside no sculptures were more famous than Arria and Pætus and Papirius and his mother. He noted, however, that Winckelmann had disproved both identifications (1764), suggesting for the first Canace, condemned to death for incest with her brother, and for the latter Electra and Orestes. The casino in the garden contained Guercino's *Aurora*, 'the finest fresco perhaps in the world'. At the end of the century, finally, Stolberg mentioned Mars reposing with Cupid, a Faun playing a flute, and a Bacchus 'inimitable for softness and beauty'. He was also critical: 'Pætus and Arria' were not Romans, but rather a German, Gallic or Thracian general killing his wife and himself. As for Guercino's *Aurora*, the goddess was not beautiful, and the chariot was too heavy![103]

One of the jewels of the Renaissance was the VILLA MADAMA, on Monte Mario, planned by Raphael for the Medici from 1518. In 1535 it passed to the Farnese and took its name from Margerita of Austria. It remained with them apart from a brief return to the Medici (1549-1555) until 1731, when it was acquired by the Bourbons of Naples (1731-1913), during which time it suffered appalling neglect, and devastation in the endless upheavals at the end of the eighteenth century until the mid nineteenth. It subsequently passed into private hands and was lovingly restored by Maurice Borges and Count Carlo Dentice de Frasso, until it was acquired by the state in 1940. Montesquieu paid attention to the villa in 1729, noting the paintings and the architecture and the wonderful views. Burney named it the villa Rafaele; to reach it cost him a 'monstrous long, hot and dusty walk' from piazza del Popolo. He also mentioned Raphael's frescoes and Giovanni da Udine's grotesque paintings. His main interest, however, lies in the fact that the villa was occupied by an English musician, (Charles) Wiseman, who had been there for nineteen years, and that he gave concerts for important visitors, such as the duke of York.[104]

In the VILLA MATTEI, Joseph Addison noted two statues of actors, which he had found nowhere else. A fairly detailed but select catalogue was given by de Blainville. The identifications of many of the portraits may be fanciful, but the taste and quality of the collection are apparent. By the time of the earl of Pembroke's visit in 1779 it was a different story:

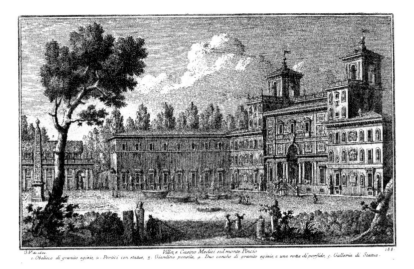

Giuseppe Vasi, Villa Medici, *1761*

once reckoned among the finest in Rome. All the good things sold, many in England. In the Garden on a Lawn, a bad Tomb, an Obelisk, and at the end, a head of immense size, said to be Alexander, belonged to a statue, 93 palms high. The head is reckoned very perfect.

The obelisk still stands in the villa. The height of the Alexander statue would be more than twenty metres. Goethe provides our final glimpse. There was an attractive reward for those who completed the pilgrimage of the seven main basilicas in Holy Week: a ticket for entertainment in the villa Mattei, and those who were thus admitted received bread, wine, cheese or eggs, and were allowed to picnic there; the favourite spot was the small amphitheatre. The grandees watched the spectacle from the Casino.[105]

Another of the grand villas was the MEDICI. Blainville, as usual, is the first of our eighteenth century visitors. He singled out in the gallery a Bacchus, Ganymede, and Marsyas, noting that 'the peasant overhearing the conspiracy of Catiline' (in reality the Arrotino) was

The Arrotino *(knife-sharpener), part of a group of Apollo and Marysas*

now in Florence. In the gardens were two granite basins from the Baths of Titus, an obelisk, statues of a seated Roma, and Niobe and her children (see ill. opposite). Berkeley in 1717 described the villa as 'stripped of its best furniture and neglected'. In the garden he particularly noticed the lion by Flaminio Vacca, the two granite basins, and the sixteen figures of Niobe and her children, 'dug up in the garden'. Breval, similarly, described the palace itself four years later as being in a 'very ruinous and neglected condition'. He asserted that the Niobid group came from the vigna Caro, outside porta S Giovanni. De Brosses in 1740 gave a more cheerful picture:

> Do not miss visiting the Villa Medici near the Church of the Trinity. You will find a building covered over with antique bas reliefs, a pretty garden, an obelisk formerly in the Circus of Flora, several tasteful fountains, especially one with a lion, an artificial hill shaped like a pyramid, tree covered, and with a little castle at the summit, marble pillars and antique statues in the apartments. Nor will you forget to look at the Niobe and her children, by Praxiteles or Phidias, I am blessed if I know which of the two! It is a very celebrated work, but there exist finer. The Venus of Medici was here formerly, now she is at Florence; she got broken on the journey. May the careless idiots be confounded for their stupidity. However, she has been so carefully put together again that no one could guess she had been broken.

De Sade, musing on the public nature of the gardens of the villa, thought them private enough for trysts. The highest part of the garden was called Parnassus. He also noticed the obelisk, found at S Maria sopra Minerva in the 1560s, erected in the villa *c.* 1570, and shortly now (1789) to be removed to Florence, and the façade decorated with reliefs and statues, notably the four barbarian kings. He gave as usual a very detailed listing, but with little discrimination, except for the frequent label 'mediocre'.[106]

The VILLA PAMPHILI on the Janiculum (see ill. overleaf) had been established in 1630. Baron Karl Pöllnitz described it in 1721 as 'the most beautiful spot in the environs of the city'. 'The gardens have an air of grandeur and symmetry... The outside and inside of the house are equally clad in marble reliefs, of admirable workmanship.' The statues were rather damaged, because their genitals had been rudely

Niobe and child

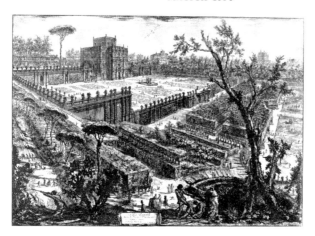

G. B. Piranesi,
Villa Pamphilii,
1776

covered with plaster, but the prince changed his mind, and the worker removing the plaster was too energetic! Caylus asserted that there was little to see inside the building, apart from a grisaille by Giulio Romano (his *Bacchanal*), a Seneca, and the stucco ornament of the eastern apartments, as well as the view from the terrace. The park contained deer and very pleasant walks bordered by pines. Berkeley also found the villa delightful, with the gardens 'neat, spacious and kept in good order', but it was the 'prospect, with the variety of risings and vales,' that constituted its beauty. Half a century later, Anne Miller rounded on the garden as laid out in very bad taste: no flowers in parterres, and the hedges 'clipped to the quick'. Of the statuary she singled out a Vestal and Clodius in women's clothing (famously at the Bona Dea festival). Miller was in a minority about the gardens: de Sade accounted them a little later 'very pleasant, planted with all possible taste and almost everywhere different'. The collection contained two large ancient tombs with excellent reliefs, statues of 'Jules Augusta Imperator', Julia Domna, the famous Clodius, a Nile in basalt, busts of Socrates and Demosthenes, Cupid as Hercules, an Hermaphrodite whose male characteristics had been so concealed as to spoil the whole effect, and a Titian *Venus*. Pembroke found many of the busts and statues falsely named and the gardens in old taste, but highly regarded in Italy.[107]

The VILLA PERETTI-MONTALTO-NEGRONI (see ill. Vol. I), finally, founded by Sixtus V on the Esquiline, passed to the Negroni for most of this century (1696-1784). Since it fell a victim to commercially motivated destruction in the next century, descriptions of this gem are precious. De Blainville provides one in 1707:

> Including the vigne or vineyard, it is about three Miles in Circuit, and contains many fine groves of Cypress, Bay, Orange and Lemon-Trees, interspersed with beautiful Fountains and Jets of Water, the principal of which has a large Basin at least sixty Paces in Circumference.
>
> There are two large Palaces in the Villa, and both adorned with a vast Number of Statues. The mostly admired among them are those of Marius and Marcellus sitting in their Curule Chairs, by the hand of Apollonius; the Statue of Livia, wife of Augustus; of the goddess Nænia...; and a Gladiator of black Marble, for which, 'tis said, the King of France offered ten thousand Crowns.
>
> Here are also a great many very curious Busts; and among others, those of the first Brutus, of Pyrrhus, king of the Epirotes, of Scipio Africanus, of Caligula, of Nero, of Cardinal Montalto, and of Sixtus V done from the Life. As to Paintings, they are innumerable, and done by the most celebrated Masters, such as Raphael, Carache, Guido and others.

A little more than thirty years later de Brosses dismissed the villa as 'in wretched repair'. When de Sade saw it in 1775, it was for sale and ruinous. In the vestibule of one building Zuccari's frescoes were being ruined by damp and neglect. Under another were the seated statues of Marius and Sulla. The figures on the principal fountain were all broken, and the two fine sarcophagi were being used as pots for orange trees. At the same time de la Platière declared that the villa was 'absolutely abandoned, everything valuable withdrawn, dispersed and sold'. Riesch in c. 1780 could still, however, mention the seated consuls, a victor in the circus, the veiled head of Paris, a child on a tiger, a caryatid, and Mercury with his lyre. In 1787 Smith left a remarkable description of the park, 'ornamented with rows of the finest cypresses to be seen, planted about the year 1580 by Sixtus V, while cardinal. They are now in the full vigour of their growth, by no means inclining to decay.'[108] It was a symbol of a reprieve. In 1789 marchese Camillo Massimo bought the villa and began restoring it.

It was Johannes Tischbein the artist who best understood the importance of the villas:

> In general the villas inside and outside Rome are pleasant places which can lead the soul which is drifting downwards and entangled in the confusion and difficulties of the busy world back to itself. Here one is easily reconciled with oneself and the world, and returns from the demanding struggles to satisfaction and a true enjoyment of happiness in the abundance and beauty of Nature.[109]

The fate of the Roman villas in the next century was determined by those who had not the faintest inkling of these ideals.

ANTIQUITIES

Jerome Richard in 1761 was critical of Roman attitudes, especially those of the aristocracy, towards the classical past: 'In general they know little about it, but the admiration excited by these traces of magnificence which they regard as their patrimony, flatters them.' Charles Dupaty in 1785 was more direct: 'The Italians preserve their ruins as beggars keep open their sores': to attract tourists. Alternatively, as Montesquieu put it, 'modern Rome is selling ancient Rome, piece by piece'. That was in 1729. In 1740, Horace Walpole gave chapter and verse:

> by the remains one sees of the Roman grandeur in their structures, 'tis evident that there must have been more pains taken to destroy those piles than to raise them. They are more demolished than any time or chance could have effected. I am persuaded that in an hundred years Rome will not be worth

seeing; 'tis less so now than one would believe. All the public pictures are decayed or decaying; the few ruins cannot last long; and the statues and private collections must be sold, from the great poverty of the families. There are now selling no less than three of the principal collections, the Barberini, the Sacchetti, and Ottoboni.

Lady Mary Montagu reported: 'Here is a statue of Antinoüs lately found, which is said to be equal to any in Rome, and is to be sold; perhaps the Duke of Bedford might be glad to hear of it. I do not hear of one valuable picture that is to be purchas'd.' Jean de la Platière in 1777 noted the departure in progress of the Farnese collection for Naples. Antiquities were 'an inexhaustible mine', but were 'daily being devastated'. Laws to protect them were eluded in an infinity of ways by the powerful and the rich. A favourite method used by aristocrats was to make a copy to replace anything they wished to sell. Moszyński in 1785 described the frenzy of sale:

> They wanted to sell me the most beautiful rooms of the Baths of Titus for the paintings, but apart from the fact that it is already quite ruined, I remembered the embargo (on export) and I will limit myself to just one picture if I can get it cheaply so that you [King Stanislaus of Poland] can have at least one good piece of ancient painting. Because as they say they want to sell these rooms, they will soon be stripped, and it is impossible to get any of them at Naples. The king of Sweden [Gustav III] has bought a lot and is still buying; he has just paid 2000 ducats for the famous Endymion. There is a Venus which is undoubtedly the most beautiful after the Medici and the Capitoline Venus. They refused 17,000 *scudi* once, then they wanted to sell it. The king of Sweden offered 3,000 but was refused. At present the owner is without money and would sell it for 1,000, but at the moment there are no English or Swedes or Russians at Rome.

As early as 1729 Montesquieu stated that 'it was necessary to pass a law in Rome that the major statues are furniture and can only be sold with the house where they are, under pain of confiscation of the house and other effects of the vendor. Otherwise, Rome will be completely stripped.'[110]

De la Platière also described the flourishing restoration trade, not that requiring artistic taste or skill, but the joining of pieces, the hiding of breaks, the making of veneers, inlays and mosaics, the restoration of vases, columns and even obelisks, the imitation of cameos and engravings (he noted that the Calcografia, or State Engraving office, sold engravings, but that they were all retouched, yet the English were crazy for them, which sent up the prices). Marble for the restoration trade was available in abundance from the ruins.

Montesquieu mentioned also the production of counterfeits, especially coins. Copies were taken by a mould, but were usually recognisable by being under weight. A Florentine had perfected a system for overcoming this, but the lettering was still not convincing. Worn coins were often retouched.

There was, on the other hand, a legitimate industry in plaster casts. The most famous collector of these was Goethe. He had casts of the Rondanini Medusa and a colossal head of Jupiter; the latter caused a commotion in his lodging when the landlady's cat was found 'worshipping' it, with its paws on the god's chest and licking its beard. To these he added the Ludovisi Juno. The casts were, in fact, often too large and too heavy to take home.

And who in Rome was interested in the antiquities? De Brosses in 1740 gave a depressing picture:

> Regarding antiquarians in Rome, there are not so many as you would be likely to imagine. The nobles cultivate letters but little, although they have palaces overcrowded with rarities and curiosities. The Colonnas, the Pamphili, the Chigi, the Giustiniani, the Borghese are like so many Turks in their seraglios, and the ecclesiastics are more occupied in accumulating money than in teaching religion. Out of the whole College of Cardinals there are not half a dozen of any learning.

De Brosses named as worthy antiquarians at this time only Cardinal Alessandro Albani, Giuseppe Assemani and Giovanni Bottari, both of the Vatican library, Francesco Ficoroni, and Antonio Borioni.[111]

What was the attraction of the Roman ruins? Robert Gray (1791) is one of the few to address the question directly. The churchman drew moral lessons:

> The pleasure received on beholding the ruins of ancient Rome… must be derived principally from the reflections which they suggest; generally speaking the ruins have little beauty in their present appearance…
>
> The common spectator, who glances over the vestiges of Rome merely as objects of sight, is soon wearied, but the intelligent traveller who dwells with improving meditation on the changes which the city has suffered, and on the moral causes which have effected them, feels considerable satisfaction in this wonderful place and finds every object pregnant with instruction.

The poet John Dyer, author of the *Ruins of Rome*, focussed on their charm:

> There is a certain charm that follows the sweep of Time, and I can't help thinking the triumphal arches more beautiful now than they ever were, there is a certain greenness, with many other colours, and a certain disjointedness and moulder among the stones, something so pleasing in their weeds and tufts of myrtle, and something in the altogether so greatly wild…

There were, of course, the literalists. Vincent Arnauld, paradoxically, was an historical dramatist:

> I could not rediscover the chasm of Curtius in the pool of greenish water, the Forum in the Campo Vaccino, the Golden House in the brushwood which covered the Palatine, the Via Sacra in the path bristling with brambles and thistles which crosses the vast solitude where once the destiny of the world was decided, and where today one gathers only to buy and sell cattle.[112]

The Golden house was not, of course, on the Palatine. On the other hand, Arnauld experienced some annoyance in seeing the modern use of the classical monuments: the Inquisition in the temple of Minerva, the College of Apothecaries in the temple of Antoninus in the Forum, the altar of Jupiter now that of the Bambino (Aracœli), the temple of all the gods (the Pantheon) now all saints, the theatre of Vespasian (the Colosseum) a calvary. 'That seemed to me not only a profanation, but also a usurpation.'

The most famous visitor of this century was Edward Gibbon. For him there were no problems with imagination:

> At the distance of twenty five years I can neither forget nor express the strong emotions which agitated my mind as I first approached and entered the *eternal* City. After a sleepless night I trod with a lofty step the ruins of the Forum; each memorable spot where Romulus *stood*, or Tully spoke, or Cæsar fell was at once present to my eye; and several days of intoxication were lost or enjoyed before I could descend to a minute or cool and minute observation.[113]

Particular categories of antiquities were singled out by some visitors. For Joseph Addison it was statuary:

> The workmanship is often the most exquisite of anything in its kind. A man would wonder how it were possible for so much life to enter into marble, as may be discovered in some of the best of them; and even in the meanest one has the satisfaction of seeing the faces, postures, airs and dress of those that have lived so many ages before us.

Benjamin Hobhouse was puzzled by sarcophagi: why did so many of them show Endymion and Diana, Meleager and the boar, the Rape of Persephone, or indecent Bacchantes and satyrs? An Irishman explained: 'The world was then as now; the majority of mankind were either hunters, drunkards or fornicators. Thus the funeral ornaments bear a relation to the lives of the deceased.' And the ever curious Addison drew attention to one of the most sumptuous classes of antiquities:

> The most valuable pillars about Rome, for the marble of which they are made, are the four columns of oriental jasper in St

Paulina's chapel at St Maria Maggiore; two of oriental granite in St Pudenziana; one of tra[n]sparent oriental jasper in the Vatican library; four of Nero-Bianco, in St Cecilia Transtevere; two of Brocatello, and two of oriental agate in Don Livio's [Odescalchi] palace; two of Giallo Antico in St John Lateran, and two of Verdi Antique in the Villa Pamphilia. These are all entire and solid pillars, and made of such kinds of marble as are nowhere to be found but among antiquities, whether it be that the veins of it are undiscovered, or that they were quite exhausted upon the ancient buildings. Among these old pillars, I cannot forbear reckoning a great part of an alabaster column, which was found in the ruins of Livia's portico. It is of the colour of fire, and may be seen over the high altar of St Maria in Campitello, for they have cut it into two pieces, and fixed it in the shape of a cross in a hole of the wall that was made on purpose to receive it; so that the light passing through it from without, makes it look, to those who are in the church, like a huge transparent cross of amber.[114]

Visitors at this time, moreover, had special ways of viewing antiquities. The most famous account of this is given by Goethe:

Nobody who has not taken one can imagine the beauty of a walk through Rome by full moon. All details are swallowed up by the huge masses of light and shadow, and only the biggest and most general outlines are visible. We have just enjoyed three clear and glorious nights. The Colosseum looked especially beautiful. It is closed at night. A hermit lives in a small chapel and some beggars have made themselves at home in the crumbling vaults. These had built a fire on the level ground and a gentle breeze had driven the smoke into the arena, so that the lower parts of the ruins were veiled and only the huge masses above loomed out of the darkness. We stood at the railing and watched, while over our heads the moon stood high and serene. By degrees the smoke escaped through holes and crannies and in the moonlight it looked like fog. It was a marvellous sight. This is the kind of illumination by which to see the Pantheon, the Capitol, the square in front of St Peter's, and many other large squares and streets.

The custom of visiting the great Roman museums by torchlight seems to have still been fairly recent in the eighties of the last century, but I do not know when it first started.

There are several things to be said in favour of this kind of illumination: first, each work of art is seen by itself, isolated from all the others, so that the spectator's attention is exclusively focussed on it; second, in the bright light of a torch, the finer nuances of the work become more distinct, the confusing reflections (particularly annoying on highly polished statues) disappear, the shadows become more marked and the illuminated parts stand out clearer. But the greatest advantage of all is that only such illumination can do justice to statues which are unfavourably placed. Laocoön in his niche, for example, can only be seen properly by torchlight, for no direct light falls on him, only a reflected light from the small circular Cortile del Belvedere, which is surrounded by a colonnade.

The same applies to the Apollo, the so called Antinoüs (Mercury), the Nile, the Meleager and, above all, to the so called Phocion, because by torchlight the exquisitely carved body becomes visible through simple transparent drapery, something which cannot be seen at all by daylight.[115]

The classical centre is the FORUM (see ill. opposite). After pages on the remains, de Blainville in 1707 declared that 'scarce anything is remaining here but Heaps of Frightful Ruins, apter to excite Horror, than Admiration in the Spectator'. He identified the temple of Castor and Pollux, for example, with SS Cosma e Damiano, and that of the Deified Vespasian with the base of Domitian's equestrian statue. Charles de Brosses in 1739, however, agreed with him: 'Everything is in a miserable condition and in the utmost disorder – a mighty pile of ruin. An avenue of trees has been planted, which makes the desolate place look still more abandoned.' He was amazed that no excavations, clearances, preservation or decoration had been attempted. The surgeon Samuel Sharp noted the cattle market in the Forum every Thursday and Friday. James Boswell, whose guide was Colin Morison,

Gian Paolo Panini, The Forum, *1747*

described 'the wretched huts of carpenters and other artisans' on the site of the Rostrum, (the speakers' platform) and thought the Temple of Castor part of Caligula's fabled 'portico' from Palatine to Capitol. Anne Miller dismissed the Forum as 'this foul cow market'. At the end of the century, the botanist James Smith declared the Forum 'a dirty, desolate place' and Count Frederick Stolberg found it still 'full of cattle and hogs'. The uniformity of this condemnation and rejection by the eighteenth century visitors is striking.

John Moore the physician tried to imagine where all the ancient monuments stood, but then thought the space between the Palatine and Capitol so circumscribed that he 'found it impossible to make the Roman Forum larger than Covent Garden'! Even with the best will in the world, there were distractions. A vivid picture of the area is given by the lawyer Friedrich Meyer in 1783:

> It is in vain that the imagination tries to enjoy these monuments – it is at every moment troubled by the sound of bells, the lowing of herds, the cries of merchants, the tumult and riot of the populace incessantly occupied in games.

G. B. Piranesi, The Arch of Titus, *with the Farnese Gardens on the Palatine on the left,* 1748-78

Most outrageous of all, however, was the radical lawyer Charles Dupaty: 'I took a pleasure in trampling underfoot the Roman grandeur. I enjoyed walking on Rome.'

Another lawyer, Johann Volkmann, is the exception. In 1758 he noted the alley of trees. 'For the lover of antiquity a solitary promenade in this space is very important; he can exactly depict the location of the old buildings according to our description, and at the same time reflect on the great revolutions in Rome and the transience of earthly things.'[116]

The ARCH OF TITUS disappointed Addison in that he found no representation of the temple at Jerusalem. He noted that some believed, however, that the composite pillars of the arch imitated its pillars. De Sade recorded the Jewish aversion to passing under the arch, and that they had bought permission to use a side path. Perhaps confusing this arch with that of Constantine, de la Platière declared it built by Trajan. Isaak von Riesch, chamberlain to Stanislaus of Poland, described the arch as loaded with 'superstitious and tasteless ornaments'! Hobhouse in 1784 found it 'in ruinous condition'. The ARCH OF SEVERUS was, in de Blainville's view, 'infinitely more remarkable and beautiful than that of Titus'. He recorded that Bellori and Baronio had suspected that the name of Geta had been erased from the inscription. Volkmann noted that the main arch in 1758 was filled to half its height, the lateral arches to two thirds. Always critical, he declared the main opening too big, the attic too low, the inscription too large. De Sade thought that the arch commemorated Severus' victories over the Cimbri and Dacians, whereas it was the Parthians. By 1775 the two lateral arches were completely blocked, but the central one was still 'easily passable'.[117]

The only BASILICA to be seen was that OF MAXENTIUS (see ill. overleaf), misnamed the Temple of Peace of Vespasian – after his victory over India, stated Lady Miller. Of the eight original columns only one remained, transferred to piazza di S Maria Maggiore in 1613-1614. De Brosses waxed eloquent over this: 'I cannot describe to you what this temple was like, but I know that this isolated column is the most beautiful architectural fragment that exists, and that it gives me as much pleasure to look at as at any complete building, whether ancient

Giuseppe Vasi, The Arch of Severus, 1752

G. Vasi dis. in.
Parte di' Campo Vaccino
1. Arco di Settimio Severo 2. Colonne del supposto Tempio della Concordia 3. Colonne nel Clivo del Campidoglio 4. Colonna sola 5. Muri del Campidoglio 3:

VEDUTA DEGLI AVANZI DEL TEMPIO DELLA PACE

G. B. Piranesi, Basilica of Maxentius, *1757*

or modern, for it represents the very highest perfection to which architectural art has ever attained.' He had to record that the column was damaged by lightning in 1739. Volkmann described a visit to the basilica in 1758: there was a garden on the roof where one had to proceed with caution, for there were large holes in the vaults! More fell every day. To reach the basilica one passed through a poorhouse of the Mendicanti, where one hundred-and-twenty orphan girls made woollen material, valued at the considerable sum of 12,000 Taler per annum. Pierre Grosley at the same time described the basilica as being used as a stable for cattle. One wonders what possessed von Riesch to suggest that the 'temple' must have been as big as St Peter's. On some the truth began to dawn: Johann von Archenholz in the late 1770s declared that 'the ruins bear not the least resemblance to a Roman temple'.

Behind the Palatine was the nearby FORUM BOARIUM (see ill. opposite), the 'cattle market'. There were two temples, the so called temple of Vesta (the little round temple by the Tiber) and the so called temple of 'Fortuna Virilis', in reality that of Portunus, the harbour god. It was the 'temple of Vesta' which was the favourite. De Brosses was appalled that the colonnade had been bricked in and the temple converted to a chapel:

> How interesting and delightful it would have been had this lonely little building been left in its former state, with its open colonnade, its cupola, its simple altar in the centre, on which burnt the sacred fire; with five or six young vestals, clothed in white, with rosy crowns, lovelier than cupids, who approach the altar with reverential steps, their faggot of aloe-wood in their hands, in the fashion of the honest Guebrians [Zoroastrians], and pronouncing the sacred formula as they make a lowly reverence, 'Behold, Lord Fire, Eat!' I'faith, they should have left a little of paganism in Rome for our benefit, and I vow we should not have abused our privilege.

The 'Arch of Janus' in the Forum Boarium incited de Sade to complain of the false nomenclature: it was simply an assembly point

Giuseppe Vasi, The Forum Boarium, *1754*

for merchants. During his visit (1775) an excavation was conducted at the foot of one of the pillars, but after reaching fifteen feet its base had not been discovered, which showed the elevation of modern Rome. De la Platière thought that it was this arch on which the *fasti* (lists of consuls) were exhibited! One of the few to notice the much more interesting Arcus Argentariorum (Arch of the Bankers in honour of Septimius Severus and his family) was de Sade.

Little interest was shown in the Bocca della Verità. Edward Wright told an amusing story (his guide was Ficoroni). 'If the Party that would clear himself was known to be guilty, or that it was resolv'd that he should appear so, the Priests conceal'd behind were ready with a hot iron and burnt his Fingers when put into the mouth'!

Nearby was the Theatre of Marcellus. Given how little remained in its original state, John Breval's enthusiasm is striking: 'this magnificent Pile', 'the noblest Building, I may venture to affirm, that was ever applied to that purpose in any part of the World'. De Sade, for example, stated that it was hard, from its present state, to recognise what it had once been.[118]

The IMPERIAL FORA were almost completely buried, and therefore usually wildly misplaced, if noticed at all. The temple of Mars Ultor, for example, was commonly identified with the church of SS Luca e Martina (from an imagined connection of the latter with Mars). George Berkeley described the remains as they were in 1717: 'The wall is noble, of rustic work, like the palaces in Florence, vast stones heaped upon one another, with an irregular jutting out here and there. It now makes part of a nunnery. The pillars that remain are of white marble, fluted, very large.' He named it the basilica of Nerva. The Forum of Nerva beside it comprised 'some pillars and entablatures... with rilievos, and a statue of Minerva in the wall'. This naturally he called the temple of Minerva.[119]

Of Trajan's forum the only thing to be seen was the column (see ill. opposite), as cleared by Sixtus V. Addison was uncertain whether Trajan's ashes had been placed on the top (where could they have been more nobly lodged?) or at the base. Breval in 1721 commented on the damage to both this and the arch of Aurelius: 'No part of them has receiv'd near so much Damage as that which lies expos'd to the

Giuseppe Vasi, The Column of Trajan, *1752*

Tramontane [northerly] Wind, which eats away visibly some of the noblest antiquities in Rome.' No wind ever did as much damage to Rome's antiquities as human vandalism. Sixtus V's arrangements had much degenerated by *c.* 1721. Jonathon Richardson described the column as being in a pit full of 'Filth and Nastiness'. Being an artist, he noted acutely that the figures in the relief were a little larger at the top than the bottom, and that the relief was 'pretty high', because it was meant to be seen at a distance. De Brosses found, for his taste, the pedestal to be 'the finest part, especially that portion of it adorned with sculptural laurel wreaths'. A testament to the taste of the lawyer Meyer is found in his judgement of Sixtus' placing of a statue of St Peter on the column: there was 'no monument in Rome where he less deserves to be'. There was finally a very negative assessment, by Hobhouse in 1784: 'what an injudicious expenditure of national money': the figures were, in his view, 'a confused mass'.[120] A virtuoso and path-breaking example of relief narrative was thus so easily dismissed!

François Boucher, Imaginary Landscape with the Palatine Hill from Campo Vaccino, *1734*

Apart from the Forum, the other main classical site was the PALA-TINE. If the former dismayed some visitors, what would the latter do? It was 'no more than a Heap of dismal Ruins', stated de Blainville. Breval in 1721 noted the excavations of the duke of Parma, which had been kept a secret: a beautiful 'Bathing Room' had been found three years earlier and demolished for its materials, as well as a statue of a contemplative elder Agrippina, reflecting on her recent banishment! Montesquieu in 1729 visited the Palatine with Cardinal Melchior Polignac and noted that all marbles and columns had been stripped, but that the excavator, Francesco Bianchini, had thoughtfully set up an inscription describing the one-time treasures. De Brosses in 1740 described the palace of Augustus as 'a harbour for bats, owls and snakes'. Ownership had passed from the Farnese to the king of Naples, who refused to protect the ruins. He then described the Aula Regia: 'a vast hall, formerly encrusted with marbles and adorned with columns and Corinthian pilasters of green and yellow marble… the niches contained statues'. Boswell was so carried away at these sights that he was 'seized with enthusiasm' and began to speak Latin! De Sade described the situation in 1775, by which time there were three owners: the king of Naples owned the side overlooking the Forum, a French abbot (Rancoureuil, whose first name is one of the best kept secrets) owned the middle, where he made constant excavations, and the German College owned the side overlooking the Circus Maximus. In the first section, the Farnese Gardens, 'the lowest part of the population now comes to get drunk on the ruins of the homes of the masters of the universe' and here the 'Baths of Livia' were discovered in 1736. The French section was usually inaccessible, but de Sade described the recent discovery of two richly decorated large round rooms. Hobhouse reveals the impression made by the paintings in the 'Baths of Livia' under the triclinium: 'small chambers, the walls of which are ornamented with paintings either of foliage or small well designed figures in the most graceful and easy attitudes. Some of these figures are executed in gold colour on an azure background, others in azure on a gold ground.' Marianne Starke warned that the baths were 'too damp and close for Invalids! Give 3 or 4 *paoli* to the man who finds the lights.'[121]

After the Palatine, the visitor might turn his or her steps to the Capitol. MARCUS AURELIUS' EQUESTRIAN STATUE (see ill. Vol. I) was, properly, a focus for the traveller. De Blainville began by setting the record straight. It will surprise us that the identity of the emperor was contested: some thought him Antoninus Pius, Lucius Verus (Marcus' co-emperor), Septimius Severus or even the Republican Metellus Pius. It can only be Marcus, argued de Blainville with impeccable logic: compare his coins and his reliefs in the Capitoline Museum. The eulogies were almost unanimous: for Breval, 'the noblest equestrian statue in the world', for Karl Pöllnitz 'the most beautiful and most perfect piece that perhaps was ever made of this kind', and it pleased Tobias Smollett more than anything in the Belvedere collection – and he noted a further identification, with Constantine, because it had originally stood by the Lateran palace. There had, of course, to be critics. Given the famous story about Michelangelo and the horse,

Jean Baptiste Labat contrarily declared the emperor too static, too inanimate – so much for Michelangelo's fancy – and a certain Falconet was said to have written a book of 200 pages to prove that the horse was not fine: in fact, the sculptor Etienne Falconet's *Observations sur la statue de Marc Aurèle*, Amsterdam 1771 (210 pages). To this James Smith replied that the length of his arguments was a strong presumption of his being wrong. It is in keeping with the Roman ability to find a sinecure for everyone that there was a custodian of the horse, paid 10 *scudi* p.a.[122]

The TARPEIAN ROCK continued to be the subject of very contradictory – and often humorous – comments; that was because of argument over whether it faced the Forum (as all sources attest) or the other way (towards piazza Montanara). Breval in 1721 declared:

> From the strictest observation I could form of this Place it is even to this Day both steep and high enough to break a reasonable Neck (notwithstanding what the learned Montfaucon affirms to the contrary), for it is one hundred and thirty Roman palms measur'd, which come but little short of as many English feet.

Breval's calculations are wildly astray. The palm was 22 cms, so 130 palms were a little more than 28 m, or 93'. He noted that the Caffarelli coachman had 'made the experiment' while he was drunk, and been killed. This presumably located the Rock on the Montanara side. From this point the antiquarians battled it out. Wright also in 1721 was shown the rock by Ficoroni, who attacked Montfaucon for saying that there was little precipice left: it was 60'. Moore quoted James Byres' measurements: 58' perpendicular, but the ground had risen 20', so it was originally about 80' high. Stolberg, being conducted by Aloïs Hirt, reported his view that the Rock was on the western side (piazza Montanara), where it was now 'highest and almost perpendicular', whereas most visitors were shown the eastern (Forum) side.[123]

Leaving the Forum, one was confronted by the most imposing classical monument. A major interest with the COLOSSEUM (Flavian Amphitheatre) (see ills opposite and p. 126) was the number of spectators which it could hold. The modern estimate is that it could

Gian Paolo Panini, The Colosseum, 1747

accommodate about 50,000 spectators. 87,000 seated and 15,000 standing[124] was de Blainville's estimate. That was nothing in comparison with its technology. 'An Infinity of invisible Pipes were artfully placed within the Walls, by Means of which a perpetual perfumed Rain or Dew gently fell upon the Spectators' and the statues in the building were 'artfully, and by Means of imperceptible Channels, made to sweat all Sorts of the most delightful Perfumes'! Pöllnitz had the strange idea that the senators sat at the top, this being the most 'elevated' position. The decoration continued to arouse fantasy: according to Charles Thompson (1731), 'It was adorned with Statues representing all the Provinces of the Roman Empire; in the Middle whereof stood that of Rome, holding a golden Apple in her hand.' De Brosses agreed on a capacity of 90,000, comparing it with the theatre at Verona, one-third the size. Modern life, however, intruded. 'In the galleries which envelop the exterior of the Colosseum are the booths of a number of small trades-people, who here display their wares, which hang from sticks placed in the holes from which the bronze rivets have been torn out.' Walpole told a wicked story: 'A propos du Colisée, if you don't know what it is, the Prince Borghese

Giovanni Volpato, The arena of the Colosseum, *1780, showing the Stations of the Cross and a friar preaching*

[Camillo, 1693-1763] will be very capable of giving you some account of it, who told an Englishman that asked what it was built for: "They say 'twas for Christians to fight with tigers in."' A rare word of criticism was voiced by Volkmann in 1758: the columns of the top level seemed to him too small in comparison with the lower ones, and the columns in the arcades were too widely spaced, seeming too weak to support the vaults. He reduced the capacity, appropriately, to 34,000. He was contradicted by Boswell. 'It is hard to tell whether the astonishing massiveness or the exquisite taste of this superb building should be more admired.' Its state in 1765, however, left much to be desired. 'It was shocking to discover several portions of this theatre full of dung. It is rented to people who use it in this fashion.' Smollett stated that it could contain 100,000 spectators, although he noted that Fontana's measurements, allowing one and a half feet for each, suggested 34,000. Smollett rightly used the Colosseum for a long account of the cruelty of the Romans. Moore in 1775 was guided by

James Byres who presumably then is the source for the statement that the name Colosseum came from a statue of Apollo, that the capacity was 85,000, that gladiators were fed richly in order to bleed more freely (a misunderstanding, it seems, of Tacitus), and that thumbs up was the signal for death. William Beckford was outraged by the contemporary use of the arena: there was 'a vehement desire in me to break down and pulverize the whole circle of saints' nests and chapels, which disgrace the arena'. He preferred 'a dark arcade, overgrown with ilex' where he could reflect on the Roman past: 'triumphal scenes, but tempered by sadness'. Dupaty similarly saw in its dimensions 'the work of a people, sovereigns of the universe, and slaves of an emperor'. 'How ferocious was the very indolence of the Romans! It could find no amusement but in blood.' And the end of the century saw the first bizarre projects for restoration. The Pole August Moszyński proposed to demolish half of the building and use the materials to restore the other half.[125] It could then be used, amongst other things, for stores of oil and grain.

Between the Arch of Constantine and the Domus Aurea de Brosses was shown the DOMUS CICERONIS (the house of Cicero): 'a low and poor looking entrance gate… the squalid atrium of some wine merchant'! It is interesting that more attempts were not made by fanciful ciceroni to show dwellings of famous Romans.

Of the META SUDANS (see ill. Vol. III), de Blainville in 1707 recorded that only an 'insignificant fragment' remains, and no water was running. It was still fancifully thought to have been where the gladiators of the Colosseum washed.[126]

Next to the Colosseum was the ARCH OF CONSTANTINE (see ill. overleaf). This was the most commented on of all the arches. Addison searched for any evidence in the sculptures of Constantine's 'vision', to no avail, and noted the 'hint' at it in the inscription (*instinctu divinitatis*). He declared it 'not only the noblest of any [arch] in Rome, but in the world'. De Blainville repeated the old story about the damage to the heads of the statues by Lorenzo di Medici: 'the whole of Rome are ready to swear the Truth' of this. It is interesting, therefore, to have de Brosses blaming 'the barbarians' for this damage; the arch had, however, been restored in this century. It was generally

Abraham Ducros, Arch of Constantine, c. *1790*

recognised that this arch was a mélange of various periods. Jean-Jacques Barthelemy declared that this, properly speaking, was the arch of Trajan 'revu et corrigé', but admitted that he was following the views of the famous French architect, François Blondel. De Sade, similarly, stated that the upper portion belonged earlier to an arch of Trajan, but was 'transported'. He also noted the removal of one of the eight columns by Clement XII (1730-40) for the organ of S Giovanni in Laterano – thus the Church treats Constantine, 'who betrayed his conscience for politics, and to whom Christianity owes what it is today!' Perhaps taste had changed by the end of the century. Dupaty in 1785 declared that the arch 'no longer commemorates anything but the decline of arts under Constantine'[127] – shades of Bernard Berenson!

In the Campus Martius to the west of the Corso were many things to see. THE PANTHEON (see ill. opposite) as ever was a favourite, but few visitors offer anything besides admiration. Berkeley drew attention to the contrast between 'the grandeur, the nobleness and the grace' of the granite pillars in the portico and 'the beauty and delicacy' of the *giallo antico* columns within. It seemed to de Brosses half buried, and the piazza was dirty and squalid, with a market held around the fountain; he thought that the *oculus* had a diameter larger than the height of the columns in the portico (so it may seem, but the former is 28', the latter 40'); the fine porphyry sarcophagus in the portico, taken by Clement XII to be his tomb in the Lateran, was thought by de Brosses to be that of Agrippa, but it was found in the nearby temple of Isis. Volkmann decried Benedict XIV's whitening of the cupola in

Canaletto,
The Pantheon,
1742

1756 by means of 'hanging scaffolding' as very damaging; he pointed to the double gable, because the height of the columns had been lowered, which improved the portico by bringing the columns closer to each other; and at his time the climb to the *oculus* seems to have been normal. Abbé de Saint-Non agreed: after the whitewashing, the Pantheon looked like a 'big caffe'! Smollett had much to protest about: the portico corresponded badly with the 'simplicity of the edifice'; he could not see what others meant by the beauty of the rotunda; he did not think the interior was well lit; and the ground level had been lowered by Alexander VII, so that there was no descent whatsoever. De Sade returned to the more usual emotion: on seeing this famous temple, the heart breaks and the tears flow. He had two cautions: the 'windows' above the frieze are modern (this cannot be maintained) and the doors are not original (this is generally admitted). Thomas Jones in 1779 climbed to the oculus, but found it 'a Situation more dreadfully trying to weak Nerves than the Ball on the Cupola of St Peter's'. Archenholz in the late 1770s was still appalled by the setting: the Pantheon 'stands upon a little spot where the women roast fishes all day long, and sell other provisions'. The last word may go to Smith: 'a calm and solemn tranquillity is diffused over the mind on entering the Pantheon which I never felt before in any situation' and Stolberg: 'Place yourself in the centre of the Rotonda and all your ideas are aweful. You are inspired with a profound sense of the noble simplicity which everywhere meets your eye. Before you rise the ages that have passed away and the races of men that have descended to the dust since the foundation of this temple.'[128]

Another major interest of visitors to the Campus Martius was the MAUSOLEUM OF AUGUSTUS (see ills Vols I and III). It was at this time owned by a Portuguese, Marchese Correa. De Blainville, who entered the tomb, recorded the danger of its demolition at Correa's hands to enlarge his house, but this was prevented by Clement XI. The comte de Caylus described it as a temple turned into a garden, noting the thickness of the walls and the great galleries. At the same time Berkeley saw the vaults and some 'scattered vases, statues and bas-reliefs'. A more detailed description was provided by Grosley in 1758. The mausoleum was a round tower 40' in diameter, divided into two stories 'the first with a double wall of prodigious thickness', the upper crowned with a vineyard, where Grosley used to go to meditate on 'the vanity of human grandeur'. By the time of de la Platière's visit in 1787 it was used as a stables and storeroom by the famous hotelier Damon, who rented carriages, but still had a garden on top. A more repulsive use had been devised by the end of the century, as recorded by Hobhouse in 1784: 'The only public amusement during my residence of six weeks was a combat between men and buffaloes in the amphitheatre, once the mausoleum of Augustus.' It was also a market: Moszyński saw 'in the funerary niches pieces of beef, pork and lamb hanging, and sacks of flour standing there'. Goethe calculated the capacity of the bull-ring to be 4-5,000.[129]

The third major attraction of the Campus Martius was the COLUMN OF MARCUS AURELIUS. It was most valuable, in Addison's opinion, for the confirmation of the 'Rain miracle', attested also by coins and a passage in Claudian. Others less learned than he followed the current denomination, ascribing the pillar to Antoninus Pius. Richardson suggested that the scenes had been sculpted in drums before erection, because some of them did not match. Montesquieu noted in 1729 that the real column of Antoninus had now been found – but that was in 1703. De Brosses repeated a tall story obviously told to him that one side of the pillar is blackened because the Goths 'in revenge of the victories pictured on this column over their countrymen burnt these bas-reliefs, being unable to overthrow the pillar'. The foes of the Romans were not the Goths but the Germans, and the pillar could easily have been thrown down by determined vandals. De Brosses did not climb this column, being told that the stairs were 'ruined and impracticable'. One who did climb it was Jones in 1778, to smoke a pipe and drink a flask of wine there! As for the COLUMN OF ANTONINUS PIUS de Brosses described it in 1740, lying on the ground near Monte Citorio (see ill. overleaf). 'It was unearthed some thirty years ago, and it will be raised when Heaven pleases. I had to squint through a palisade to see it, but I could distinguish the bas reliefs upon it.' De Sade gave this account in 1776:

It is totally broken and incapable, they say, of ever being

Giovanni Paolo Panini, The Lottery in Piazza di Montecitorio, *1743-4, before the fire. The base of the Column of Antoninus Pius can be seen to the right*

restored. It is in a kind of iron cage when it was proposed to repair it and set it back on its base. Both were found much earlier buried while digging the foundations of the nearby house of the Fathers of the Mission. The pedestal rests in the piazza of the Palace of Justice (Montecitorio).[130]

The shaft had, in fact, been ruined by fire in 1759, and the base was removed to the Vatican in 1789.

There was one other classical monument in the Campus Martius which every visitor knew – because it was the first one seen by them in the city: the HADRIANEUM (see ill. opposite), then the customs house, so notorious to all visitors. De Brosses made the same criticism as he had made of the 'temple of Vesta' in the Forum Boarium: 'What a disgrace, instead of leaving these exquisite columns in their majestic loneliness, to have bricked them up with a monstrous wall, in which they are practically embedded'![131] They remain so to this day.

The QUIRINAL hill was primarily visited as the site of the papal

residence. There were, however, classical attractions. The Quirinal
HORSETAMERS (see ill. overleaf) formed a famous sculptural group.
De Blainville followed the main view that they were found in the time
of Sixtus V in the Baths of Constantine on the same hill, and referred
to a tradition that they were given to Nero by Tiridates of Armenia –
a tradition which he rejected. Etienne Silhouette protested that it was
thought sufficient to claim that a work was by Phidias or Praxiteles
(as in this case) to assume that it must be beautiful; to the contrary,
he found the attitudes forced and the necks of the horses too long for
their bodies. Montesquieu agreed. The American painter Benjamin
West, on the other hand, constantly revisited this group. He found
the action of the human figures 'so majestic', while in his view the
smallness of the horses was deliberate on the part of the sculptor, 'to
augment the grandeur of the men'. Another critic was de la Platière:
the figures were so much restored they were more modern than
ancient; he judged them 'mediocre'. By the end of the century perhaps

Giuseppe Vasi, The Hadrianeum, *1752*

G. B. Piranesi, The Quirinal Horsetamers, *1750*

the general view had changed. Marianne Starke stated that they were 'esteemed the finest pieces of sculpture in Rome'.[132]

Very few mentioned the Quirinal TEMPLE TO THE SUN of Aurelian (see ill. Vol. I). It was generally regarded as the Baths of Constantine. The most interesting notice is by Walpole, who mentioned two immense fragments of Parian marble, part of the frieze, which the Colonna had wanted to sell to a stonecutter for 5,000 *scudi*, but Clement XI forbade it. Walpole agreed, on a very important ground: 'Is it not amazing that so vast a structure should not be known of, or that it should be so entirely destroyed?'[133]

There are finally some classical monuments which can best be discussed in categories, as they were scattered over the city. Among the grandest remains were the baths.

What are now known as the BATHS OF TRAJAN on the Oppian were from the sixteenth century miscalled the 'Baths of Titus'. Berkeley described them in 1717:

The ruins above ground are pretty unintelligible. They are of brick, as the other thermæ, but [from] the stucco, &c. one may see they were encrusted anciently with marble, as the other baths do likewise appear to have been. At some distance under ground we saw eight large galleries or halls, that were anciently reservoirs of water for the baths of Titus. The walls are covered with plaster as hard as stone, and in many places encrusted with a sort of tartar from the water.

This was also the name given to the DOMUS AUREA, 'where Raphael was wont to copy the antique paintings in fresco and the arabesques, which are now almost all perished. It was in this place that the ivory coloured statue of the Mealeager and the group of the Laocoön were discovered,' wrote de Brosses. De Sade combined the two monuments. There were the baths on which S Pietro in Vincoli was built, with the nearby Sette Sale, cisterns which furnished, he thought, not only the baths but also the *naumachiæ* (mock naval battles) in the Colosseum, and then 'an infinity of underground rooms… partly filled by rubbish from nearby gardens, partly covered with earth'. The largest vault was of immense depth and 25' wide, lit by windows in the vault.[134]

The most visited were the BATHS OF CARACALLA (see ill. overleaf) to the south. The comte de Caylus offered historical deductions: 'What remains is brick. One can see that this was previously better clad, and one can make an estimate of it from the magnificent columns and marbles which the Jesuits have taken or excavated from this building, which they use for ball games. What one can see of it is not very much; I climbed up to the highest point.' In 1721 Breval observed workmen digging, and finding an abundance of arms, legs and fragments of marble and alabaster. A strange story began to circulate that the marble seats found in such baths were to allow so many people 'to bathe separately', in this case 1,600 claimed Thompson. Smollett suggested that 2,300 people could bathe at the one time without being seen by one another, and that the pipes were of silver and the lamps of crystal. Despite her classical education, Marianna Starke in the last decade of the century declared that 'most of the apartments destined for bathing are buried under ground, and the

Abraham Ducros, Baths of Caracalla, *1780s*

whole building is in so imperfect a state as to be scarcely worth a minute observation'.[135]

The BATHS OF DIOCLETIAN (see ill. opposite) on the Esquiline had other attractions: the tradition that they were built by Christians and the fact that Michelangelo had built a magnificent church into them. Berkeley measured the eight pillars of granite in the church and found them fifteen feet in circumference. Breval noted that eighteen of the best busts in the Farnese collection were found here and that Queen Christina 'turned up a great part of it without any success'. Part of the baths was occupied by the public granaries built, he claimed, by Clement X. This was rather the work of Gregory XIII in 1575, but it was Clement XI who enlarged them in 1705. Stolberg in 1792 had the benefit of a lecture on the baths from his guide Aloïs Hirt, who stressed their importance to the Romans for both mind and body, with four halls for philosophers, poets and orators, Greek and Latin libraries, and temples to Minerva and Mercury, patrons of science and bodily exercise.[136]

The ruins of the CIRCUS MAXIMUS (see ill. Vol. III) were almost invisible and attracted little attention. De Blainville described them in 1707 as 'all cover'd over with Kitchen Gardens'. De Sade in 1775 lamented that 'where fifteen thousand spectators once were easily accomodated in the seating, now only the outline remains, without the least race to show any remains of its magnificence'; the site was now used to grow cabbages and salad.[137]

The CIRCUS OF MAXENTIUS along the via Appia was universally known as that of Caracalla (see ill. Vol. I). In 1717 Berkeley reported seeing a good part of the wall and the metæ (turning-posts) standing, with two towers at one end and the imperial box along the side. Lady Philippina Knight unkindly wrote of dining at a house adjoining 'the stable of Caracalla'. Such were the pretensions of that emperor, which were still accepted. This was the mausoleum of Maxentius' son Romulus. The old story of the pots in the walls of the circus being for acoustic reasons was retold by Archenholz. By c. 1780, however, Riesch was able to declare that the round building was not a cavalry hall but a tomb.[138]

The city since the end of the sixteenth century was famous for its OBELISKS. Berkeley summed up brilliantly: 'the Roman emperors in their greatest glory valued themselves upon bringing them from Egypt; and the most spirited of the popes looked upon it as the greatest event of his life to be able to place one of them on its pedestal'. In connection with the Montecitorio shaft, de Blainville saw parts of the

Filippo Juvarra, Baths of Diocletian, c. *1710*

horologium in a cellar near S Lorenzo in Lucina where it was discovered in 1463 while digging the tomb of Cardinal Filippo Calandrini, and where it still lies. The obelisk itself, discovered in 1512 near S Lorenzo in Lucina, was partly visible to Breval in 1721 in a cobbler's cellar, 'to which it serves as a Wall on one side'. It was reerected by 1792. Goethe described it as 'lying in a courtyard amidst dirt and rubble', 'now in fragments, and some sides have been damaged, probably by fire'. He ordered wax impressions of sphinxes, men and birds. Stolberg's guide Aloïs Hirt told him it had originally belonged to the pharaoh who oppressed the Israelites, and was therefore without hieroglyphs because of his disgrace! It in fact was the work of Psammetichos II (594-589). The Pincian obelisk (erected in 1822) was discovered in 1740. De Brosses in this connection noted ominously that the French king was given anything which he wanted. In the Barberini gardens he saw the obelisk in three pieces, which he thought came from the Circus of Maxentius; in fact it was from near S Croce. De Brosses' project was to buy it and set it up in piazza San Luigi as a memorial to his and his friends' visit to Rome. In 1783 Mary Berry saw preparations for the erection of the obelisk of the Quirinal. The 'Horsetamers' had to be turned from being parallel to facing outwards from each other; 'workmen were polishing the pillar, and mending it where it had been broken'. Goethe, finally in 1787, was present during the digging of the foundations for the erection of the obelisk of Trinità dei Monti.[139]

We have visited the mausoleum of Augustus in the Campus Martius. There were, finally, many other last resting places of the grand and the obscure which the eighteenth century travellers were anxious to see. The great MAUSOLEUM OF HADRIAN (see ills Vols I and III), in its modern guise as Castel Sant'Angelo, was described in detail by Berkeley in 1717: rooms decorated by Perino del Vaga, Giulio Romano and Polidore Caravaggio, an archive containing the 'Donation of Constantine' (proved a mediæval forgery by Lorenzo della Valle in 1440), the treasury, and the armoury. He mentions two prisoners: a Spanish archbishop, recently arrested, and a Greek archbishop, imprisoned in 1703 (Giacomo Alii). Although other visitors stressed the fort's weakness, Montesquieu more insightfully stated that it was what made the

G. B. Piranesi, Santa Costanza, *1748-88*

popes masters of the city. It was true, on the other hand, that, as Smollett stressed, 'it could not hold out half a day against a battery of ten pieces properly directed', and it could not longer serve as a refuge now that the popes lived on the Quirinal.[140]

Outside the city were two more imperial mausolea. That of COSTANZA on the via Nomentana was frequently visited. The famous porphyry urn was still in place. De Blainville told the story that Paul II was taking it for his tomb, but he died (1471) while it was being removed and his successor Sixtus IV replaced it. Caylus declared that the 'temple of Bacchus', as it was known, was not magnificent, but so much had been taken to adorn the neighbouring church; the sarcophagus he liked only for its stone. Berkeley claimed that the body of Constantia had been taken out and buried under the altar. He recognised that the true identity of the monument had been found, but Keysler noted that some thought it the tomb of Cicero's daughter Tullia, and others another Tullia, the wife of Tarquin II, last king of

Rome (such the fantasies that a name evoked). De Brosses also rejected the general high admiration for the sarcophagus: he found the figures 'rudely worked and lacking finish. It is folly to attempt to carve so hard a stone.' De Sade liked it better and declared it the sarcophagus of Constantia, Constantine's daughter, which he imagined had originally been in the mausoleum of Hadrian, but her body was stolen by the barbarians. Julius II wished to be buried here: 'it is always a kind of enjoyment for an old pope to think that after his death his ashes will be in the same place as those of a pretty virgin' was de Sade's comment. The other imperial mausoleum outside the city, that of HELEN, Constantine's mother, on the via Casilina, was rarely visited. Keysler in 1730 recorded that the sarcophagus, which pope Anastasius IV (1153-4) was going to use for himself, was now in S Giovanni Laterano.[141]

It would be logical here to include also the tomb of CÆCILIA METELLA on the via Appia, but no visitor gave more than the standard description, apart from the note that the urn was now in the palazzo Farnese.

The most special tomb in Rome, and therefore deserving its own category, was the PYRAMID OF CESTIUS (see ill. Vol. I). The old misunderstandings continued. Because Cestius had been an *epulo*, a priesthood which provided feasts for the gods, de Blainville became fantastical: 'History tells us that this man was not only one of the greatest Eaters, but one of the hardest Drinkers of his time in all Italy'! The paintings inside the tomb were said to have 'preserved their freshness extremely well'. Caylus reported in 1715 that the Senate had the key to the door and for some few years no one had entered. De Brosses in 1740 did enter, guided by marchese Galli, only to find that the 'famous little antique paintings… have almost totally disappeared'. Further misunderstandings proliferated: such a great tomb for a mere triumvir (*sic*): 'what European monarch has built himself so expensive a mausoleum as this one?' (Many!) By Smollett's account in 1765, Cestius had been promoted to consular status (yet another proof that no one could be bothered to understand the inscription); the paintings were described as 'almost effaced'. De Sade made a serious allegation: some paintings had been cut out and taken to the Kircher Museum.[142]

G. B. Piranesi, Columbarium of the Arruntii, *1757*

De Sade draws our attention to two COLUMBARIA which he locates in the same garden as Minerva Medica (at this time, villa Magnani), one for a family, the other 'communal'. The bodies had been cremated and placed in urns in the niches. He calls the family the Arruncii; we now rather read Arruntii (*CIL* 6.5931f); of the other cemetery he cites C. Clodius Triumphus (*CIL* 6.5898).[143] The columbarium of the Arruntii had been discovered in 1735, and was illustrated by Piranesi (*Antichità romane* vol. 2). The other cemetery, opposite, was found in 1731.

Few, finally, sought out an infamous site: the CAMPUS SCELERATUS. De Blainville visited these tombs of the unchaste Vestals, which he located at the end of Sallust's Circus, between the Baths of Diocletian and the Pincian. De Sade located them in the villa Mendosi near the porta Salaria, and described entering the 'vaults' and 'cellars', their entrances covered with thorns and shrubs, and the danger of snakes. The campus was, however, not inside the porta Salaria, but the porta Collina of the Servian Wall.[144]

COLLECTIONS OF ANTIQUITIES

Apart from the many palaces and villas, the main collection of antiquities was housed in the CAPITOLINE MUSEUM. De Blainville in 1707 thought the lion devouring a horse was the finest thing in the Conservatori, while the 'greatest rarity' was the head of Brutus, 'indisputably antique and the only one of its kind in Rome'. In the Palazzo Nuovo he joked about how Lassells had thought the *lex de imperio Vespasiani* (the law conferring powers on Vespasian in 70) was the Twelve Tables (a mere five centuries earlier). Caylus stated that the 'most beautiful piece' was an Agrippina (see ill. opposite), but that the reliefs of Marcus Aurelius were superb. Breval offered notes on some provenances: the Horse and lion came from outside porta Ostiense, and was repaired by Michelangelo; Hadrian in a toga from S Stefano Rotondo on the Cælian; the four statues of Isis from the villa Verospi under Clement XI; and the She-wolf from the Forum Boarium under Sixtus IV. Silhouette singled out the She-wolf, the Fasti, the *lex de imperio*, the Arretino (still called the slave overhearing the Catilinarian conspirators) and the Spinario (see ill. Vol. I). Thompson in 1731 noted that the inscription of Duilius was at the foot of the stairs leading to the Capitol. De Brosses' description in 1740 brings the collection to life:

> Let us enter the apartments. Here is the statue of Marius – a unique statue, although there exist busts of him. It has been here since time immemorial, and is traditionally known to be his portrait. Here, too, is the Gladiator (il Mirmillone), an exquisite work in the highest style of antique art. No more perfect figure can be imagined, nor a more touching expression; this comes from the gardens of Sallust, the pope having bought it some time ago from the Ludovisi family. Here is a torso; the head is supposed to have been that of Virgil. What a shame to think of all the medals struck to commemorate emperors and kings, and not one struck in honour of the most illustrious man of antiquity! Would you not prefer one medal of Virgil to five hundred of Tiberius? But why this should be the torso of Virgil

is not known. Here is the bronze Wolf giving suck to the twins; this, too, has been here for ages. I remarked with satisfaction the mark of the lightning which has run along the side of the leg, and which partly melted it, when it was struck in the year of Cicero's consulate [63 BC]. You know how much he made use of that event in his third harangue against Catiline. A little further on is the statue of Leo X in bronze, with his apoplectic fat neck, and one is not surprised, after seeing this, that he died suddenly in his forty-seventh year. I regret it, for he loved the arts, knew much about them, and if he had lived to the usual age of the popes would have brought together many beautiful things. In the same apartment are the original Consular Decrees, written on marble fixed on the walls; these are called the Capitolian Marbles, and are by far the most curious things here. Among many other inscriptions are some of great value; that, for instance, relating to the consulate of the two Gemini [AD 29], during which Consulate our Saviour was crucified, and that in the Regia containing the ratification of what Commodus had done before his advent to the throne, &c.

Seated Agrippina (*Capitoline Museums*)

It is amazing that de Brosses mistook the date of Jesus' crucifixion as 29 instead 33. A most detailed catalogue was offered by Volkmann in 1758, but he made hardly any comment, save principally that the Conservatori contained the biggest collection of statues in Rome and that one should tip the keeper 3 *paoli*. Smollett admitted that he visited the museum only once, but especially liked 'a bacchanalian drunk', Leda and the swan, an old hired mourner 'very much resembling those wrinkled hags still employed in Ireland and in the Highlands of Scotland, to sing the *coronach* at funerals', Antinoüs, the two Fauns, and above all, the Dying Gladiator (see ill. Vol. III): 'the attitude of the body, the expression of the countenance, the elegance of the limbs, and the swelling of the muscles', not to mention the back muscles and the spine. Burney noted that the Castor and Pollux were not admired. The hands and feet of the colossal statue were then thought to be those of Apollo, brought from Pontus by Lucullus. The seated Agrippina was 'to the last degree exquisite: such drapery and expression as I never saw in sculpture'. He naturally paid great attention to any musical instruments: a faun with his pipe, Apollo with a very large lyre. A woman's perspective is provided by Lady Anne Miller: she found Zeno's portrait (founder of the Stoics) 'very ugly and is so characteristic of the idea I had formed of him, that I am persuaded it must be extremely like what he was'! Venus emerging from the bath was bound not to be missed: 'esteemed a powerful figure here, yet I think, was she dressed, she would appear too plump for the present taste'. Riesch declared that the Dying Gladiator was a dying herald – because Winckelmann said that statues were never made of gladiators. The mosaic of the doves (see ill. Vol. III), on the other hand, was the most 'accomplished' one could find. Goethe took the opportunity to recommend again seeing statues by torchlight. The so-called Pyrrhus was 'a piece of excellent workmanship', and the half-length figure of a draped Venus was 'splendid', while the nude Venus was 'the most beautiful statue of its kind in Rome'. For Smith the head of Medusa and the relief of the head of Mithradates in relief were 'above all praise', while the mosaic of the doves 'was acknowledged to be the best thing of the kind which we have received from the ancients'. Stolberg, accompanied by Hirt, particularly noticed at first the head of Brutus, perhaps Etruscan, 'serious, powerful, noble' and the Spinario, 'one of the most beautiful works of art that have descended to modern times'. On a later visit, he declared the mosaic of the drinking birds 'a most animated and inimitable expression of lovely nature', but the Venus did not compare with the Medici version, and he disagreed with Hirt who declared that the Dying Gaul was the one killed by Manlius, because the depiction did not, in fact, agree with Livy.[145]

There were also private collections not belonging to famous families. Grosley in 1758 visited the collection of GIUSEPPE ASSEMANI, keeper of the Vatican Library 1739-68, noted for its cameos, especially a Cleopatra in agate onyx. His items came from Arabia, Egypt and Judæa.[146]

Addison in 1701 mentions mosaics of gladiators in the collection of a cardinal, whom infuriatingly he does not name. These showed a *retiarius* (net and trident man) fighting a Samnite, who, although completely enveloped in his opponent's net, eventually won, and a *pinnirapus* (crest-snatcher) armed like a Samnite, and his antagonist with two *pinnæ* (feathers) on his helmet.[147]

Addison also mentioned 'one of the finest statues in Rome', the Meleager with a spear and the head of a boar on one side, of Parian marble, 'as yellow as ivory'. This belonged to the FUSCONI (now in the Vatican). De Blainville described the Meleager and an equally famous Venus as belonging to the PICHINI collection, a family related to the Fusconi. Arundel had offered 20,000 *scudi* for the two.[148]

In the palazzo CESARINI Addison saw busts of all the Antonine family, excavated two years before, near Albano, supposedly in a villa of Marcus Aurelius. They were all 'incomparably well cut'.[149]

The same visitor also mentioned a collection belonging to ANTONIO POLITO, where he examined various bowls (*pateræ*).[150]

Only two of our eighteenth century visitors mention EXCAVATIONS. The first is de Sade, who in 1775 mentions such works at Marmorata, below the Aventine. The discoveries included entire walls and very solid brick buildings (presumably the famous warehouses), and nearby, appropriately, a mass of broken marble. 'The profusion is such that bases and capitals of columns of the most beautiful marble and the most delicate workmanship today serve as tables of the leaser of this vigna and the stairs of his house are of the same.' The other excavation was the famous one in 1777 in the villa Peretti:

> July 5th Went with Tresham to see the Antique Rooms just discovered, by digging for antient Bricks, in the Villa Negroni – The painted Ornaments much in the Chinese taste – figures of Cupids bathing &c and painted in *fresco* on the Stucco of the Walls – The Reds, purples, Blues & Yellows very bright – but had a dark & heavy effect – NB Tresham made a Purchase of these paintings for 50 Crowns, to be taken off the walls at his Own Expence –

Mary Berry in 1784 saw the same thing. The digging had reached 35 palms (nearly 8 metres). 'They had got out a number of broken columns, pieces of marble and some medals.'[151]

CONTEMPORARY ROME

The basic statistics are given by Jean-Baptiste Labat at the beginning of the century. Rome then contained about 140,000 inhabitants, including 8-10,000 Jews. There were forty bishops, 2,646 priests, 3,556 monks and 1814 nuns, not to mention 393 courtesans, and the city contained eighty one churches. Montesquieu in 1729 quoted as his source the marchese Bolognetti: 144,000 (an increase of 24,000 since 1675), of whom about only 10% had both mother and father born in Rome. By 1776 John Moore gave 170,000, with 9,000 Jews, but de la Platière at the same time calculated 130-140,000, rising to 150,000 if one included foreigners. In the 170,000 Dupaty in 1785 included 10,000 mendicants, and calculated the clergy at one sixth.

In 1805 the Swiss naturalist Charles de Bonstetten gave very detailed population figures for the eighteenth century, showing an increase from 138,000 in 1716 to 166,000 in 1796. More important, however, was his breakdown of these totals into males and females, revealing a grave imbalance: men exceeded women by 25%, so that, as Bonstetten put it, half the population engaged in 'illegitimate amours'. Some two thousand immigrants arrived each year.[152]

De Brosses explained the effect of the population distribution:

> Although the town is large, it has not the air of a capital, and the life here resembles more that of one of our provincial towns than that of Paris, where all is tumult and variety... Spacious as Rome is, a third part is about all that is occupied. Here you cannot sneeze without its being known; gossip is rampant, but you can do just as you please, and I think that on the whole there is no more agreeable or more comfortable town in Europe; and I would sooner live here even than in Paris.

At precisely the same time (1740), Horace Walpole gave another view:

> I am very glad that I see Rome while it yet exists: before a great number of years are elapsed, I question whether it will be worth seeing. Between the ignorance and poverty of the present Romans, everything is neglected and falling to decay; the villas are entirely out of repair, and the palaces so ill kept, that half the pictures are spoiled by damp.

In the 1770s, Martin Sherlock identified 'munificence, hypocrisy and sadness' as the three chief characteristics of the city: the grandness of the palaces and churches; the hypocrisy because there were 'as many courts as cardinals' and women were 'reserved in public, wanton in private'; and the sadness from the lack of public entertainment, the small population, the sirocco wind, and the common wearing of black. He summed up the main sectors of the population as 'prelates effeminate, nobility illiterate, and the people wicked'. Robert Gray, who was to go on to be bishop of Bristol, agreed. Rome was

> a sad mixture of magnificence and dirt, a slave of ecclesiastical pomp and wretched poverty, a city of spiritual pride and hideous beggary, where vice and sin of every kind predominate, where prostitution holds out its lures at every window, where

assassinations are daily committed in the face of day and known murderers beg for charity under the porches of every church.

And Montesquieu adds a keen insight: 'What is special at Rome is to see a city where women do not give it its tone, as they do everywhere else. Here, it is the priests.'[153]

The first impression of the eighteenth century city was the STREETS. Labat declared the three running off piazza del Popolo to be the most beautiful in the city: bordered by beautiful houses, important palaces and magnificent churches. They were also, however, badly paved, extremely dirty and 'interlarded' with many poor houses which disfigured them. They therefore became very muddy in winter and very dusty in summer, when water carts were employed to keep down the dust. The Romans, he claimed, had no knowledge of street sweeping, relying on Providence and rain. The paving broke up, because the small stones had no firm foundation. By day was one thing; night was another. There was no lighting. Lanterns were, of course, carried but anyone could demand: 'Turn away the lantern!' if they did not want to be recognised. Sherlock went so far as to say that it was 'the worst lighted city in Europe', given that there were no flambeaux.[154]

Visitors of all nations complained of the DIRT. One would expect Tobias Smollett, of course, to complain:

> This great plenty of water, nevertheless, has not induced the Romans to be cleanly. Their streets, and even their palaces, are disgraced with filth. The noble Piazza Navona, is adorned with three or four fountains, one of which is perhaps the most magnificent in Europe, and all of them discharge vast streams of water: but, notwithstanding this provision, the piazza is almost as dirty as West Smithfield, where the cattle are sold in London. The corridores, arcades, and even staircases of their most elegant palaces, are depositories of nastiness, and indeed in summer smell as strong as spirit of hartshorn. I have a great notion that their ancestors were not much more cleanly.

Jean Marie de la Platière agreed: Rome was the filthiest city. There was 'ordure in every ally, in the porticoes of palaces, on the stairs, in the corridors, up to the doors of antechambers. And the odour of urine especially attacks the nose and affects the heart everywhere.' The Romans did not notice, or claimed that all this was a valuable antidote against malaria. Johann Archenholz declared that 'filth infects all the great places of Rome except that of St Peter's': the entrances to palaces and houses were 'receptacles of the most disgustful wants'.[155]

There were ways to gain a more savoury impression of the city. De Brosses listed the view from the Janiculum as one of the three highlights of Rome: 'when the sun begins to decline is the time to look down on this crowd of domes, towers, and golden cupolas, churches, palaces, verdant trees, and sparkling waters. No view of Paris equals this, although I must allow that our suburbs are far superior to those of Rome.'[156]

Trying to put the unpleasant impressions behind us, we may visit some of the main features of the city, apart from churches, palaces and villas. The BORGO drew de Brosses' attention:

> The whole space might with advantage be cleared between the bridge and the colonnade, and the ugly little buildings which separate the Borgo-Vecchio from the via Transpontino should be taken down, and a fine avenue of trees planted, or, if possible, a colonnade built.[157]

That plan was to be carried out two centuries later.

The CORSO is best described by Goethe: lined with high and, for the most part, magnificent buildings, to which its width bears no relationship; for it was 'barely sufficient for three carriages to drive abreast'. Every Sunday and holiday all the 'eminent and wealthy Romans' for an hour or more before sunset drove their carriages up and down in one long unbroken line, between piazza Venezia and the ponte Milvio. The carriages kept to their left, but ambassadors and the Young Pretender had the right to drive down the middle in either direction (!) between the two lines. As soon as the evening bell was rung, however, total disorder ensued as each driver sought the quickest way home. Anne Miller described cattle being killed at the doors of the butchers in the same street.[158]

We have, unfortunately, only a brief – but vivid – description of one of the most famous haunts of the traveller, the ENGLISH COFFEE HOUSE (*caffè degli Inglesi*) in piazza di Spagna: 'a filthy vaulted room, the walls of which were painted with Sphinxes, Obelisks and Pyramids, from capricious designs of Piranesi, and fitter to adorn the inside of an Egyptian Sepulchre, than a room of social conversation'.[159] Such was the judgement of the artist Thomas Jones.

We are indebted to the Swedish naturalist Johann Ferber, who provides an extensive list of plants to be found at Rome, for giving us an impression of GARDENS in the city. 'The beauty of the Italian gardens and views is partly owing to spontaneous forests or planted tufts of deciduous trees and evergreens, whose variety is extremely pleasing to the eyes.' The trees included oak, plane, poplar, ash, elm, beach, chestnut, pines and cypresses. In Rome there was a Botanical Garden belonging to the University, 'well provided with plants, sufficiently spacious, though planted without much respect for symmetry'. In 1772 the Inspector was the surgeon Liberato Sabati. The professor of Botany, abate Giovanni Maratti, lectured here, and together they were publishing *Theatrum horti romani* (in fact, Maratti's *Flora romana* was published posthumously in 1822). In 1787 the English botanist James Smith said of the botanical garden on the Janiculum near the aqua Paola: 'we never examined one more indigent'.[160]

Rome was famous for its FOUNTAINS. De Blainville declared that the most beautiful was in the piazza Navona, 'the most magnificent in all Europe', followed by the aqua Felice, with the two granite lions from the temple of Serapis and the other two of marble by Flaminio Vacca. Montesquieu singled out the aqua Paola, in the form of a huge portal, and summed up by saying that the Roman fountains were superior to those of Versailles (see ill. opposite). De Brosses declared that three things made all the trouble of a visit to Rome worthwhile: St Peter's, the fountains, and the view from the Janiculum. His favourites also were the piazza Navona and the aqua Paola, and during his visit (1740) the Trevi fountain was being transformed from a 'neglected and rustic' water into one of the most handsome. By 1780, when Isaak Riesch visited the city, the Trevi fountain could be assessed. He found much to criticise, as often with new art: Ocean's legs were 'too turned', he was too tight in his niche, the horses were poorly done, the Tritons

G. B. Piranesi, View of the Fountainhead of the Acqua Paola on Monte Aureo, *1751*

looked rather hard, and horses do not naturally walk on rocks! De Sade especially liked the Triton fountain in piazza Barberini when the water froze, because of the way the water formed a kind of turban on his head. Charles Duclos agreed that there was nothing to equal the magnificent fountains, and went so far as to declare that by comparison, the Seine was a drain! The aqua Paola also caught Goethe's eye, for its happy device of the use of a triumphal arch for the entrance into the city not of a conqueror but a peaceful benefactor. Someone, of course, had to protest that it would have been better to have the water emerge more naturally over a pile of rocks, to which the answer was that the water was not natural, but brought by an aqueduct.[161]

A notable feature of Rome was the JEWISH GHETTO (see ill. overleaf), established by Paul IV in the 1550s. In 1761 Christopher Hervey, who strongly disapproved of Italian tyranny, judged that the Roman Jews were better off than those in Spain and Portugal, but he pitied them greatly nonetheless. 'If persecution alone can prove a religion, that of the Jews has more right at present to be true than any.' De la Platière

Giuseppe Vasi, Piazza Giudea *(the entrance to the ghetto at the right rear), 1754*

attended a Jewish funeral, and everything was explained to him; he bemoaned the Jews' situation. Friedrich Meyer recorded the new repressive measures of Pius VI in 1775: reclusion at night was transgressed on pain of death, the Jews were banned from convents, churches, and hospitals, forbidden to have Christian servants, suffered corporal punishment for using a horse or carriage, and were to conduct burials in silence and not to have a tombstone, but at least their forced naked race in the Carnival had now been suppressed. Charles Dupaty in 1785 gave their numbers as 7,000 and contradicted Hervey: the Jews were 'more miserable here than in other parts of Europe'. The weekly sermons continued, in which 'a missionary loads them with insults, and for the slightest inattention a sbirri [*sic*: *sbirro*, a policeman] bestows on them a caning'. Archenholz gave their numbers as 10,000 and described them as all living 'in real slavery'.[162]

The various piazze attracted comment, and show us a different society two centuries ago. PIAZZA NAVONA (see ill. opposite) was a major public space. De Blainville declared it 'unquestionably the most magnificent' square in the city. The Jewish clothing market was held here twice a week, recorded Labat. In summer it was flooded to a depth of three feet an hour before sunset. Karl Pöllnitz described the crowds hanging out of the surrounding windows and standing around the edges, shouting when a carriage took water or tipped over. And at the other end of the piazza might be a Jesuit preaching to penitents. De Brosses remarked on the piazza's dirtiness, because of the vegetable market. Johannes Tischbein liked to visit the Thursday market, in search of cheap antiquities, but he was always forestalled by the agents of the antiquarians. The other space which inspired most comment was PIAZZA DEL POPOLO (see ill. Vol. I), the entrance to the city for most visitors. De Blainville stated the essential: 'it must be confessed that on entering Rome by this gate [porta Flaminia] the prospect which presents itself gives a very high Idea of the City'. Berkeley remarked on the effect intended by Sixtus V, who set up the obelisk, so that 'your prospect shoots through these three streets', the middle

Gian Paolo Panini, Piazza Navona, *1756. The piazza is flooded and crowded with carriages, which are proceeding around the perimeter in two files going in opposite directions, apart from a few individualists in the middle. The surrounding balconies are crowded with spectators*

one (the Corso) 'carrying the eye... almost to the Capitol'. Johann Keysler enthused:

> The large noble area, an astonishing obelisk, a superb fountain, two beautiful churches exactly resembling each other, three fine streets running in a direct line, as if they were drawn from the centre of the obelisk; all these must have an uncommon effect on the mind of a stranger at the first view.

The two churches had been remodelled to seem to constitute a pair in the 1670s. Dr Charles Burney in 1770 did not even mind being held up by the customs so that he could feast his eyes on 'this grand and noble spectacle' of the piazza, the obelisk, the two churches and the three streets. There were, however, less enthusiastic appraisals. Pöllnitz complained that on the left after S Maria were 'very bad houses or sheds' and on the right hay stores and poor huts. And Duclos complained that the piazza did not measure up to the place Vendôme with its noble and uniform architecture: here there were low, irregular houses, most of them stables or grain stores. The explanation of the contrasting views was provided by de Brosses:

> Nothing can give a finer idea of the grandeur of Rome than this first sight of the town: but one must always look straight ahead – not to the right or left hand of the square; if you do so you will see on the right hand only some ugly large barns, and on the left the Church of S Maria, a poor building, and near it a row of very small buildings, so that although the Piazza del Popolo contains some fine things, it can scarcely be called a very beautiful one. Such contrasts are common here: it is either palace or hovel.[163]

The great transformation of the piazza by Valadier had to await the nineteenth century.

Most travellers stayed in or around the PIAZZA DI SPAGNA, as they done since last century. Pöllnitz was again critical. It was too narrow and too long, and still only half-paved. The stairway had cost 60,000 *scudi*, but he thought the money ill-spent: it was Gothic in taste, and although only five years old, was already falling into ruin. It was, however, already an attraction: everyone came in the evening 'to breathe a lot of dust and the worst air in Rome'. One was beset by beggars and in danger of being run over. Charles Thompson a decade later in 1731 agreed: the piazza was 'far from handsome', but it was the rendez vous of all the Beau Monde. Every evening women arrived in coaches for an hour or two to be greeted by men, but those on foot were almost choked by the dust or crushed between the coaches.

Today the main feature of the piazza is the steps. They were built by Francesco de Sanctis between 1723 and 1726. Their forgotten history is recalled by the travellers. Wright in 1721 saw the models for the work, 'which indeed is much wanted... [T]he ascent (to the church) was not only rude and wild, but troublesome and difficult.' By 1729 Montesquieu recorded the stairway as finished, paid for by an old legacy from a French auditor of the Rota. 'It is a bad work; part fell last winter during a flood.' He returned to the subject. It was in bad taste, he declared, without any kind of architecture, and only the first ramps could be seen. It needed some fine columns. In 1739 de Brosses revealed that 'this gigantic work has been carelessly done, and it is already going to pieces'. The French benefactor referred to by Montesquieu is revealed as Cardinal Melchior de Polignac, but Cardinal Pierre de Tencin in vain also claimed the right to be mentioned in the inscriptions.[164]

About the TIBER de Blainville was scathing. It was 'a pitiful, paultry stream... Catullus, Virgil, Horace and Ovid and all their Brethren must have been real Gascons to boast as much as they do of this river.' It is 'every Day up to the Ears in the vilest Nastiness and Filth'. It could also be dangerous. He recorded that in the floods of 1598, 1500 people perished. Twenty years later (1731), Keysler agreed: the water of the Tiber was 'so thick and foul that it is not fit for horses to drink till it has stood two or three days'. Thomas Spence met the flood of 1740. De Brosses identified another problem:

> There are no quays along the banks of the Tiber – an immense fault in so ornate a town. Owing to this the portions of the city near the river are the worst by far – that of the Jews a perfect

Gaspar van Wittel, The Tiber near the Porto di Ripa Grande, c. *1711*

kennel. If quays were built they would be the greatest benefit and ornament that could be given to the city.

The 'quays' which de Brosses desired were the embankments constructed from the 1870s. Sherlock was driven to comparison: 'There is not a river in Europe less beautiful than the Tiber, not a character in history more dreadful than that of Augustus.' Goethe's courage then may be appreciated: 'In the evening I bathed in the Tiber from a well appointed and safe bathing machine.'[165]

It is significant that few travellers offered comments on TRASTEVERE. Apart from St Peter's they rarely ventured there. Archenholz is an exception: 'rude, unpolished manners joined to bodily deformity are the common attributes of the inhabitants of this part', as well as 'having recourse to knives upon the smallest incident'.[166]

The workings of the GOVERNMENT called forth a torrent of criticism from the travellers. Duclos in 1767 described it as 'one of the worst in Europe': factionalised and self-seeking. No reform was possible of areas such as agriculture and justice. And the abbé Gabriel Coyer had described the pope as 'the most absolute sovereign in Europe'. Under Pius VI, however, these French commentators began to change their tone. De la Platière declared that Rome had the most moderate government in Italy, citing the lowest taxes and greatest freedom.

Dupaty admitted that the pope was notionally absolute, but noted that he was limited by the poverty of his revenue, the smallness of his army, the power of the police, and the powerlessness of the tribunals. Finances were a matter of 'fraud and rapine', justice was perverted by asylum and patronage. He summed up Rome as the most secure political state, the most peaceful social state, and the most wretched civil state. As for political stability, Dupaty wickedly used the metaphor of the infamous Roman lottery: 'The greatest fault the popes can commit against the Romans is to live too long, to retard the drawing of a lottery in which everyone has tickets, and which contains prizes for everyone.' The Pole Moszyński, finally, focussed on foreign policy:

> The pope is no longer, so to say, the centre of neutrality and mediation. He is no longer the arbitor, but the injured party. Ministers do not negotiate and are sometimes the most ignorant of all. Roman policy is entirely limited, moreover, to not yielding to the stronger and a few little intrigues, in which the main movers are the coachman, the valet, the maid or the singer.[167]

The other major determinant of foreign policy was the ARMED FORCES at the state's disposal. Many commented on Rome's inadequate defences. Archenholz at the end of the century described the army as 2,000 men, and the navy as five ships in very bad condition. In 1761, however, Hervey noted that the papal fleet was setting out against the Turks. 'The papal galleys, the *St Peter* and *St Paul*, to which has been lately added the *St Prospero*, go out every summer to cruise against the Turks and the Moors.'

There was also the SWISS GUARD. Hervey declared that the officers were subservient to the commander-in-chief of the papal forces, an ecclesiastic, Monsignor Piccolomini. Archenholz recorded the guard's notorious 'rudeness and stupidity'. One so abused an Englishman that in revenge he shot the first one he came across; another, when ordered to prevent anyone entering the Vatican Library, because the pope was coming, blocked the pope. Staszic was his critical self: 'The papal Swiss seemed to me like harlequins. Whatever does this mean? The pope ought to be surrounded by people dressed decently for the Church and not for the theatre.'[168]

Various visitors mentioned the POLICE, commonly known as the *sbirri* (spies). Labat claimed that the *bargello* (chief) had three hundred spies at his command. One visitor who had personal experience of them was Michel Merville *c.* 1720. He was stopped by a midnight patrol, armed with swords, guns and long rods with hooks (to catch those who tried to run away!). Rome, he claimed, was safe by night, although the *bargello* had only one hundred men. Another duty was to ask travellers how much they were paying, to see that they were not overcharged. This reassuring testimony is, however, undercut by his claim that all Jews, all cake-sellers (*ciambellari*) and all watersellers were spies! Christopher Hervey saw the advantages: 'I do not think there are any cleverer [spies] than those of Rome, or that any government has better intelligence of the little things that pass in their state than this.'[169]

'In Rome there is nowhere as convenient as churches for prayer and murder,' declared Montesquieu. If you do not like the look of anyone, you simply get a servant to stab him two or three times and run into a church. He will come out wearing the uniform of some prince or cardinal (and so be safe). He quoted the case of a monk, who shot his confessor and sought religious asylum. This institution was the main encouragement to murder. Richard noted that there were few cities where so many CRIMES attracted the death penalty, but that the criminal justice system was impossible to understand: the nature of the courts, the resort to protection, and the difficulties of proof all meant that most criminals escaped. As for the crime rates, Richard recorded that between December 1761 and July 1762 there were twenty stabbings. In June and July, however, he claimed, the government took no notice, regarding this as a 'necessary result of the fermentation of the blood'. Duclos suggested that often a thief was punished more severely than a murderer. He refers to the *strappado*, whereby the guilty had his arms tied behind him, was raised to a considerable height and then dropped, usually dislocating the shoulders. Meyer stated that assassination was rife, but that compassion usually went to the assassin: 'Poverino – ha amazzato un uomo!' (Poor fellow – he's killed a man!). Festivals were the most dangerous time for personal injury; another major cause was the ubiquitous gambling. Archenholz also commented on the frequency of stabbings, but commended the governor, Ferdinando Spinelli, for his reduction of them, when faced with the difficulty that murderers took up residence in the porches of churches for weeks. Goethe recorded that there had been four murders in his quarter (by piazza del Popolo) in three weeks, instancing that of a Swiss, whose killer uncharacteristically stabbed himself instead of taking sanctuary. Stolberg in 1791 calculated that there were five hundred murders a year, but Pius could not reform the police (a strange way to state the problem), because of the system of seeking sanctuary in churches, not to mention taking refuge with ambassadors and cardinals. Alongside these more fatal crimes, Hervey in 1761 recorded a more amusing one. His dog was stolen, but was seen in a coffee house, where the holder claimed that he had bought it. Hervey simply hired a Spanish *bravo*, who soon recovered the dog. And poor Thomas Jones was twice robbed at his lodgings: first of a hat and silver buckles, then most of his linen, all his silk stockings, and 20 golden louis. The culprit was the amorous daughter of the owner, whose advances he had not returned, but nothing could be done about it. The punishment for murder, where carried out, was hideous. Hervey recorded in 1761 that three women had been killed, and Cardinal Camillo Paolucci's coachman was arrested. He was defended by the advocate of the poor (an early system of legal aid). He was executed, quartered in piazza Sant'Angelo, and his head set over the porta Angelica. 'You cannot imagine how eager the people of Rome are to see such a melancholy kind of spectacle. They have been taking places even tonight (the night before), and windows in St Angelo's square... let at I know not how much money.' Burney was horrified at another execution in 1770:

> I was got about half way thither, when I met a great number of people, which increased every moment, till at last the street became impassible either in latitude or longitude, and I was quite hemmed in, and what should come close by me 10 minutes after, but a cart with 2 priests, masqued, and a poor devil in it going to the most disgusting execution in the world. He had murdered a woman, by throwing her out of the window, or some such thing, and was to be amazzato, knocked

on the head; to have his throat cut and have his hands and feet amputated while he was panting and bleeding. It seemed by the account I had of it more like another murder, than the execution of justice. He seemed more dead than alive when I saw him, and will run in my head a long time – the procession was very solemn. There were priests on foot of all orders – singing the Service of the Dead in canto fermo – and the 2 in the cart were Venetian noblemen devoted by the rules of their order to this dreadful task of attending criminals. They are called *Confortori*. One held close to his eyes a crucifix while the other talked to him.

The state of prisons may be imagined, but Labat gives an account of one for children aged ten to sixteen at S Michele a Ripa. He described the workroom, where they were kept, chained by a foot, from morning to evening, spinning cotton or knitting stockings and bonnets. They were 'not spared bread, water and the whip'. The main prison was, of course, Castel Sant'Angelo. Here, for Staszic,

three things caught my attention and made me think: 1) a review of soldiers commanded by a monsignor; 2) an immense building designed for the tomb of a single man: certainly this vain man must have believed that he would be different from everyone else in death; 3) those guilty of treason are here shut away by order of the Holy Father before being judged… Confronted by this tomb of the living, prisoners of despotism without judgement being pronounced, I compared this action with the holiness of those the pope represents. The fortress revealed itself to me as terribly dark, more horrible than seemed to me Spielberg at Brno or Sant'Elmo at Naples.[170]

Rome was the capital of Christendom. Visitors did not fail, however, to detect contradictions. 'As to the Italians, and more especially the Romans, I can aver that I scarce ever met a Man of Parts among them, who could be called a true Believer,' noted de Blainville. And the adaptation of paganism to Christianity disturbed Spence. By the Lacus Curtius was built S Maria Liberatrice in the Forum. The temple of

G. B. Piranesi, The Gothic Arch, *from* Carceri d'invenzione *(*Imaginary Prisons*), c. 1750*

the twins (Castor and Pollux) was now S Teodoro, so he thought, where women still took sick children. The temple of Juno was now S Maria Maggiore, where women still came to pray for children, and nearby a temple of Diana had become St Anthony's, both patrons of animals. Robert Gray also listed many churches established in temples and other pagan buildings, even S Agnese in piazza Navona in 'some public stews'.[171]

The major aspect of Church government which was noticed by travellers, however, was the INQUISITION. Pöllnitz, who can be critical of the Church, declared that this was 'the mildest court in the world'. No honest person had anything to fear; the gravest crimes against the Church required only repentance for absolution – for example, the man who married his daughter! The German Protestant Keysler, however, recommended that 'every prudent traveller should be on his guard, as rather to talk too little than too much'. At the same time he noted that the English were not insulted when they did not kneel at the elevation of the Host. De Brosses returned to a more reassuring view, describing the meetings of the Inquisition each Wednesday at the Minerva: twelve cardinals and a secretary. 'The liberty to think on religious matters, and sometimes even to talk on those subjects, is at least as great in Rome as it is in any other town that I know' (more was revealed than de Brosses realised by his distinction: freedom to think without freedom to express one's thoughts is no freedom). 'It is said [*sic*] no one is imprisoned unless proof of his fault is thoroughly established, and thus the delinquents who accuse themselves of their free will are always pardoned. All takes place in the greatest secrecy.' The abbé Richard stated that the court required 'positive and evident proofs – and once established there is no way to escape the rigour of its laws'. The accused was never told what he was accused of. Perhaps the last word may go to the politician de la Platière: 'the wise man [*sic*] can always live safely in Rome: he breathes the air of freedom; he feels himself in the patrie du monde'.[172]

Allied to this matter was that of CENSORSHIP. The customs were notorious for seizing a vast array of literature as subversive. Lady Mary Montagu several times referred to the inconveniences of postal checks. Hervey in 1761 mentioned the imprisonment of Pagliarini the bookseller for publishing an anti-Jesuit tract, *Wolves in sheep's clothing*. He was eventually freed and went to Portugal, where he found royal employment (there the Order had been banned in 1759). Staszic saw what was coming:

> The best books are banned. What does Rome expect? In all the countries of Europe they read and think, while in Rome, if they don't read and think, surely Europe will think of them.[173]

A seemingly more positive side of ecclesiastical institutions was CHARITY. Labat described at length the Company of the Rosary which gave dowries to girls (50 *scudi* for those marrying, 100 for those entering the Church) in the chapel in S Maria sopra Minerva. Samuel Sharp, however, noted that one young Scottish woman, who had the patronage of the Chevalier, attended so many of these ceremonies as to amass 2,000 *scudi*, and better off girls were reported to pay substitutes to parade on their behalf. De Brosses dilated on the pernicious effects. Charity was one of the vices of the government, encouraging laziness and begging. 'When a poor man's daughter has the protection of a bastard of a Cardinal's apothecary, she is enabled to collect a dowry from five or six different churches, and then farewell to any work... Some good for nothing fellow will marry her for her dowry.' Duclos denounced the dowry system for girls going into convents, when 'depopulation was so striking', as 'castration by monasticism'. More highly regarded were the hospitals for the sick, old, weak, and incurable. All nations had established one for their pilgrims, but here all the sick and all abandoned children were taken. There were also famous orphanages, which did not refuse anyone. Labat noted that the children in these institutions rarely went out, but that when they did, the children walked in pairs, and that carriages stopped to let them pass. With such institutionalised charity, Richard made an insightful observation: there was no charity among individuals. 'The neighbour sees his neighbour fall and does not think he ought to help him up.'[174]

The ECONOMY of Rome creaked at the seams. Montesquieu, not unexpectedly, paid it considerable attention under Benedict XIII. As with many other matters, his notes are scattered and not organized in this account. He commented on the poverty: no cardinal spent more than 2,000 French *livres* (400 *scudi*) on his table, and the marchese Mancini, who had a small picture gallery, gave his servants neither wages nor food, forcing them to live on what they could make showing the pictures. The state lost money because of payments to foreigners, who provided almost all the capital for the banks, and because there were no manufactures. Money came in, on the other hand, especially from Spain and Portugal. Naples sent 500,000 *scudi* worth of wine and fruit each year. There had been an attempt to ban the import of cloth, to protect Roman manufacture, but cardinals and ambassadors fraudulently circumvented it, and the pope lost only his 10% duty. The Roman state was almost the only one to pay for minting money. Benedict had run up a debt of three million *scudi* and cut off the sources of money. The revenue was given as three million *scudi*, of which the Camera Apostolica owed nearly two million; the rest went on state expenses. Income included about one million from Rome itself, and 240,000 from the secret treasury, including the Datary. Some taxes had been removed while expenses had increased, because of the pope's 'exorbitant indulgence' towards the Benedictines, and repairs to the buildings of the Camera Apostolica. Thus Montesquieu. Richard made observant comments in 1761. 'In general the inhabitants of Rome fear work.' His contemporary Duclos agreed: the main profession was sloth. The city depended on the income from foreigners. As for industry, all cloth came from abroad, all carriages came from Milan, and the main item of manufacture was candles. Moszyński in 1785 gave an economic summary:

> The Camera Apostolica is in debt up to its eyes, and prints paper money to help… A few miserable manufactures in silk and a little wine and oil are the total production and trade, and if there were not barter in paintings, antiques and marble work and this lot of foreigners who bring their money here, there might not be a poorer country in Europe. Ten or twelve great families and a few bankers are rich, the rest are modestly off or in poverty.

As de la Platière put it: 'it is rare to be rich, but everyone always wishes to appear so'. Duclos reported that the people were very poor, although food was not costly – but 'everything is dear for the poor'. There were beggars at every turn, but he found both aristocracy and poor very generous. Very few of the middle class lived on commerce or industry. Riesch in 1780 provided some prices: grain was 640 *livres* (130 *scudi*) per *rubio* (a little less than 300 litres), wine was eighteen *paoli* a barrel; lamb cost three *bajocchi* per lb; beef four; veal five; and oil was thirty-two *bajocchi* per *bocal* (a jug, *c.* two litres). He noted that manufactures were limited to some velvet, cloth, cotton and silk; almost everything was imported, and the customs were high. Despite some variation in statistics, we may therefore sum up by saying that manufactures and commerce were minimal, income relied on tariffs, ecclesiastical dues, and foreigners, and poverty was widespread.

De Blainville was informative on the FOOD SUPPLY. The main granaries were in the Baths of Diocletian. The pope had a monopoly on grain, all of which had to be sold to him and was then resold at 100% profit. Each year the same amount had to be bought by each baker; returns were bought back at 50% of the purchase price. The old was then mixed with the new and resold; and the selling measure was 20% short of the buying measure. So bread was light and of poor quality, and the production of grain was falling. This whole system had been established by Donna Olimpia under Innocent X, but Livio Odescalchi, nephew of Innocent XI, made two million *scudi* from grain.[175]

Montesquieu commented on another aspect of the Roman 'economy': 'public SIMONY rules at Rome. The crime has never been seen to reign so openly in the government of the Church. Base men are everywhere put into office.'

Equally infamous was the LOTTERY. The Romans were mad about it, and many lost everything. Each drawing earned 70,000 *scudi* and paid out 10-12,000. Some gamblers even paid women to dream winning numbers for them!

In this list of bizarre sectors of the economy, one cannot finally omit the ART TRADE. Moszyński set the scene. He was collecting for Stanislaus II of Poland. He had bought for about 100 ducats various 'bagatelles': marbles, tables, vases and statues. He complained of the Romans' skill in patching up and falsifying paintings and statues for which they asked ridiculous prices. For one small piece he valued at 150 ducats (300 *scudi*) they asked 1000. Even the English had stopped buying. One could not rival the collections formed over two centuries, and now Cardinal Albani and Clement XIV had exhausted everything. Moszyński saw a copy of a Viennese Correggio, claimed to be original, offered at 1500 ducats; even a Batoni cost fifty ducats (although he *did* charge). And a passable marble statue cost 400-500 – but the English and Russians paid it. At the same time Goethe mentioned some purchases. Tischbein found in the convent near porta del Popolo a *Deposition* by Daniel da Volterra, and Angelika Kauffmann bought it for 1,000 *scudi*. And Count Josef Fries bought an Andrea del Sarto *Madonna* for 600 sequins (1200 *scudi*).[176]

The monetary system itself excited comment. To quote Mary Montagu in 1740: 'I cannot help mentioning what is more curious than all the Antiquitys, which is that there is litterally no money in the whole Town, where they follow Mr Law's System, and live wholly upon Paper. Belloni, who is the greatest Banker not only of Rome but of all Italy, furnish'd me with 50 sequins, which he solemnly swore was all the money he had in the House. They go to market with paper, pay the Lodgings with paper, and in short there is no Specie to be seen, which raises the price of everything to the utmost extravagance, nobody knowing what to ask for their goods.' John Law (1671-1729), Scottish banker, devised the 'Mississippi System' – which collapsed; Girolamo Belloni was especially powerful under Benedict XIV (1740-58). De la Platière in 1776 described the system near breaking point. The *cedule* (paper money – in reality IOUs) were exchangeable at the banks, but only up to 10 *scudi* at a time! This was only with interminable formalities and enormous crowds (de la Platière spent two hours). These *cedule* were filthy and tattered from their endless circulation. It was Pierre Grosley, however, who explained that, when you received your 10 *scudi* out of, say, 200, a new note was issued for the remaining 190, payable only in eighteen months' time!¹⁷⁷

Armed with these notes from travellers on government and economy, we turn to Roman SOCIETY. After the pope (on whom see 'portraits' below) came the CARDINALS. Pöllnitz almost felt sorry for them. Cardinalates were sold for sums ranging from 30,000 to 80,000 *scudi*. Cardinals led terribly sequestered lives, with barely an hour in a day to themselves. When they went out, they had to have three carriages, and if two cardinals met, the senior had precedence. Leopold Mozart in 1770 wrote to his wife that 'You cannot conceive how conceited the clergy are here. Any priest who has the slightest association with a cardinal, thinks himself as good as he, and each cardinal, when on business connected with His Holiness, drives with a cortege of three or four carriages, each of which is filled with his chaplains, secretaries and valets.' Etienne Silhouette noted that the popes ruled through nephews and other confidants, so that the cardinals had only an appearance of power. If we wish to have some idea of the grandeur and importance of the cardinals, however, the abbé Richard's description of the promotion of cardinals in November 1761 is stunning. He described the palace of Cardinal Jean Rochechouart:

Giovanni Paolo Panini, The Piazza Farnese Decorated for a Celebration in
Honor of the Marriage of the Dauphin, *1745*

The principal facade of the palace where the cardinal lived was
decorated with a grand order of Corinthian architecture as high
as the building. Between the columns in niches were placed
statues of the four cardinal virtues with spirits and emblems
relating to them. Above the door which divided the order into
two equal parts was a large niche supported by four columns on
which was placed the statue of Religion leaning on the Church
of France, represented by a little temple placed on a globe with
the arms of France; above were the arms of the pope and below
those of the cardinal with the sash of the Order of the Holy
Spirit. This decoration ended with beautiful vases, figured flares
and intermingled spirits. The whole building was of a solid
frame painted in the colour of rarest marbles and the capitals
and bases of the columns were gilded, as most of the decorative
reliefs. The statues were made of a little frame covered with
plaster to which were given the colour and glow of marble.

In front was a large semi-circular gallery, decorated with
the same taste, large enough to contain one hundred musicians, who formed two choirs of instrumental music and who

responded so that the symphony did not stop. Above this orchestra some metres of the wall of a house were built to make a wide balcony in a big room where the cardinal and ladies could view the facade at their ease. This loggia was lined with red damask strewn with gold lilies; the front was decorated with two twisted columns painted in *lapis cæruli* and hung with a gilded garland. They supported a large pediment with the arms of France. At the other end of the palace which gave on to the opposite quarter was a symphony of hunting horns, hautebois and basses which announced the main festival.

For three days the house was full of clergy and nobility who were continually served refreshments of every kind: glacés, confitures, sorbets, fruits, all in profusion. Richard was astonished at the stomach capacity of some people who gorged while at the same time not hesitating to fill their pockets with anything dry! There were two or three hundred carriages in the neighbourhood, and seven or eight hundred liveried servants. As for the rest of the hierarchy, Richard commented on the poverty and ignorance of the poor clergy, in comparison with the pride and greed of the 'regulars', who were regarded, he claimed, as 'demi gods'.[178]

Among the ARISTOCRACY, in 1721, Pöllnitz reported that the Colonna were the most powerful, after the eclipse of the Pamphili and Orsini; they held the office of Constable by inheritance. The Borghese were the richest, with an income of 116,000 *scudi*. Despite that, Walpole in 1740 was impressed with the nobility's parsimony and the sad lives of the women:

You may judge of the affluence the *nobility* live in, when I assure you, that what the chief princes allow for their own eating is a testoon a day; eighteen pence: there are some extend their expense to five pauls, or half a crown: Cardinal Albani is called extravagant for laying out ten pauls for his dinner and supper. You may imagine they never have any entertainments: so far from it, they never have any company. The princesses and duchesses particularly lead the dismalest of lives. Being the posterity of popes, though of worse families than the ancient nobility, they expect greater respect than my ladies the countesses and marquises will pay them; consequently they consort not, but mope in a vast palace with two miserable tapers, and two or three monsignori, whom they are forced to court and humour, that they may not be entirely deserted. Sundays they do issue forth in a vast unwieldy coach to the Corso.

Twenty years later Richard recorded that the Colonna and Orsini were the two leading princely houses, and never appeared in public together to avoid problems of precedence. Then came the Conti (eight popes) and Savelli, although they had passed into the Orsini, in the same way as the Barberini had merged with the Colonna, and the Pamphili with the Doria. Stolberg at the end of the century was fierce: most of the aristocracy were 'ignorant', with 'that arrogance which sleeps in barren ignorance'. And they did not educate their daughters, which meant that 'domestic happiness is rare'.

As for the LOWEST CLASSES, Meyer in 1783 declared that nowhere was there such a gap between them and the upper classes. They were without education, moral culture or employment. In a rather convoluted discussion, Jones suggested that in Rome there was greater freedom of speech between the classes. 'By this humble familiarity, the Lower Orders acquire an open unembarrassed manner and a certain Urbanity in their behaviour and Conversation little short of the higher.'[179]

It was a French visitor (appropriately) who tells us most about the Roman WOMEN. De la Platière found them very badly and dirtily dressed and not perfumed, which he attributed in part to their diet: fennel, garlic, onions, condiments and lots of wine. They were very proud, and formed long lasting extramarital attachments. Much power came from their dowries. Cicisbeism was useful to both sides, leaving the husband free, and flattering him that his wife was desirable. It is reassuring to have another picture at exactly the same time. The artist Thomas Jones was much impressed at 'the elegant manners of the women, even among the lower Order, both at Rome and in the surrounding districts – the Ease and gracefulness of their deportment, perhaps, may be attributed to the genial warmth of the Climate, and the variety of Antique Statues which are perpetually before their Eyes'! Another Frenchman resumed the complaints: Dupaty noted that the women all wore wigs and white paint (he refers obviously to the upper classes) and declared that they were 'in a state of the grossest ignorance in an art so important as that of dress'. The German Archenholz, however, found the Roman women 'interesting' for their wit, gravity and dialect, but he noted that they in turn found the black coat of an abbé 'irresistible'. This was the sober dress assumed by men with intellectual or professional status. Richard calculated that one-third of the population wore 'ecclesiastical habit': curials, lawyers, doctors, professors, even some merchants. Johann Herder found this black silk garb so useful that he had a suit made up.

The main commentator on marriage was Montesquieu, and it is a bleak picture. The leading people do not marry, he claimed, and married men were only the trustees of the mistresses of those in government. When a girl marries, her husband looks around for a cardinal or priest for her; there was nothing so frequent as the sale of women for money or protection, because the lower bourgeoisie never worked.

The most famous women of Rome were the courtesans. Michel de Merville was very anxious to scotch the idea that the pope received money from them: they were tolerated, but everything was done to keep young women out of that profession. They suffered many disabilities: they were not to ply their trade during Lent, they were registered, they were not to mix with other women, they were not to travel in carriages, they were forbidden communion, they were not allowed to make a will, and they were buried separately. In short, all the standard cruelty and hypocrisy. It is Boswell who of visitors tells us most of prostitution:

> Then to girl near Cardinal Protector of France; charming. Sister a nun. Mother, who sells daughters, talked of 'vocation'. Much enjoyment… Be Spaniard: girl every day.[180]

Several French visitors commented on the quality of FOOD in Rome. Labat praised the excellent quality of meat (lamb and veal) and fruit. De Brosses half agreed:

> On the whole, food is good here; but not game, which is poor; but common articles are good, such as bread, fruit, and butter.

Meat, especially beef, is as superior to that of Paris as the latter is to that of our provincial towns. The soups of vermicelli and macaroni are excellent. As to compotes, the best are those of citrons cut into slices and boiled in water with a little sugar and a compote of apples. I am disappointed regarding Italian fruit. They have a lot of what they call 'agrumi', a noun which includes all the bitter kinds of fruit, and which the Genoese call 'bad fruit'. I have often heard them say, 'We have only got bad fruit here.' This seemed strange, accustomed as we are to think so highly of oranges and lemons. 'They are very well to look at,' they said to me, 'but not to eat; apples and pears are far better. What is the good of a fruit one cannot eat raw?' In France fruit is more varied and on the whole better than in Italy, with the exception of figs, grapes, and melons. The Bologna grapes are incomparable, but I have not eaten in Italy such good plums and peaches as we have in France.

He even provided a recipe – for the puddings he had enjoyed at the Monte d'Oro:

Take a large quantity of beef-marrow, a good deal of bread crumbs steeped in milk, frangipane, cinnamon, and Corinth raisins, all mixed up together, and place in a fine napkin, then cook it a second time in a pie-dish to raise a crust; then, if you are so disposed, eat a lot of it. Martialot was an ass not to place this dish at the head of the 'Cuisinier français'. To my taste, the Corinth raisins are unnecessary.[181]

English friends said that they had never tasted better, even at the Houses of Parliament!

Food for the mind was provided in Rome in many forms. There was the famous university, the SAPIENZA. Labat was fascinated with the dramatic defence of theses by three people, who all studied their roles, and acted them in public. Keysler stated that there were thirty professors but few students, and that the Jesuits monopolised the education of the youth. Richard attended the lectures of François Jacquier in experimental physics, and also knew Thomas Leseur (mathematics),

Cesare Pozzi (same) and Benedetto Stai (eloquence and Roman history). A much less reassuring picture was given by the Polish Illuminist Stanislaw Staszic in 1791:

> There were few lectures in chemistry and physics; Chemistry once a month, Natural History twice, but without the Museum, Physics once a week. Complete domination by Theology and Law. Latin, Theology and Law occupy the whole time and the whole life of the young people and all the talents with some ambition.

The other most famous educational institution was the COLLEGIO ROMANO. Berkeley saw in the court a list of books studied, and noted that the only Greek volumes were Homer's *Battle of the Frogs* and Aesop's *Fables*! Anne Miller claimed to be in 1771 only the second woman allowed to enter – after Queen Christina – by special order of the pope. The COLLEGE FOR THE PROPAGATION OF THE FAITH was also visited by travellers. De Brosses wickedly described it as

> where missionaries are fattened for the cannibals. A couple of Franciscan fathers stewed in their own juice would be undoubtedly an excellent ragout for these people, nor is a stewed Capuchin to be despised, and must taste as good as a fox after a sharp frost. The Propaganda contains a library, and a printing press furnished with type used for printing every Oriental language, and here small Chinamen are educated like singing larks in order to catch others; we often go there and have endless discussions with the fathers on China. [Filippo] Monti, who will soon be a cardinal, is the librarian of the Propaganda; he is a man of worth, and is deeply versed in Oriental literature.

That was in 1740. When Jacob Björnstahl came in 1772 the secretary was Stefano Borgia, and the college was printing texts in twenty-seven languages.[182]

Rome was famous for its LIBRARIES. The Vatican library has been described under the Vatican palace. The Angelica, Björnstahl informs us, bought Passionei's library for 32,000 *scudi* (16,000 ducats) – a collection which he had formed 'partly by various legal means, and partly by theft'. Named after Cardinal Girolamo Casanate was the Casanatense (otherwise called the Minerva). Labat described it as containing 20,000 volumes. The upper levels were reached by a spiral staircase of olive wood. It was open to the public every day 8-11, and 2-5. Labat incredibly states that silence was observed by some fifty readers. In 1740 de Brosses declared:

> The finest library in Rome is that of the Minerva; the building is spacious, bright, convenient, in two stories, like the King's Library in Paris. It is open to the public, and is nearly always full of readers. I found there some excellent MSS of Sallust, which are being collated for me. One is well attended to, and with celerity.

Richard gave a total of 80,000 volumes and mentioned some of the treasures: the Pontifical of Capua (ninth century), letters of Seneca, Petrarch and Dante, Nicholas Jenson's *Decor puellarum*, 1462 (one of the very earliest printed books), a botanical collection in twelve volumes, and the unpublished manuscript of Giovanni Pinaroli's *Polyanthea Thecnica*, a treatise on instruments. De Sade was especially impressed with this library. The librarian, Giovanni Audiffredi (1714-94), an astronomer(!), told him that it contained 70,000 volumes, but suspected that the date of Jenson's book was five or six years too early, and might have been a misprint.[183]

There were also the ACADEMIES. The ARCADIA was founded in 1690. It was visited in *c.* 1720 by Merville. It met in the Bosco Parrasio on the Janiculum, or if too hot, in the gallery of cardinal Corsini. The best Latin poet was abbé Casoni, small and almost blind; the best Italian poet Giovanni Battista Zappa d'Imola, son-in-law of the painter Carlo Maratta. The abbé Coyer was taken to a meeting in 1764 where some English were admitted, in celebration of which a poem had been composed which was read out, in which England defeated France! Coyer protested bitterly. Some reacted with scorn. Archenholz declared: 'nothing more despicable can be imagined': the real *literari* refused to attend. In 1784 Mary Berry found a 'crowd of abbati in a room much too small for the company. The subject for the evening was the Passion of Our Saviour. I heard a number of sonnets read: one treated the subject in a ludicrous style, and the whole room went into repeated roars of laughter.' Our most detailed description of an eighteenth century meeting is, however, the induction of Goethe in 1787:

> The function at which I was admitted took place as follows: In the anteroom of a decently appointed building I was presented to a distinguished ecclesiastic, who was to act as my sponsor and introduce me. We entered a large hall, which was already rather crowded, and took our seats in the middle of the front row, facing a high desk. More and more spectators kept arriving. An imposing elderly man took the empty chair on my right, who, to judge from his clothes and the respect with which he was treated, must have been a cardinal.
>
> Speaking from the desk, the custodian made a few general introductory remarks and then called on several persons by name, who recited either in verse or in prose. After this had gone on for quite a time, the custodian delivered an address, which I shall omit because it was almost identical with the diploma I received and which I reproduce below. When this was over, I was formally declared a member, and everybody clapped loudly, while my sponsor and I rose to our feet and returned the applause with many bows. Then he too made a well-turned speech, which was not too long and to the point. This was again applauded and then I took the opportunity to thank various members individually and say some polite words. I also did my best to make the custodian feel highly satisfied with his new fellow-shepherd.

A much less flattering account was given by Staszic a couple of years later:

> The Arcadians read one after the other verses in honour of their late President. This institution has something strange about it in its very name, but when I heard the laments of the shepherds for the loss of their shepherd, their sentiments seemed to me ridiculous and childish, unworthy of serious men.[184]

Jacques-Louis David, The Oath of the Horatii, *1786*

The FRENCH ACADEMY could not fail, of course, to catch the eye of President de Brosses. It was then (1740) housed in the palazzo Mancini, Corso 270-2. The students occupied the ground floor, the director the second. De Brosses was not impressed with the current students of painting, but thought that there were promising sculptors. The students were fortunate to have a large gallery of the most celebrated statues of antiquity. The situation was transformed nearly fifty years later:

> The exhibition of the French Academy at the end of the month was an important artistic event. The *Horatii* by David converted everybody to the French School, and stimulated Tischbein to begin his life-size picture of Hector challenging Paris in the presence of Helen. The works of Drouais, Gagneraux, Desmarais, Gauffier and St Ours also created a sensation, and Boquet made a name for himself as a landscape painter in the style of Poussin.

The painters' academy was that of s LUCA. De Sade gave an extensive catalogue of the paintings. It was also visited by Goethe. He mentioned its most famous relic: the skull of Raphael, which he thought authentic. 'An exquisite bone structure in which a beautiful soul could walk about in comfort'! He could not tear himself away, and through Johannes Reiffenstein, the Russian agent, managed to have a cast made of it and sent to Germany, which he loved to look at and reflect upon.[185] When Raphael's tomb in the Pantheon was opened in 1833, his skeleton was found still to possess its skull.

Alongside the academies were the SALONS. Pöllnitz in 1721 was infuriatingly coy about the women who were the hostesses. That of Mme B. (*sic*) was attended by lots of attractive women, but the baron was upset that one could not approach them without 'un petit collet', ecclesiastical dress. The same situation prevailed at Mme S. (*sic*). He therefore preferred the soirée of Cardinal Corsini, that is, Lorenzo (1652-1740), cardinal from 1706, later Clement XII, who lived in piazza Navona from 1713. Pöllnitz was more forthcoming in his letters: the most attended salons were those of the signore Corsini (the pope's nieces), the duke of Santobuono and Countess Bolognetti. At the last, women listened to abbés 'nonchalantly leaning on the backs of their chairs', then people played cards such as Tarot, Pazzica, Primiere, and Melchiade. In 1740 de Brosses found the assemblies disagreeable socially because strangers were ignored. He therefore frequented only the houses of Mme Bolognetti, Mme Patrizi and Mme Piccolomini: 'the last is still handsome, although no longer young, and she is most courteous and affable to the French'. The meetings began at nine and ended at midnight with supper. At least in this way, within a week, one met all the best company in Rome.

Twenty years later Richard described the most brilliant and attended *coversazione* as that of Cardinal Prospero Sciarra Colonna. Cardinal Domenico Orsini held one in the morning in the Farnese gallery painted by Carracci, and it was attended by women even 'en petite robe' and 'en coiffeure négligée'. Of female presidents he named Princess Palestrina, Princess Doria, marchesa Bolognetti and marchesa Patrizi. Moore was amused by the conventions. He spent the mornings seeing the sights and two-three hours every evening at *conversazioni*.

Everyone was constantly on the move to avoid boredom, and one was announced by servants when moving room to room. Women were not to be accompanied by their husbands: 'familiarities between man and wife are still connived at in this country, however, provided they are carried on in private'! At Cardinal Bernis' everyone was served coffee, lemonade and iced confectionary. De la Platière agreed about the brilliance of Bernis' receptions, catering for two or three hundred people. Also in the late 1770s Sherlock noted Bernis' weekly assembly and daily dinner, but 'of all the grand assemblies here, that of M. de Bayenne, auditor of the Rota of France, has the most amusements' (literature, politics and music), while the marchesa Margharita Bocca-Paduli (*sic*) had 'the most agreeable and the best chosen' coterie, and she was 'witty, handsome and as amiable as a French woman'! A final judgement is offered by Stolberg:

> Here the animation of the Italians is displayed in its full force. To listen to their voices, to observe their attitudes and gesticulation you would imagine they were discussing the most momentous questions: but when you approach and listen to their discourse, you are amazed that the subject is so trifling.

This, however, is undercut a few pages further on: 'Were I to live in a foreign country, and condemned to spend my life in a great city, it is probable there is no place I should prefer to Rome': because of the social life, the ease of *conversazioni*, and the animated conversation.

Concerning intellectual life in general, Moszyński was unimpressed:

> I think that one should at Rome seek mainly only for the material; for regarding science and politics, which were previously so praised, one would now find a great void. There are some men of letters, but they are very rare, uncommunicative, and very devoted to their work. The others who claim to be scholars do so only for their own advantage.[186]

The matter of salons and *conversazioni* naturally leads us on to one of the highlights of Rome, its MUSIC. Those in Rome in 1707 and 1708 had a treat. Georg Friedrich Händel was in town. On 14 January 1707 he played the organ in S Giovanni Laterano, amazing everyone by his skill. His memorialist Mainwaring records his relations with Cardinal Pietro Ottoboni, who had his own orchestra, in which Arcangelo Corelli played the first violin. Händel composed for them, but Corelli complained that he could not play the overtures, whereupon Händel snatched his violin and gave a demonstration. Here he also met Domenico Scarlatti, with whom he had a famous competition: judgements varied about who was superior on the harpsichord, but Scarlatti owned himself defeated on the organ. In Rome, Händel composed the *Resurrection* and one hundred-and-fifty cantatas. The oratorio was finished in April 1708 and immediately performed at the palace of marchese Francesco Ruspoli in Santi Apostoli on 8 April; we have the accounts (528 *scudi*), including the hire of a bed for Händel. Of his own performances in 1770 Mozart tells us only that he played some concertos. Two months after he and his father left, Dr Charles Burney arrived in September. It is not unnaturally to the great musicologist that we owe our most detailed picture of music in Rome at this time. His first concert was at Mr Beckford's – not the writer, but his cousin of the same name, who was an historian:

> Mr Beckford's concert, consisting of 12 of the best hands in Rome, led by Celestini – and 3 voices, viz Signor [Tommaso] Cristofero of the Pope's chapel who sings very much in Guarducci's way and is little inferior to him in delicacy, Grassetto – a boy made a eunuch by his own choice against the advice of his friends in order to preserve his voice, which is a very pleasing one, and he is moreover in other respects a very promising singer; and a buffo tenor, a very comical fellow. – Here was a great deal of company – among which [John Sackville] the D[uke] of Dorset, Mr. Layton [Leighton], Abbé [Peter] Grant, Mr [Thomas] Jenkins, Mr Vyse, etc. etc.

Musicians mentioned only by first name or by *noms de théâtre* are very hard to trace. Eligio Celestini (1739-1812) was a violinist and composer. Next Burney heard Pietro Crispi (1737-97), maestro di capella, play many of his own compositions, and (Pietro?) Mori's *Te Deum* at Santi Apostoli. Crispi then invited him to an evening concert:

There was a pretty good band and much company, among which the Marchese Gabrielle at whose house I had been a day or two before – several of his things were performed as well as of Signor Crispi – but neither of them has any originality of style or thought. No one sung [*sic*] while I was there but Madame Crispi, who has facility of execution and some taste by dint of practice – but her voice is false and coarse. After the company was gone she and her husband sung some of the Marchese's *Duettini*, and Crispi with a young professor played on 2 harpsichords some sonatas written by the former for one harpsichord accompanied by 2 violins and base – it was caw me, caw thee, between the two authors. From hence to the D. of Dorset's who made a concert *for me* on purpose that I might hear a girl sing who is much admired at Rome as a promising subject, but by some accident she could not come. However there was a good deal of English company and a very agreeable concert – the Grassetto and [Domenico] Corri sung very well.

The duke of Dorset provided another concert at Albano, where Bacchelli, called la Mignatrice, sang: 'she has a very sweet voice with infinite taste – has a good shake, great flexibility… and embellishes and changes passages better and more at her ease than any female I ever met with'. And she was by profession a painter (la Miniatrice = the miniaturist) And yet again, the duke produced another concert: 'there was an excellent German flute player from Saxony, a good tenor from Naples, [Francesco?] Torelli Veronese, and the Mignatrice. They sung [*sic*] songs and duets most exquisitely, accompanied by Celestini, Corri etc.' In February 1788 the senator, Count Abondio Rezzonico, gave a concert in his palace. The performers were Mme von Diede, 'a famous pianist', Christoph Kayser, also a pianist, and 'a lady who sang a popular aria'. Elisabeth Vigée le Brun in 1789 heard the celebrated Brigida Banti (1759-1806): 'she was very small and ugly, with such masses of hair that her chignon was like a horse's mane. But what a voice! none could equal it for strength and compass… [S]he was very curiously formed: she had a high chest, shaped like a bellows; she permitted us to see this strange formation after the concert when a few ladies and myself withdrew into an adjoining room.' She also heard Girolamo Crescentini (1766-1846): 'His singing and voice were perfection; he took a woman's part, and was clothed with a panier, like those worn at the court of Versailles, which made us laugh heartily.' Crescentini succeeded Marchesi in the affections of the Romans.[187]

Perhaps the most famous singers in Rome were the *castrati*. Richard recorded that the operation was now not allowed before the age of consent: ten or eleven years of age! The chief actor at the Argentina was a *castrato* who was paid 1,000 *scudi* for six weeks. Archenholz recorded the remarkable fact that there were 82 *castrati* at St Peter's on the saint's day in 1780, and that there were two hundred of them in Rome, all from Naples.

Goethe, on the other hand, throws light on the level of popular music in Rome: 'There are always groups of people in the streets until the small hours, who play music and sing. One sometimes hears duets which are as beautiful as anyone hears at the opera or a concert.' There was a striking illustration of this. Goethe's favourite composer was Cimarosa. Some friends were able to arrange for a private concert with singers and musicians from the theatre. A large crowd gathered outside his lodging in the Corso to hear, and applauded rapturously. Then somehow a carriage with orchestral players came by, and 'a fine bass voice, accompanied by all the instruments, began singing one of the most popular arias from the same opera'.[188]

Many visitors attended the THEATRE. Berkeley in 1717 saw a tragedy on Caligula where, 'amongst other decorums, Harlequin (the chief actor) was very familiar with the Emperor himself'. Montesquieu in 1729 provides the essential survey. Women were not allowed on stage, so that *castrati* often took their parts (every traveller comments on this, usually unfavourably). He mentions that at the Teatro Capranica there were two famous *castrati*, (Mario?) Mariotti and Chiostra: 'the most beautiful creatures I saw in my life', with one of whom a young Englishman was desperately in love for a month. Famous singers were Faustina Bordoni (contralto), Senezino (Francesco Bernardi, castrato), Turcotta (Marta Turcotti?), Farsallino and Carlo Scalzi. The Capranica was one of only three theatres: the others were the Grand, called del' Liberti (in fact, the d'Alibert in via del Babuino, burnt down in 1863) and La Pace (in the homonymous street). The whole population

Giovanni Paolo Panini, Musical feast given by the cardinal de La Rochefoucauld in the Teatro Argentina in Rome in 1747 on the occasion of the marriage of Dauphin, son of Louis XV, *1747*

was mad for music and the theatres were packed. More details were given of the Alibert by Pöllnitz: he declared it the only beautiful theatre, with seven rows of small boxes and a parterre which could hold nine hundred people. He praised the voices, judged the music ordinary, and the dancing frightful. Of composers, Leonardo Vinci (1690-1730) had just died, leaving Haas (called Saffone), the incredibly prolific Johann Hasse (1699-1783), husband of Bordoni, and Niccola Porpora (1686-1767). Spence noted the two peculiarities of the opera: the custom of moving from box to box and the ban on women performers: 'half the dancers are boys dressed like women, and the queen and all the ladies of the play are eunuchs. You'd be surprised to see how much they all look like women, and how well they manage the fan.' In 1740 de Brosses hired a box at the Capranica for the winter, but one paid for a ticket as well. He used it once, for *Merope*, but what a disaster:

> I had an uncomfortable seat; the scenery was very unfinished, the orchestra was tipsy, the parts were badly performed, and the actors were suffering from influenza, Merope being simply abominable and Polyphante deserving a good thrashing. The next day the Governor of Rome clapt the manager into prison and the actors as well.

The subscriptions were not refunded but given to the employees. 'All the indemnification I had was having heard [Angelo] Monticelli [castrato], for he alone knew his part. He played and sang like an angel; he is one of the best voices in Italy of the kind they call *voce di testa*, of marvellous charm and power.' Hervey in 1761 saw a satire of English, French, Spanish and Italian characters. The Englishman (My lord Roastbeef) was very generous, but spoke little – and that with his teeth closed. Coyer was astounded that the opera lasted for five hours. There was, moreover, the same inattention on which Spence had commented:

> In France we go to listen and follow the play; here it is for conversation or to visit box to box; no one listens, they go into raptures only at the arias… and all attention is also given to the obligatory recitatives, more affecting than the arias.

With women not allowed to perform, Dorine 'has a foot an ell [*c.* a metre] long, with sinewy arms and traces of beard'! Comedies were far from free of indecency. Coyer, to his credit, was upset at ridicule of Judaism. He saw one Pulchinella as a Jew and a rabbi wildly wielding a circumcision knife. Jones in 1777 tells us more about comedy:

> [Gioacchino] *Garibaldi* at the *Valle* theatre was esteemed the best Tenor, and he certainly was an excellent comic Actor – At a little Theatre called the *Pace*, appropriated to farcical representations were two famous Buffos, *Fallope* & *Prospero*, the former, I was told, was very much admired by Our *Garrick* – To

my fancy, a certain vacant stare & an inflexible irrisibility of Countenance, seemd to be his chief excellence as an Actor, but I must own, that as the greatest part of what he spoke was extempory, I can not pretend to decide upon his merits – I understood, however, enough to know that many of his jokes were too gross to be suffered by the One Shilling gallery in London – All the female Characters are represented by Young Singers call'd *Musici*, & perform their parts to Admiration – I was confidently told, that ladies of the first quality, not only lend them their richest habiliments on the Occasion, but take great pleasure in dressing them for the Stage.

Smith praised the serious opera at the Alibert: 'the decorations and ballet are superior to anything met with anywhere else'. Goethe, finally, summed up the theatrical life of Rome at the end of the century:

The Aliberti and the Argentina give *opera seria* with ballets between the acts; the Valle and the Capranica comedies and tragedies with comic operas as intermezzi. The Pace does the same, though its standards are lower, and there are many other minor kinds of performance, down to puppet shows and tight-rope dancers.

The great Teatro di Tordinona, which burned down and then collapsed the moment it was rebuilt, is no longer there, unfortunately, to amuse the people with its historical melodramas and other spectacular shows.

The Romans have a passion for the stage, and in the old days were all the more ardent theatre goers during Carnival because this was the only season at which they could satisfy it. Nowadays, at least one playhouse is also open during the summer and autumn.

He attended the Comic Opera, where he saw Cimarosa's *L'impresario in angustie*. At the beginning of 1787 he revealed

I am already beginning to shudder at the thought of the forthcoming theatre season. Next week seven theatres will open. Anfossi [Pasquale Anfossi (1736-97) composer] himself is here and will perform *Alexander in India*. Cyrus will also be given and a ballet, *The Conquest of Troy*. This would be something for the children.[189]

There were also grand BALLS. Goethe again gives the best description:

> The dances at these balls are usually danced after the English fashion, in long rows, the only difference being that their few steps usually pantomime some typical action; for example, the falling out and reconciliation of two lovers, who part and meet again.
>
> Their ballets have accustomed the Romans to an emphatic style of gesture, and, even in their social dancing, they love expressive movements, which to us would seem exaggerated and affected. No one dares to dance unless he has studied it as an art. The minuet, in particular, is treated as a work of art, and it is only performed by a few couples. The other dancers stand in a circle round such a couple, watching them with admiration and applauding when their dance is over.

Given the seriousness of such occasions, one understands why visitors did not attend. Gray was an exception in 1740 – but he did not dance.

> Figure to yourself a Roman villa; all its little apartments thrown open, and lighted up to the best advantage. At the upper end of the gallery, a fine concert, in which La Diamantina, a famous virtuosa, played on the violin divinely, and sung angelically; Giovannino and Pasqualini (great names in musical story) also performed miraculously. On each side were ranged all the secular grand monde of Rome, the Ambassadors, Princesses, and all that. Among the rest Il Serenissimo Pretendente (as the Mantova gazette calls him) displayed his rueful length of person, with his two young ones, and all his ministry around him. 'Poi nacque un grazioso ballo', where the world danced, and I sat in a corner regaling myself with iced fruits, and other pleasant rinfrescatives. [190]

We may conclude with general observations on the CHARACTER OF THE ROMANS by the eighteenth century visitors. Pöllnitz, critical as usual, noted the Roman who had never passed the Milvian Bridge who will tell you that nothing equals the pleasures of Rome! He found that they understood much more about respect than politeness. Their manners at table were extraordinarily bad, and he claimed that they rarely changed clothes each day. They were not as jealous as usually made out to be, but were very avaricious. Richard was equally critical: 'more representation than reality, more surface than depth, more appearances than being… How many does one see without education, without knowledge, and without talent who because they are born into a distinguished rank, regard themselves as demi gods… [T]hey exist only to live in idleness.' Modern Romans were flattered by the classical remains and traditions, of which they knew little, but believed that they were their heirs. These French verdicts were echoed by Archenholz: 'By an astonishing change of things we find among the posterity of the most famous, valiant and freest people of the antique world, obscurity cowardice and slavery united in the highest degree.' The pride of the population he found pitiful. There was great pretence in dress and the owning of servants, but thousands lived on handouts, and 'indolence and indigence' were notorious; the city was 'the real paradise of beggars'. Moszyński agreed: 'If you wish to know the character of the people, here it is in a few words: much suspicion, even more hypocrisy and avarice; everything is for sale, as long as secrets and appearances are maintained.' Dupaty summarized succinctly: 'the cultivation of the mind here is as much neglected as that of the earth'.[191]

WITNESSED EVENTS

De Blainville was present at the COMMEMORATION OF JAMES II OF ENGLAND on 24 September 1707 in S Lorenzo in Lucina (see ill. overleaf). He had died in France in 1701. The eulogy was delivered by the Jesuit Carlo de Aquino with vastly exaggerated rhetoric:

Alessandro Specchi,
The catafalque for James II
in S. Lorenzo in Lucina,
*1701. This gives some idea of
the extraordinarily elaborate
funerary arrangements seen
in Rome for very important
people up to the nineteenth
century*

The ceremony was certainly magnificent in every Respect. The whole Church was hung with Black and illuminated with an infinity of White Wax tapers. A vast Multitude of Trophies, Emblems and Motto's [*sic*] adorned, not only the Castrum Doloris, or Burning Chapel, but also the Walls and the Columns of the Church, with the Arms of England on all Hands.

De Blainville fulminated against the hundreds of inscriptions, many of them mendacious: 'zelando zelum Dei', when he 'put all Europe in an Uproar, in order to come at an absolute Power, which he had no manner of right to'; 'Lover of Victory and Truth', of the man who betrayed the religion and laws of his country.[192]

Michel de Merville told of the EXECUTION OF ABBÉ CÆTANO VOLPINI in the second half of 1719. Clement XI seemed very appreciative of his poetry, but was in fact using him to spy on Prince Grillo, who was arrested by the Inquisition, but jumped bail and fled to Venice. Volpini was very unhappy with his commission, and did as little as possible, until Clement realised and stripped him of his pension. Volpini then offered his services to Count Galassi, Imperial ambassador, as well as to Cardinal Troiana Acquaviva, ambassador of Spain, in addition to writing satires against Clement's attraction to Clementina Sobieski. Clement revealed Volpini's double game and had satires against the Empire and Spain secreted in the luggage of the Venetian courier, who was then arrested. The Congregation to try Volpini delayed, suggesting clemency, but he was condemned; Clement wept on signing the death warrant. In the same year Merville also recorded an outbreak of MALARIA. One could not leave or return to the city, or leave the rooms one already had. The effects were felt up to forty miles around the city.[193]

On the death of Clement XI, the CONCLAVE for his successor occupied MARCH TO MAY 1721; his successor was Innocent XIII. Merville noted that the death of a pope was a calamity for his relatives and ministers, who lost all power. Everyone then began flattering the *papabili* (the electable cardinals) and their connections. The vital officials were the conclavists, the staff of the cardinals. They knew everything which transpired in the conclave, but on the other hand they were imprisoned the whole time, suffered the extremes of heat and cold and any sickness, and were made culprits for their master's faults. Albani's party favoured Fabrizio Paolucci (secretary of state), and hoped to elect him before the emperor's supporters arrived, but his conclavist insulted another cardinal who therefore did not vote for him the next day. Giulio Alberoni then arrived; crowds had awaited him outside porta del Popolo for a week. The cardinals were, however, very opposed to admitting him to the conclave, because he had not completed formalities for his appointment as a cardinal. By May the people favoured Michelangelo Conti, but his numerous and powerful nephews alarmed the other cardinals. Merville joked that the election of a cardinal with poor relatives would cost much more.

Here his letters break off. Conti was elected. Edward Wright also arrived close on the death of Clement XI. 'Immediately after a Pope is chosen, the Mob run and rifle the Palace he had when Cardinal; and such as have a prospect of being chosen do therefore remove the richest of their Furniture beforehand.'[194]

On the death of Innocent XIII, the CONCLAVE to elect Benedict XIII (Pietro Orsini) lasted from MARCH TO MAY 1724. Montesquieu did not arrive until 1729, but he had an account of it from Cardinal Melchior de Polignac. It is, not unexpectedly, one of the most detailed accounts of a conclave which we possess. The French and Spanish had twelve cardinals, the Germans three. Fabio Olivieri had been agreed upon by all the European courts, a secret which Armand de Rohan revealed (abbé de Vaureal produced the bon mot that the electors came bearing an olive branch, a pun on Olivieri's name). Olivieri's chances were thus finished. 'What ever did I do to the French', he cried, 'to lose ten papacies?' The courts next agreed on Bartolomeo Piazza, so the Albani opposed him. Melchior de Polignac then arrived, and was passed from one cardinal to another when he wanted to know what had so far happened. He did, however, confer with Annibale Albani, who assured him that he would never agree to have Piazza's election forced upon him. Rohan thereupon told Polignac that he was writing to the French court to say that Piazza would be elected the next day! He also told marchese Monti in Bologna, and everyone sent letters congratulating Piazza's brother. The next day, to mock Rohan, the Albani gave seventeen votes to Pietro Orsini, and the day after, seventeen votes to Fabrizio Paolucci. The votes increased for Orsini, and he was elected, despite his protestations of incompetence.[195]

The next year, 1725, was a JUBILEE. The poet John Dyer was present at St Peter's,

> in the midst of a most unnatural uproar, with the cries of many strange penances around me. And I'll assure you that a Lord Mayor's show is infinitely preferable to that of opening the holy door. It was very silly, for after a great length of the most wretched pageantry, the pope reached the door and beat it down with three strokes of a hammer, three good prayers,

and the most successful force of three of four lusty fellows, who pulled and hauled with ropes and crows of iron, to pull down the little wall on a carriage of low wheels, and they wheeled it away to be broke into 10,000 pieces, to be dispersed for pence and halfpence to all the corners of Europe.[196]

On the death of Benedict XIII, another lengthy CONCLAVE, FEBRUARY-JULY 1730, was required for the election of Clement XII (Lorenzo Corsini). Baron Karl Pöllnitz recorded this. Giuseppe Imperiali would have been elected, but was vetoed by Spain. Gianantonio Davia was then proposed, but he was accused of being a Jansenist; in fact he was anti-Jesuit. Meanwhile Lorenzo Corsini, who feared a German veto, wrote to the Grand Duke (Giovanni) and Grand Princess, who secured him the emperor's favour, and the Camerlengo Annibale Albani was won over; Francesco Barberini, however, refused. Albani then went to Alvaro Cienfuegos, who supported Carlo Colonna, begging him on his knees and in tears not to oppose Corsini. The French became suspicious that the Germans were not objecting to him, but they agreed if they could name the Secretary of State (to be Antonio Banchieri) Many well informed people thought that the Germans were tricked, because the French appointed both the pope and the secretary. The ceremony to enthrone Clement lasted five hours. Johann Keysler also observed these events and described Benedict XIII lying in state for four days with a foot protruding for the faithful to kiss. In the conclave the 'apartments' of the cardinals were 18-20' square, divided into a bedroom, dining-room and lobby. They were partitioned from each other only by cloth, so that everything could be heard by neighbours. He estimated the cost of the conclave at 200,000 *scudi* (£50,000).[197]

CLEMENT XII'S POSSESSO was held on 19 November. According to Pöllnitz it was a poor affair, more magnificent in illustration and description than in reality: it gave the impression of 'a masquerade seemingly ill suited to the court of the vicar of Jesus Christ'. The duke of Parma always had to erect a triumphal arch in the Forum, made of cardboard(!), but heavy rain a few days before had ruined it. Most of the cardinals and priests were too old for horseback, and the 'order of march' was poorly observed, with sometimes gaps of sometimes fifteen or even thirty minutes.[198]

Pöllnitz was also present at the FUNERALS of CARDINAL JACOPO BONCOMPAGNI and PRINCE FRANCESCO RUSPOLI in 1731. He was amazed at their lying in state exposed. No members of the latter's family were present (it was not a Roman custom), but the mourning was very closely observed, with women in black from head to foot.[199]

On 11 January 1740 CARDINAL GIANANTONIO DAVIA died. De Brosses declared that his interment and catafalque in S Lorenzo in Lucina would be a fine sight. 'He was highly thought of in the Sacred College, although of strongly suspected Jansenist tendencies.' He might have been elected pope in 1730 but for Cardinal Henri de Bissy. 'The pope, who is dying, on hearing of the cardinal's death, said, "This is now the second time we are found in competition together. I carried it off on the first occasion, but it has pleased God to call him first in this one."'[200] The DEATH OF CLEMENT followed on 6 February. De Brosses was a remarkable witness:

> I am now starting for Monte Cavallo, and I hear the bell of the Capitol tolling, whilst the drums are being beaten in our quarter.
>
> I have just returned from the Pontifical Palace, where I saw a sad image of human grandeur. All the rooms were open and deserted, and I passed through them without seeing a cat till I entered the pope's chamber, whose corpse lay on a bed, watched by four Jesuits, who were reciting, or pretending to recite, prayers.
>
> The Cardinal Camerlengo [Annibale Albani] had come at nine o'clock to do his duty, which consisted of tapping with a small hammer several blows on the brow of the defunct, and calling him by his name, Lorenzo Corsini; finding that he gave no answer, he said, 'This is why you are mute,' and, taking off the fisherman's ring from his finger, he broke it, according to custom. Apparently every one followed him out immediately after. As the pope's corpse has to remain a long time exposed in public, the face was shaved and the cheeks rouged to hide the pallor of death. He looked certainly better than when I saw him alive. The features are regular, and he was a handsome old man.

The embalming takes place tonight, after which there will be much to keep the town in a ferment, such as the funeral obsequies, the catafalques, and the preparations for the conclave.[201]

De Brosses was clever enough to forecast a longer than usual CONCLAVE for a successor, and it took from FEBRUARY UNTIL AUGUST 1740 to elect Benedict XIV (Prospero Lambertini). In May, Horace Walpole had some gossip to report:

Other feuds have been between Cardinal Portia [Leander Porzia] and the faction of Benedict the Thirteenth; by whom he was made cardinal. About a month ago he was within three votes of being pope. He did not apply to any party, but went gleaning privately from all, and of a sudden burst out with a number; but too soon, and that threw him quite out. Having been since left out of their meetings, he asked one of the Benedictine cardinals the reason; who replied, that he never had been their friend, and never should be of their assemblies; and did not even hesitate to call him apostate. This flung Portia into such a rage, that he spit blood, and instantly left the Conclave with all his baggage. But the great cause of their antipathy to him, was his having been one of the four, that voted for putting Coscia to death; who now regains his interest, and may prove somewhat disagreeable to his enemies; whose honesty is not abundantly heavier than his own. He met Corsini t'other day, and told him, he heard his Eminence had a mind to his cell: Corsini answered he was very well contented with what he had. 'Oh,' says Coscia, 'I don't mean here in the Conclave; but in the Castle St Angelo.'

With all these animosities, one is near having a Pope; Cardinal [Vincenzo] Gotti, an old, inoffensive Dominican, without any relations, wanted yesterday but two voices; and is still most likely to succeed. Cardinal [Lorenzo] Altieri has been sent for from Albano, whither he was retired upon account of his brother's [Cardinal Giovanni Battista] death and his own illness; and where he was to stay till the election drew nigh. There! there's a sufficient competency of Conclave news, I think...

…Don't talk of our coronation; 'tis never likely to happen. The divisions are so great between the Albani and Corsini factions, that the Conclave will probably be drawn out to a great length. With Albani, are his uncle's creatures, the Spanish and Neapolitan factions, and the *zelanti*, a set of cardinals, who always declare against any party, and profess being solely in the interest of the Church. With Corsini are the late Pope's creatures, and the dependants of France.

Gray returned to Rome from Naples at the end of June and could add some details:

The Conclave we left in greater uncertainty than ever; the more than ordinary liberty they enjoy there, and the unusual coolness of the season, makes the confinement less disagreeable to them than common, and, consequently maintains them in their irresolution. There have been very high words, one or two (it is said) have come even to blows; two more are dead within this last month, [Serefino] Cenci and Portia; the latter died distracted: and we left another (Altieri) at the extremity: Yet nobody dreams of an election till the latter end of September. All this gives great scandal to all good catholics, and every body talks very freely on the subject.

Charles Duclos, who was in Rome in 1767, wrote that Pompeo Aldrovandi constantly received thirty-three votes (one short!). His enemy Albani pretended to be won over, and when Aldrovandi wrote him a note about it, Albani used this to accuse him of intrigue. Aldrovandi then had his supporters vote for Lambertini to exclude Albani.[202]

At the end of 1740 Thomas Spence recorded one of the worst FLOODS. After reaching Rome, he could not visit St Peter's or the Pantheon.[203]

In September 1745 FRANCIS of Lorraine was elected HOLY ROMAN EMPEROR at Frankfurt. Although Charles Duclos was not in Rome until twenty-two years later, he had an account from eyewitnesses of the repercussions. The Austrians in Rome celebrated by dressing up a boy of about twelve whom they carried around crying 'Viva l'imperatore!' At the French ambassador's Cardinal Frederic Rochefoucault gave them money, but at the Spanish Cardinal Trojano Acquaviva was enraged. Shots were fired, and some twenty people killed or wounded. Acquaviva had a thousand *bravi* and four canon to defend the palace. The mob planned to blow up the palace and were led by a mason called Giacomo, but he was persuaded to desist. Benedict XIV did nothing about Acquaviva.[204]

On the death of Benedict XIV, the CONCLAVE occupied MAY- JULY 1758. Again Duclos, who visited Rome during the reign of his successor, Clement XIII (Carlo Rezzonico), provided some notes. Giuseppe Spinelli was vetoed by Spain and Carlo Cavalchini by France, although he was not aware of it. After an offer to back Cavalchini was vetoed, Spinelli induced him to support Carlo Rezzonico, who was elected.[205]

12 November 1758 was the POSSESSO OF CLEMENT XIII, observed by Pierre Grosley. The procession was three miles in length, from the Vatican to S Giovanni in Laterano. The pope was preceded and followed by two thousand horsemen: cuirassiers in damask armour with an embroidered mantle on their right shoulder and a plumed helmet. The Roman barons were all in black, each preceded by four pages, with grooms at their stirrups and twenty footmen in livery. The cardinals wore their hats fastened under their chins, and mantles which covered their horses' bodies. The pope came on a beautiful white mule. The whole population was on its knees to receive the papal benediction.[206]

In February 1761 Christopher Hervey recorded that a ship arrived in Rome with eighty Portuguese JESUITS from Brasil. This was one result of the expulsion of the Jesuits from Portugal. Apart from doctrinal conflicts with the Jansenists, Franciscans and Dominicans, the Jesuits were feared for their political power. They were finally accused of attempting to assassinate Jose I of Portugal and expelled from that kingdom in 1759, from France in 1764, from Spain and the Holy Roman Empire in 1767, and dissolved by Clement XIV in 1773. Hervey also recorded in January 1760 the expulsion from Lisbon of the papal nuncio, Cardinal Filippo Acciaiuoli, and the retaliatory departure of the Portuguese ambassador to Rome, Francisco Almada.[207]

In June 1761, Hervey recorded various DEATHS: the marchesa Gabrielli, beloved of a rich Englishman, Thomas Stevens; she died from dancing while pregnant at the villa Borghese. Hervey saw her laid out in church 'with the little embrio placed upon her bosom'. And Cardinals Giuseppe Orsi, Antonio Banchieri, and Raniero Delci (d'Elci) all died.[208]

Clement XIII died on 2 February (Jeudi Gras) 1769 during Carnival. Festivities were therefore terminated, as Louis Dutens observed. The people were resigned ('The pope is dead, we will make another' was the traditional refrain), but the nobility was greatly excited, visiting all the cardinals. For an idea of the catafalque, Dutens recommended reading Herodian's account of funerals of Roman emperors! Albani[209] directed the CONCLAVE, assigning cells to the cardinals; their complaints so exasperated him that he declared them all fools (*minchioni*). Albani himself had an apartment with a window looking on to a little courtyard. Here Dutens came to visit him and bring him news: he used to let down a little basket to collect letters! So much for the supposed isolation of the election.[210] The conclave from FEBRUARY TO MAY 1769 concluded with the election of Clement XIV.

In the same year, 1769, Dutens recorded the VISIT OF THE EMPEROR in disguise as Count Falkenstein. This was Joseph II, archduke of Austria and the Holy Roman Emperor 1765-90. He went about the streets attended by only one gentleman, with many stories told of the tricks he played while incognito. He was very popular at Rome, and was called 'Re dei Romani' by the crowds, when his disguise was penetrated. 'You are our legitimate sovereign,' they cried. Prince Bartolomeo Corsini gave a dinner for five hundred guests, all with individual settings, and Prince Andrea Doria gave a ball. More details are given by Charles Mayer. The visit occupied 15-29 March. The emperor arrived during the conclave, to which he was instantly introduced. He stayed at the palazzo Sforza. He complimented Cardinal de Bernis for his work for peace in Europe and alliances with France and Austria. He was entertained by Prince Andrea Doria, the Venetian ambassador, Prince Emilio Altieri, Duke Bracciano (an assembly and ball), Prince Corsini (dinner for six hundred guests), and Cardinal Alessandro Albani at his villa. On 26 March the facade of St Peter's was illuminated, with three thousand lamps lit simultaneously at a signal, and a horse race was held in the Corso, which he viewed from the palazzo Ruspoli.[211]

On 19 November 1775, John Moore witnessed the BEATIFICATION OF THE FRANCISCAN S BONAVENTURA (1654-1711). As a Protestant, he found the whole process of the debate between the sponsor and the Devil's Advocate long and boring. He and his friends began yawning and infected the cardinals with the same embarrassment. The only thing that kept him awake was the grimaces of the monks at the opposition's points. At the conclusion, the English felt that they had some claim on this saint, 'having done penance at his beatification'![212]

Moore also observed the POSSESSO OF PIUS VI. Prince Benedetto Giustiniani obtained tickets for him and his friends on an extraordinary vantage-point, the balcony of the palazzo del Senatore on the Capitol. That palace and the Vatican and the Lateran were 'all hung with crimson silk laced with gold'. The procession from the Lateran to the Capitol was headed by the papal horse guard, then came the Swiss guard in coats of mail and iron helmets, the barons on horseback, each with four pages, the bishops, cardinals and finally the pope on a milk white mule. The senator handed the pope the keys, which were handed back; then to the Forum, where the rabbi and Jews met him at the Arch of Titus.[213]

The artist Thomas Jones attended an ART EXHIBITION in February 1778. There was one painting: Raphael Mengs' *Perseus and Andromache*, painted for Sir Watkin Williams Wynn at his palace.

> This Picture made a Stir in Rome in proportion to the Celebrity of the Painter – & the *Exhibition* was conducted with the utmost Pomp – All the Grand Apartments of the Palace being thrown open – in most of which were groupes of Pupils making Studies after drawings pictures or Statues, according to their respective Classes – In the room where this famous piece was placed for public Admiration, decorated with a Superb frame & green silk curtain, the Senior Pupils attended in form, ready to explain the Subject, point out the different beauties of the Performance, & expatiate on the transcendent excellencies of

Bartolomeo Pinelli, A nocturnal burial in the Protestant cemetery, *1831*

their great Master – The Ceremony was indeed striking – and did honor to the Arts – but after all – the principal Merit of the piece consisted in its laborious high Finishing – The result of German flegmatic Industry – It had not that Taste, that boldness of design, or that glowing transparent Coloring, so much admired in the *Old* Italian schools – Sr *W. W. Wynne* I was told pay'd 500 Sechins for this Picture – but unfortunately, afterwards, the Ship in which it was Conveying to *England*, was taken by a French Privateer –[214]

The painting is now in St Petersburg.

The same visitor also records a BURIAL in the 'Protestant cemetery' on 8 June 1778, that of MRS PARS, wife of the artist William Pars, who accompanied Nicholas Revett and William Chandler to Asia Minor:

At the *funeral* all the English Artists who were then at *Rome* walk'd in procession with torches to the number of 18 or 20 – BANKS the Sculptor read the Service – And great Numbers of Romans attended, who behaved with the greatest Decorum, and a profound Silence was observed – The Scene was grand

& striking – The Moon, just hid behind the Tomb of *Caio Sesto*, cast her Silvery Tints on all the Objects around, save where that large dark Piramid threw its broad Shadow over the Place in which the Solemn Ceremony was performing by the dusky Light of Torches – These last Rites – performed – The Flambeaus were put out and given to Our Attendants, each of us having one for the Occasion – We then return'd by the light of the Moon.[215]

In 1779, ARCHDUKE FERDINAND of Austria (1754-1806), third son of emperor Francis I, and his wife Maria Beatrice d'Este, visited Rome. Johann Archenholz described how the Venetian ambassador invited the whole population to a masquerade in palazzo S Marco. There were 12,000 people, one could neither move nor obtain refreshment: 'the Roman population formed a line of circumvallation all round the tables'.[216]

Marianne Starke, finally, was present at the establishment of the JACOBIN REPUBLIC in 1798. She observed at the end of the previous year the grave food shortages, the debasement of coinage (it lost a quarter of its value), and visited the granaries in the Baths of Diocletian where she saw 'immense stores' of oil, but Pius VI's nephew Braschi had sold it to foreigners. Then came the riot in which Matthieu Duphot was shot by the papal troops (28 December, 1797). In an attempt to avert retribution, there was procession after procession of suppliants until 23 January 1798, when news came of General Berthier's march on Rome. There was then a procession of priests, nobles and women, barefoot and uncovered, from S Maria in Valicella to St Peter's. 'All Rome attended this procession.' Pius issued an edict ordering the population to remain quiet and declaring that the French were his 'friends' ('one of the most disgraceful that sovereign ever issued'). The Trasteverini brought gunpowder and carried stone to roof tops – to avenge insults to any Roman women! Berthier declared Pius 'superannuated and beneath my vigilance'. Pius declared himself satisfied if his life were saved. On 9 February piazza del Popolo was filled with anxious priests and the via Flaminia with Jacobins to welcome the French. A city of 180,000 inhabitants was thus taken without a shot by 5-6,000.[217]

PORTRAITS

CLEMENT XI Albani (1700-21) (see ill. opposite, left) is described by
Jean Labat:

> very tall and very fat, he had a long full face, pendulous cheeks,
> a sad appearance, a pale complexion, dull eyes, and if ever he
> failed to shave, he seemed like a dying man... [N]o-one had
> more wit, insight, commonsense, judgement and prudence
> than he; he was delicate in thought and in his manner of
> expression; he was fine and skilful, and although everything
> about him seemed of an extraordinary simplicity, nothing was
> more studied, or carried out with more policy, although with
> the most natural manners.

He did not enrich his nephews, often took confession in St Peter's,
and easily granted private audiences.[218]

Montesquieu had nothing good to say of BENEDICT XIII Orsini
(1724-30) (see ill. opposite, right):

> He is much hated by the people; even his devotion is scorned,
> because it makes them die of hunger. Besides he has shown
> everywhere too much favour for Benevento – all the money of
> Rome goes there...
>
> He knows nothing of the affairs of the world. His world is
> the kingdom of Naples and the Ecclesiastical State.

Montesquieu also comments at length on his enmity to Cardinal
Andre de Fleury. Benedict wanted all the bishops in France to be monks,
but Cardinal Melchior de Polignac had to point out the differences
between France and Italy and the distinction of the clergy in the former.
Simony was rampant, but he gave nothing to his relatives. His caprices
increased with age. He took no notice of the cardinals, but his manners
were 'angelic'. In short, Rome under Benedict was 'as sad as it was holy'.
Johann Keysler noted that he had no talent choosing ministers, quoting
the case of Niccolò Coscia. He was reputedly over generous, once giving

Left, Elias Christoph Heiss, Clement XI, *date unknown; right, Pietro Bracci,* Benedict XIII, *date unknown*

a pilgrim 1,000 *scudi*. The treasurer cannily paid it in copper, which filled ten bags, on seeing which Benedict was amazed – and gave the pilgrim only one! Baron Karl Pöllnitz likened Benedict in the hands of the Beneventans to the Holy Sepulchre in the hands of the Turks. As for his being duped by Coscia, Keysler told the story of how he was accused of visiting prostitutes; he thereupon sent an anonymous letter to the pope, telling him the time he could catch him. Benedict came – and found him deep in prayer. Pöllnitz also told how in a grasshopper plague, Benedict cursed them and banished them into the sea. Etienne Silhouette agreed that Benedict was completely under the control of the evil Cardinal Coscia; the pope himself was the simplest and most innocent of men, who did not even know the value of money (shades of Keysler's story) and preferred to discuss monkish matters with Father Antoine Feydeau, general of the Carmelites. De Brosses quoted Father Jean François Cloche, general of the Dominicans, who knew him well: he was 'like a hunting horn – hard, twisted and empty'.[219]

Left, Agostino Masucci, Clement XII, *date unknown; right, Pierre Hubert Subleyras,* Benedict XIV, *1746*

Benedict's successor was CLEMENT XII Corsini (1730-1740). He was very economical, noted Pöllnitz in the early 1730s, but losing his memory and going blind, and knew little of politics. His promotion of Vincenzo Bichi, as Nuncio to Portugal, resulted in that kingdom recalling all its subjects, with the annual loss to Rome of one million *scudi.* Silhouette described Clement as very rich, with a liking for magnificence and gambling, and a patron of art and science, but he had been very ambitious for the papacy and favoured his relatives. De Brosses saw him at the end of his life, in bed. Although for a long time he had taken no part in public affairs, de Brosses described the secretaries of state going each morning to brief him and get him to sign papers, although he was blind. It amused Clement to hear that Mme de Choiseul had given de Brosses a commission: to bring back a bone of St Peter. While cardinal he had been one of the best violinists in Italy. He summed up his own career: 'a rich abbot, a comfortable priest, a poor cardinal, and a ruined pope'. Cardinal Passionei reported to de Brosses that one morning displeasing news came to Clement from his nephews. He cried out 'Let them have what they wish, for they, after all, are the masters.'[220]

BENEDICT XIV Lambertini (1740-58) (see ill. opposite) was observed at the very start of his reign in a consistory by Joseph Spence:

> I took notice that the Pope in these private audiences looked like a man that was a master of business. He heard everybody calmly, and answered them with a great deal of ease in his behaviour. He was never in a hurry, nor ever seemed puzzled about what they said to him, or what he should say to them. This dumb show gave me the opportunity of having my eye upon him almost constantly for half an hour together, so that I could get a pretty distinct idea of his person.
>
> He is rather short than tall, and of a thickish make: his face is no good one, but he has a strong hearty look in it for a man that is not of a florid complexion. There is something droll in his face, and his eye has a particular sort of life and cunning in it: so that his look, of the two, rather diverted me more than it pleased me.[221]

CLEMENT XIII Rezzonico (1758-1769) (see ill. overleaf) was described by Jerome Richard in 1761 as

> of average height, very stout, with a full, fresh face, almost completely bald, his physiognomy full of gentleness and kindness, and with the most affable manners.

He later described his character as very retiring: he did not hold social gatherings (*conversazioni*), unlike Benedict XIV, who held one every day, often inviting foreigners, especially to discuss literature. Clement did not even visit the beautiful Quirinal gardens. As we would expect, he did not favour the theatre or balls. In 1767 Charles Duclos reported that Clement's father, a rich banker, had bought his son's cardinalate for 100,000 *scudi*.[222]

CLEMENT XIV Ganganelli (1769-74) (see ill. p. 203, left) gave an audience to the Swedish visitor Jacob Björnstahl, who reported his extraordinary affability. Although he arrived in 1775, John Moore

Anton Mengs,
Clement XIII,
1758

found strong memories of Clement. He was thought to have been remiss in etiquette, but 'an enemy to fraud and hypocrisy of every kind… He built no churches, but repaired roads all over the ecclesiastical state; he restrained malevolence of bigots, removed absurd prejudices, and promoted sentiments of charity and goodwill to mankind in general, without excepting even heretics.' He was therefore known to the Jesuits as 'the Protestant Pope'.

The most famous example of his tolerance, referred to by many visitors, was the Scottish Presbyterian. The story is first told by the American artist, Benjamin West, in 1760, when he met him in St Peter's. He had come to convert the pope (at that time Clement XIII). At the elevation of the Host, he declared in broad Scottish, 'Oh Lord, cast not the church down on them for this abomination.' Italian

Left, Christopher Hewetson, Clement XIV, *1773; right, Pompeo Batoni,* Pius VI, *1775*

priests nearby thought that it was an expression of enthusiasm! He was seized by the Inquisition, but released on the intervention of 'King James', and taken to Livorno to be shipped home. He escaped, and was again arrested and returned. The story is more commonly connected with Clement XIV. More told of the Scotsman seeing him in St Peter's and addressing him: 'Oh thou beast of nature, with seven heads and ten horns! Thou mother of harlots, arrayed in purple and scarlet... throw away the golden cup of abominations and the filthiness of thy fornication!' Clement simply had him shipped home.

Clement was most famous for the dissolution of the Jesuits, and all Romans believed him to have been poisoned. Johann Archenholz, who arrived only four years after his death, quoted the pope's surgeon, Signor B (*sic*), in confirmation of this. The limbs became detached from the corpse as it was being carried to the grave.[223]

The last quarter of the century was dominated by PIUS VI Braschi (1775-99). No one summed up the impression he made better than Friedrich Mayer in 1783:

Perhaps never has any pope so united all the external advantages admired in his person: a truly extraordinary beauty at a very advanced age [66], a dignity of attitude, nobility and grace of movement, and elegance of manners.

'Quanto è bello, quanto è santo' (how handsome, how saintly he is) was the standard Roman reaction. He had all the papal jewellery remade by Carlo Sartori. Carl Plümicke attended an audience with the Duchess of Courland in March 1785 and described Pius as 'behaving towards all foreigners, regardless of religion or race, as gallantly as any man of the world, politely and suavely, without any harm to his dignity'. He also described Pius' life, however, as very troubled and saddened by the demands of office. He was very lonely, and always ate alone, even when the cardinals were present (they ate separated from him). He was forbidden 'games, hunting and the theatre' (perhaps this tells us more about a German aristocrat's life!) His sole amusements were walking in his gardens and one or two weekly audiences. He was otherwise taken up with worldly business, many congregations (church courts) and a plethora of holy duties. The Protestant Count Friedrich Stolberg also described an audience, in 1792: 'The old man, who exercises his office with so much solemn dignity, is exceedingly pleasant and familiar in personal intercourse. I found him sitting at his writing desk: he desired me to sit by him, and conversed with me, with animation and intelligence, on different subjects.' At the very end of his reign Marianne Starke provided a much less complimentary view. She described him as marked by

> superstition and a scrupulous observance of church ceremonies, which aided by a fine voice, a graceful manner and an uncommonly handsome person, he performed with peculiar dignity. His temper, like that of his countrymen in general, is violent, and his passions are imperious.

She complimented his munificence: the draining of the Pontine Marshes, the building of the new sacristy of St Peter's, the foundation of the Pio-Clementino Museum, and the raising of three obelisks. This was counter balanced, however, by 'a boundless wish to aggrandize his family', especially his 'blind confidence in a worthless nephew' (Luigi), which was the ultimate cause of his misfortune. The end was obviously nigh.

It is of Pius VI, finally, that the story of another audience is told. Dr John Moore was accompanying Douglas, the young duke of Hamilton. It was arranged that they were to be dispensed from the obligation of kissing the pope's slipper. The party was outraged. Hamilton said that he would prefer no audience at all: 'if the most ludicrous part is left out, who would wait for the rest of the farce?'[224] From the above accounts it is obvious that Hamilton and Moore would have missed a great deal.

Following the popes, we turn to lesser figures as recorded by travellers. In fact one of the most powerful figures in Rome was Cardinal ALESSANDRO ALBANI (1692-1779) (see ill. overleaf), promoted by Innocent XIII in 1721. He had clearly upset Pierre Grosley in 1758, who described him as 'our capital repairer of antiquity... With him the most mutilated, most disfigured, most irremediable pieces recover their original beauty: nova fecit omnia [he makes everything new]: the fragment of a bust, which, even entire, all antiquaries would have disregarded as *una testa incognitissima* [the head of someone totally unknown], from him receives, with new life, a name which irrevocably perpetuates its rank.' The cause of this lies perhaps in the revelation that when the travellers expressed a desire to see his villa, 'he answered with something of a sneer, "It is not made for eyes used to the wonders of French architecture."' By 1760 he was blind, and when in that year he was introduced to the American artist Benjamin West, he asked him what colour he was and ran his hand all over his face.

From 1761 Albani was the Vatican librarian. Dr Charles Burney the musicologist was introduced to him and 'was wonderfully well received. He took me by the hand and said *Figlio mio* you shall have what you want...' Burney returned with a written list of what he wanted to see. They found Albani 'in his night cap with only a canonico with him'. He gave orders for everything, talking freely about 'English views and politicks'. 'Upon going away I found Mr Jenkins

Etienne Poussin,
Cardinal
Alessandro
Albani, *1764*

kissed his hand, he held it out to me who offered to do the same, but he would not let me. He seems a wonderfully good natured old man.' The Huguenot diplomat Louis Dutens in 1769 described him as still attended by his 'old friend' Countess Cheruffini (she bore him two daughters) and playing *minchiati* with three or four friends. He liked to talk to the English and could not stand the French (they wanted to 'bourbonize' the whole world). Albani actually favoured an alliance with England, granting them trading privileges in return for protection against Naples and Parma. Dutens drew up a plan, Albani approved, but Clement XIII died (1769). Clement XIV also approved, but the English took fright at a treaty with the pope. In 1777 Dutens gained the approval of Viscount Weymouth, and had two audiences with Pius VI, but by now England was involved in the American War of Independence. The Bohemian Franz Hartig *c.* 1775 described Albani as collector who distinguished coins and cameos by touch. Caroline, Countess de Genlis, revealed Albani's methods in collecting antiquities. She had the story from many people, including the victim, Prince Palestrina. He owned a superb obelisk, which he refused to sell. While he was away, however, Albani sent four thousand men one night to kidnap the obelisk, and given his power, Palestrina did not dare object.[225]

Alessandro's elder brother was ANNIBALE (1682-1751), the Camerlengo from 1719, seven years after his red hat. De Brosses described him in 1740 as 'terribly learned in that trade' (politics). 'He is a most masterful and terrible person, and I do not think Satan himself is more feared in the Infernal Regions than this man is dreaded here.'[226]

Charles de Brosses gives us a sketch of Cardinal TROJANO ACQUAVIVA (1694-1747) in 1740:

> Cardinal Aquaviva of Aragon is the greatest personage in Rome, and naturally fond of splendour. His great fortune enables him to indulge his taste. The Archbishopric of Monreale, in Sicily, brings him in alone annually, it is said, from five to six thousand pounds. He has charge of the affairs of Spain and Naples, which gives him great influence in Rome, as the interests of the Romans and those of the Neapolitans are nearly allied, owing to the closeness of the two States. The Cardinal has a fine presence, although somewhat heavy in figure, as he is also in mind. He is fond of amusement, of the society of ladies, and of the pleasures of the table, and at his board I have tasted sturgeon worthy of Apicius.[227]

The leading portraitist in Rome at the end of the century was POMPEO BATONI (1708-1787) (see ill. overleaf). Burney in 1770 described the whole family.

> He has a very large house and lives in a great way. He received me very politely and conversed a great deal together on the arts. We were then introduced to Madame and the Misses. He has

Pompeo Batoni,
Self-portrait,
1773-4

two daughters. The eldest is a scholar of Signor Santarelli and sings divinely with more grace, taste and expression than any female in public or private I ever heard. She was so obliging as to sing 6 or 8 capital airs in different styles, and all charmingly but her *fort* is the pathetic. She has a good shake and well toned voice an admirable portamento with great compass and high finishing in all she attempts. Indeed she does infinite credit to her master for he has contrived to unite the falset so with the real voice, that 'tis very difficult to say where it begins.

Johann Archenholz in 1778 added that Batoni went every morning to market, and that he was rude-tempered to social superiors, but very generous to the poor. It was, however, his young fellow-artist Johann Tischbein who is most revealing. Batoni gave him the highest praise. He was both kind and devout. Tischbein told of asking him why he had not finished his painting of Coriolanus, and he proceeded to tell the story of the subject and his mother, and burst into tears. He went every morning early to church, and gave liberally to beggars. Despite the sums he received for his paintings, he was poor.[228]

De Brosses was naturally much taken with the French ambassador 1732-40, PAUL HIPPOLYTE BEAUVILLIERS, duc de Saint-Aignan (1684-1776). 'He has charm, intelligence and is agreeable in conversation. He looks younger than he is... It is said that the brilliant complexion of the duke de Saint-Aignan is owing to his diet, which consists of eggs and Genzano wine.'[229]

Cardinal FRANÇOIS DE BERNIS (1715-94) was the French ambassador 1769-91. Lady Anne Miller dined with him in 1771. There were fifty guests, who, incredibly, were mostly cardinals. Bernis she described as gouty, eating only baked vegetables. In character he was witty, and learned, in physique corpulent and marked by smallpox. In *c.* 1775

Pierre Savart,
Cardinal de Bernis,
1778

Franz Hartig declared him the leading cardinal, keeping an open house and with literary pretensions – which caused a falling out with Frederick of Prussia and Voltaire. Jean de la Platière wrote a eulogy of his splendour and diplomacy. Everyone from the pope down thought that they must give France what her minister wanted and give her minister what France had the right to demand. The Countess Genlis described his legendary hospitality. She, indeed, lodged with him. He was 'a mixture of bonhomie and finesse, of nobility and simplicity'. Her servants were treated as well as she. Every day he sent to her apartment two or three times an enormous dish of ices and blancmanges. Every evening when she bathed(!), he came to chat for three-quarters of an hour. For the duchess of Chartres he gave *conversazioni* of two or three thousand people. Dupaty quoted him: 'he keeps, as he says himself, the tavern of France at the crossroads of Europe... It is difficult to be more beloved at Rome, although singularly esteemed.' Archenholz described his 'remarkable hospitality', dining artists every Friday, and strangers every other day. Johann Herder in 1788 told the same story. He was 'a very courteous, kind man, who welcomed us with a truly fatherly expression'. The table at dinner was rich, the following concert packed, 'because the whole of brilliant and upper class Rome was assembled – six or seven cardinals, hordes of princes and princesses, monsignors, foreigners etc.'[230]

Prince MARC ANTONIO BORGHESE (1730-1800) is the subject of a lively sketch by Archenholz in *c.* 1780. He was the richest nobleman, with an income of 150,000 *scudi*. He kept hundreds of horses, and owned at this time eighty-three carriages, 1700 pictures and a collection of antiquities second only to the Vatican. 'It is a pity that this prince has as little taste as any Roman nobleman, which is saying none...'[231]

One of the famous *ciceroni* was the Scotsman JAMES BYERS (1734-1817), who guided Gibbon. We learn most about him, however, from Moore in 1776. He called him 'a gentleman of probity, knowledge and real taste'. Byers calculated the capacity of the Circus Maximus at 380,000 and therefore the population of Rome and suburbs in antiquity at three millions. The Colosseum he thought could hold 85,000 – but that was from a classical source. And the Tarpeian Rock was originally 78' high. Thomas Jones the painter, in the same year, revealed that there was rivalry between Byers and Thomas Jenkins. They each held a Christmas dinner for their students.[232]

Cardinal NERI CORSINI (1685-1770) had been promoted from layman to cardinal in a month in 1730, three years before his priesthood – but he was the nephew of Clement XII. Walpole in 1740 had only the worst to report: 'The cardinal Corsini has so thoroughly pushed on the misery of Rome by impoverishing it, that there is no money but paper to be seen. He is reckoned to have amassed three millions of crowns.' In the same year de Brosses described Clement XII as blind. 'It is his nephew, Neri Corsini, a most incapable person, who directs all affairs.' It was from this man that Duclos had reported that Rezzonico bought a cardinalate for his son (Clement XIII) for 100,000 *scudi*.[233]

One of Corsini's main enemies was Cardinal CAMILLO CYBÓ (1681-1743), who pursued him for the millions 'borrowed' from the Apostolic Chamber. He claimed to have a banker at Genoa who would testify to having received three millions from Corsini. 'This Cybo is a madman, but set on by others. He had formerly some great office in the government, from whence they are generally raised to the cardinalate. After some time, not being promoted as he expected, he resigned his post and retired to a mountain, where he built the most magnificent hermitage. There he inhabited for two years; grew tired, came back and received the hat.'[234] He had been auditor-general, but resigned in 1721, retired to 'a mountain near Spoleto', returned to Rome in 1723, and as majordomo opposed Coscia, until appointed cardinal in 1729 to remove him from the post.

The vainglorious and tragic antiquarian ROBERT FAGAN (1761-1816) (see ill. overleaf) was unfortunate enough to cross Lady Philippina Knight:

> At a ball at Lady Plymouth's, a man we knew not asked Cornelia to dance. After a dance we found he was one Fagan, a painter who had refused our seeing his paintings because we were enemies to the Revolution. He is an Irish Catholic who changed his faith in England, and changed again to marry the daughter

Robert Fagan, Portrait of himself and Italian wife Maria, *1803*

of C. Ritson's valet de chambre; – a very worthless fellow Fagan is, but under the patronage of his Royal Highness. He asked Cornelia to dance a second time, she refused, and I believe said, 'No, no, not now we know you.'[235]

The leading antiquarian was FRANCESCO FICORONI (1662-1747). He guided Edward Wright in 1721, who quoted him frequently: for the correct identification of S Costanza, attacking Montfaucon for saying nothing was left of the Tarpeian Rock, for his count of 11,400 antique statues in Rome, and for the view that it was not the barbarians but the Romans themselves who removed the cramps from the stones in the Colosseum; he had a collection of cameos and gave Wright one. De Brosses in 1740 was less indulgent:

He is the regular showman [i.e. guide] here, and receives a sequin a day per person. But I will treat you better and charge you nothing. Ficoroni is said to be an able antiquarian, and he has published some books on the antiquities of Rome. He is very old, and as deaf as a post. Would to heaven he were also dumb! These people, when one takes them out with one to show one the sights, rattle off their descriptions of the things they know of – and those of which they are ignorant – like the monk who shows one the treasury of St Denis, not caring whether one is in a hurry to go on somewhere else or interested in his story. My patience was soon exhausted with this old chatterbox, and I dismissed him after the first experience.

'He is the general stranger's guide, and is well informed, but old, deaf, and a great bore.'[236]

A notorious figure was the banker HENRY FISHER (*c.* 1710-*c.* 1786). He was the agent of, among others, Lord Hervey:

And who should this Banker be, but the notorious *Fisher* who murdered his friend and benefactor Mr *Derby* of the Temple in London and which atrocious fact, with a Circumstance, almost beyond belief, is recorded in the introductory chapter to the VII book of the history of Tom Jones by H. Fielding. From England he fled to Holland & took refuge in a Merchant's counting house at Amsterdam, but being discovered, made his Escape to Leghorn, where he was employ'd by an English Merchant there – but being traced out again and an Order issued by the Grand Duke for his Apprehension; at the critical moment, he contrived to effect his Escape a second time, & got to Rome, where he turn'd Roman Catholic, & sat himself down safe under the Protection of the Church.[237]

In 1717 George Berkeley visited Cardinal FILIPPO GUALTIERI (1660-1728).

He is about sixty, a jolly well looking man, grey hair, rather low than tall, and rather fat than lean. He entertained us with a great deal of frankness and civility. We sate all in armed chairs round the fire. We were no sooner seated, but his eminence obliged us to put on our hats, which we did without ceremony, and he put on his cardinal's square cap. We discoursed on several subjects, as the affairs of England, those of the Turks and Venetians, and several other topics, in all which his eminence shewed himself a man of sense, good breeding, and good humour.[238]

One of the most talented German artists to visit Rome was PHILIPP HACKERT (1737-1807). In *c.* 1780 Johann Archenholz accounted him the best landscapist, but it is his friend Goethe who knew him best. Hackert originated the custom for the art students to show their work to each other each evening for criticism. 'He is a master at copying Nature and has such a sure hand that he never has to correct a drawing.' He was Goethe's teacher, and went with him to Tivoli, as well as taking him to the Colonna Gallery to study famous painters such as Poussin, Lorrain and Rosa.[239]

A now forgotten but then well-known antiquarian was ALOYS HIRT (1759-1837), in Rome 1782-96, who acted as *cicerone* to Goethe, Herder and Stolberg. The first left us a round picture:

> Born in Fürstenberg in 1759, he studied classical literature and, as a result, felt an irresistible urge to come to Rome. He had arrived there some years before I did, acquired a profound knowledge of architecture and sculpture, both ancient and modern, and assumed the role of a guide for such foreign visitors as were anxious to learn. Among those to whom he sacrificed much time was myself.
>
> His main interest was architecture, and, as one might expect in a city so given to wrangling and taking sides, his theories on that art provoked stimulating debates and heated discussions. Hirt's thesis was that all Greek and Roman architecture was derived from the timber buildings of earlier times, and on this he based his judgements, favourable or unfavourable, skilfully backing up his contentions with historical examples.[240]

Without doubt the most noticed visitor to Rome in the eighteenth century was JAMES STUART (1688-1766), the 'Old Pretender' (see ill. opposite). Pöllnitz in 1730 stated that he had a pension of 12,000 *scudi*, and access to the pope by a secret stairway. His son the 'Prince of

*Alexis Simon
Belle,* James
Stuart, 'The
Old Pretender',
c. *1712*

Wales' was given precedence over cardinals, but his sons had been
raised as Protestants, and every Sunday an Anglican minister preached
in the palace. Pöllnitz often dined with him and the table for twelve
was magnificently served. His wife, Princess Clementina Sobieski, was
remarkably sweet and humble, led the life of a saint, and spoke Polish,
German, French, Italian and English. His mistress was Mme Hay.
Montesquieu's first impressions were of 'a handsome and noble phys-
ionomy', and that he seemed 'sad and pious; they say he is weak and
stubborn'. He trusted only Cardinal Filippo Gualtieri, Colonel John
Hay (brother-in-law of Dunbar and Secretary of State 1725-7) and
Cardinal Pierre Tencin. The Pretender is quoted as saying that he

could not take a step without its being known in England. Montesquieu ended with an 'audience' with the Princess, and reported the breakdown in marital relations. Keysler revealed that the Pretender was known as *Rex in partibus (infidelium)*, that is, like an ecclesiastical appointment overseas in lands not under the Church's control. 'The only time he has been known to affect the least power' was when he recently encored a song at the opera! His amours in Bologna were well known; the pope effected a reconciliation with the princess by cutting off his pension. She died in 1735. Five years later de Brosses offered a nuanced portrait:

> Our last visit was to the King of England. He is treated here with all the consideration due to a sovereign. His palace is in the Piazza of the SS Apostoli, a huge but ugly building. Here the papal troops mount guard, just as they do at Monte Cavallo, and accompany the king when he goes out, which he does not often do. His household is pretty large, as several followers who have attached themselves to him live with him. The most distinguished of these is [James Murray] Lord Dunbar, a Scotsman, an accomplished person and much respected, to whom he has confided the education of his children, although Lord Dunbar professes the Anglican faith, but this may be for political reasons. The Pretender is easily recognised for a Stuart; he has it written in his face. He is tall and thin, and resembles the portraits of his father, James II., very closely, and also the late Marshal Berwick, his natural brother, only that the Marshal had a sad and severe expression, whereas the Pretender's is not only sad, but silly. He does not lack dignity in his manner, and I have never seen a prince hold a court circle with so much grace and ease. He has occasionally to appear in public in spite of the retirement in which he lives, although he has none of the actual glitter about him appertaining to other sovereigns; but he does his best to make himself liked in a town to which he owes much, and he occasionally exerts himself at public ceremonies, when his sons do the honours, while he only appears for an hour or two. He is an ultra *dévot*, and his mornings are passed in prayer at the grave of his wife in the Church of the

SS Apostoli. As to his intellect, I am unable to judge, but his appearance is not in his favour. He appears for a moment on returning from church, then he retires to his study, which he only leaves to go to dinner. He talks little, but what he says is conveyed with amiability, and he soon retires.

Thomas Gray saw James frequently at church, in the Corso, and elsewhere, especially the great ball given by the Patrizii for Prince Craon:

> He is a thin, ill-made man, extremely tall and awkward, of a most unpromising countenance, a good deal resembling King James the Second, and has extremely the air and look of an idiot, particularly when he laughs or prays. The first he does not often, the latter continually. He lives private enough with his little court about him, consisting of Lord Dunbar, who manages every thing, and two or three of the Preston Scotch Lords, who would be very glad to make their peace at home.

Thomas Spence attended the opera in 1741, and found himself in a box under the Pretender. He therefore followed the Roman custom and visited other boxes, including one opposite his own. The Pretender was with his second son, Lord Dunbar and the French ambassador Saint-Aignan (Paul Beauvilliers). He 'looks sensibly older since I was here last; he read his opera book with spectacles'. Lady Mary Montagu was anxious to say that she never once met the Pretender, although she caught sight of his sons, and left Rome early (in 1741) 'since I found that (in spite of all my Caution) if I had staid it had been impossible for me to escape suspicions I in no way deserv'd, and the Spys are so numerous and such foolish rogues, a small matter would have serv'd for accusation'. She was convinced there were attempts to concoct a sham plot; her source was Mark Parker. Samuel Sharp saw James the year before he died. From his demeanour in St Peter's, he deduced 'the extreme bigotry and superstitious turn of his mind... [H]is stature is very elegant, but his face is a little bloated and pimpled as if he had drunk too much.' Sharp noted the declining cause of the Stuarts: four 'heads of colleges' (two Irish, one English and one

Scottish) had been banished for saying mass for him as king. The economic power of English tourism was tremendous: 'the King of England has it much in his power to distress the Ecclesiastical State, by discouraging his Nobility and Gentry from coming to Rome'.[241]

On his death in 1766, James Edward was succeeded by the 'Young Pretender', CHARLES EDWARD STUART (1720-1788), who was closely associated with his younger brother Henry, Cardinal York (1725-1806). De Brosses had a long account of both of them in 1740:

> Of the two sons of the Pretender the eldest [*sic*] is now in his twentieth year, the second is fifteen: they are known by the names of the Prince of Wales and the Duke of York. Both have the family look strongly marked, but the second has a pretty boyish face. They are amiable and graceful, but both are narrow-minded, and less intelligent than princes of their years should be. The youngest is popular here owing to his agreeable presence and pleasant manners. The English, of whom there are crowds in Rome, are always eager to see these youths. They ask us to inform them where and when they are likely to meet them, and talk of the second with much interest. By English law they are forbidden, on pain of capital punishment, to enter the Palace of the Stuarts, or to attach themselves to them, but as we see a good deal of these princes we are able to give them information by which they are able to see them. The eldest son is said to be more liked in his family than the second, and is declared to have a good heart as well as great courage; it is commonly reported that he feels his situation acutely, and that if he does not come to the front it will not be owing to lack of energy.

At the same time Gray stated that he saw the two boys in the garden of the villa Borghese, 'where they go shooting almost every day'. He also saw them at a ball: 'They are good fine boys, especially the younger, who has the more spirit of the two, and both danced incessantly all night long.' Lady Mary Montagu also saw them at a ball in 1741: 'they were very richly adorn'd with Jewells. The eldest [*sic*] seems thoughtless enough... The youngest is very well made, dances finely and has an ingenuous Countenance.' By the time of the next impressions, the '45 was history and Henry was a cardinal (1747). Lady Anne Miller in 1771 was told not to address or to answer the 'King'. At the home of Duchess Bracciano he came and sat next to her!

> He is naturally above the middle size, but stoops excessively; he appears bloated and red in the face, his countenance heavy and sleepy, which is attributed to his having given in to excess of drinking; but when a young man he must have been esteemed handsome. His complexion is of the fair tint, his eyes blue, his hair light brown, and the contour of his face a long oval; he is by no means thin, has a noble presence, and a graceful manner; his dress was scarlet, laced with a broad gold lace; he wears the blue riband outside of his coat, from which depends a cameo (antique) as large as the palm of my hand... [U]pon the whole, he has a melancholic, mortified appearance.

Next evening at Princess Palestrina's he tried to teach her how to play *tarochi*! Smith, finally, in the year before his death saw him in his coach at Carnival:

> the very image of a drunken Silenus more asleep than awake, and apparently tottering on the brink of that grave to which he is since gone. The small remains of expression to be seen in his face were the appearance of good nature. He was often accompanied by his legitimated daughter, the Duchess of Albany, a lively and unaffected woman, but without any personal charms.

Charles' sobriquet was 'King of the Twelve Apostles' because he lived in that piazza.[242]

One of the most notorious antiquarians was THOMAS JENKINS (1722-98). Our fullest source is Jones, the artist in Rome 1776-7. He had mentioned that Jenkins and Byers both gave Christmas dinners and competed for attention. Jenkins had a villa at Castel Gandolfo. And when Jones was robbed at his lodgings, Jenkins took him to the governor to make an affidavit and found him alternative accommodation. 'Mr Jenkins' attention in this Affair was greater than I could have expected and claimed my warmest gratitude.' When Jones found himself equally put upon by his new landlord, however, and insisted on moving again, 'from this time I found myself declining more and more every Day, as far as decorum would permit, in Mr J-'s favour'. In short, Jenkins expected complete obedience from his clients. Goethe in 1787 described Jenkins' villa: 'an imposing house which had once been the home of the General of the Jesuits. It had plenty of accommodation for guests, salons for gay parties and covered walks where one could stroll in cheerful company.' The pickings from antiquities dealing were obviously rich. And Gray in 1791 noted that the English preferred their own company to 'being carried in crowds, under Mr Jenkins' protection, to concerts and conversazioni, at the house of princess Santa Croce or the cardinal de Bernis'.[243]

ANGELIKA KAUFFMANN (1741-1807) (see ill. opposite) was one of the most celebrated visitors to Rome in the later eighteenth century. She spoke English, and painted portraits of many English visitors. She formed a very close relationship with Goethe, who reveals intimate details:

> Considering her great talent and her fortune, she is not as happy as she deserves to be. She is tired of commissions, but her old husband [the painter Antonio Zucchi] thinks it wonderful that so much money should roll in for what is often easy work. She would like to paint to please herself and have more leisure to study and take pains, and she could easily do this. They have no children and they cannot even spend the interest on her capital: indeed, they could live on the money she earns every day by working moderately hard. But she doesn't do anything about it and she won't.

In February 1787 he recorded that she bought a painting by Titian and another by Bordone, at considerable cost, and that they inspired her to paint 'in a new style'. The most remarkable source relating to her, however, is Johann Herder, who became infatuated with her, and kept writing to his wife how much she would like Angelika! She painted his portrait: she was 'a rare and pure creature of art, a true heavenly music of grace, completeness and discretion and possessed a totally indescribable goodness of heart'! Sitting for her had been the

Angelika Kauffman,
Self-portrait, *1770-5*

most enjoyable time he had spent in Italy. A more balanced sketch is provided by the French artist Elisabeth Vigée le Brun:

> I found her very interesting, apart from her great talent, by her wit and intellectual powers. She is a woman of about fifty, very delicate, her health was destroyed by her misfortune in marrying an adventurer [the so-called Count de Horn], who ruined her. She married after his death an architect, who is also her man of business; she talked to me for some time, and very well, during the two evenings I passed with her. Her conversation is very gentle; she is very well informed, but totally devoid of enthusiasm.[244]

Dr Burney is our major source on music at Rome in this century, and his most complete portrait of a musician is that of FERDINANDO MAZZANTI:

In the evening went with Mr. Leighton, by appointment, to Mazzanti's where I had a fine dish of music and saw all his curiosities – he sings in a very rich taste, but has now but a thread of a voice. He has a great collection of Prenestine's [Palestrina's] music and has given me leave to have what I will copied. He is famous for singing the poem of Tasso to the same melody as the Baccarolli [*sic*: gondoliers] do at Venice, with infinite taste, accompanying himself with the violin. I got him to write down the melody. He has composed a great deal himself – such as operas, motets, quintets, quartets and trios for violins. He plays the violin himself pretty well, and has the best Steiner I ever saw. Has studied the theory of music very much, has an abridgement of the Modulation of Prenestina very well done.[245]

Burney is our major source on this musician, who is unknown to standard reference works.

One of the best known guides was COLIN MORISON (1732-1810), *cicerone* to Boswell, but their relations were complex. 'Disputed on religion with Morison,' wrote Boswell. 'Morison, ill-humoured Scot, disputed *matter*. He near impertinent, but kept him right. Then owned you were Catholic once, as Rouseau had been. He quite stony.' Morison himself was a Catholic. Burney found him 'admirably well informed about antiquities… to be depended on for references to classical remains and sculpture that is genuine'.[246]

The death of another famous antiquarian, MATTHEW NULTY (1716-1778) was noted by Jones:

He was an *Irishman* by birth, but had, I believe, spent the greatest part of his life in *Italy* – at one time he subsisted at *Venice* & other Cities as an itinerant Fan-painter, & if I recollect right, he told me that the late ingenious Mr Stewart (the *Athenian Stewart* as he was called) was his Associate in the same profession – however they were both very intimate, & pass'd through a great Variety of Scenes together – & he used to say that if it were not for fear of giving Offence to that Gentleman, & some other friends, he could have made a very entertaining history of their Adventures – At Rome, he occasionaly was what they call Antiquarian to some of our English Cavaliers, that is to say, a person who goes about with them to shew and explain the Curiosities and Antiquities – but not being of that oily supple disposition necessary to the Profession & disdaining the little Arts & pretensions to antient Erudition that most of these gentlemen assume – he did not find much employment in that Line – None indeed in my time – I believe he had a small Pension from some English Gentleman, whom he had formerly served in that Capacity, with which his few wants were easily satisfied – & I believe it was to this very Gentleman, that he behaved in the following characteristic manner – Having accepted of an Invitation to accompany him & his Lady to England, in his traveling Coach – when they had made about half their journey – The Gentleman happened to expatiate a little upon the Convenience of the Carriage – Old Nulty taking this as an innuendo of the Obligation he was under – order'd the Coach to stop, & out he jump'd – 'Sir says he I have traveld thousands of Miles *on foot, & can do it* again with more pleasure than in your Coach', and notwithstanding all persuations to the Contrary, walked the rest of the way to England – Poor old *Nulty* was a professed Deist & certain it is that no Philosopher, antient or modern, not Socrates himself, could have spoken with more Ease & unconcern of his approaching dissolution than what he did – After a fortnight or three weeks confinement to his Bed, he had Strength & Resolution enough to crawl to the English Coffeehouse – to take his final leave – he sat all the Afternoon – drank two half pint tumblers of rum punch, conversed cheerfully – Shook hands with us all round, & bid us adieu for ever – The next day, being the 24th of June he dyed & was buried the night following – Whether it was from Accident or Design I know not – but when the Corps was brought to the Grave – No Common prayer-book was to be found – so with a Pater noster alone it was consigned to ye Earth. – Upon which the Romans who attended, observing that we had not adhered to our usual funeral Rites – said We had lookd upon him as an Infidel as well as they themselves had –[247]

An intriguing portrait of Cardinal PIETRO OTTOBONI (1667-1740) is given by de Blainville. He was a nephew of Alexander VIII, and had an income of 80,000 *scudi*. His character was marked by gratitude and generosity: he ennobled a French wig-maker who was a favourite. Walpole told the story of the visit to Ottoboni's collection by Henry Howard, earl of Carlisle. Ottoboni told the servant who accompanied them to observe Carlisle's reactions, and the next morning all the cameos which he had admired most were sent to him. Carlisle responded by sending Ottoboni a fine gold repeater, whereupon the cardinal sent him an agate snuff box and cameos worth ten times more. He had been offered the hand of Princess Rospigliosi by her father with one million *scudi* dowry. He loved poetry, music and men of learning, and held an 'academy' every fortnight in the palazzo della Cancelleria. He also provided a concert every Wednesday; he employed Arcangelo Corelli and the singer Paolucci, and arranged the contest between Scarlatti and Händel. He died during the conclave of 1740.[248]

Cardinal DOMENICO PASSIONEI (1682-1761) received a fulsome, but not entirely uncritical account from de Brosses in 1740. He

> often ridicules to me the false air of grandeur assumed by his fellow Cardinals, of whom he has on the whole but a poor opinion, for he tells me they are an ignorant set, eaten up with ambition, who only care to attain the top of the profession in the Pontificate, and are so intoxicated by that desire that there is hardly one who does not believe he will succeed in attaining it. 'As for me,' he said, 'I do not dream of such a thing. I have all that I need, and owe no one anything. I have had to serve thirty-two years, and I was made a Cardinal when they could not do otherwise. Some of the others find fault, and ridicule my frankness and familiarity of manner, and I return the compliment by abusing them for their ignorance, their grimaces, and their shady politics.' Passionei is anxious to be considered a literary genius. This is one of the reasons which makes him so open-mouthed about the ignorance of his colleagues, among whom the only learned ones are Lambertini [Benedict XIV] and [Angelo] Quirini...
>
> I found the Cardinal stretched out at full length on a sofa, his

wig on one side and his red cap on the other. I was going to seat myself on a chair when he said, 'Come and sit here by me; you will be more comfortable.' As I made a show of resistance, he seized me by the collar and threw me on the sofa, exclaiming, 'No ceremony, if you please. You do not know me. I am not a fool, although I am the Pope's Secretary.' In this manner our acquaintance was begun. His enemies say this familiarity is all on the surface, and that his religion – for he is said to be very religious – is also as superficial; in short, that he is not to be trusted. I, however, take him as I find him, and believe him quite sincere.

Hervey in 1761 told of him *in extremis*. He was one of the three palatinate cardinals living in the Vatican. A children's catechism had been published which Passionei approved, but which the other cardinals condemned. A decree was issued forbidding it. Passionei refused to sign, whereupon Clement XIII told him to do so or resign. He did so, but fell down in an apoplectic fit, and 'entirely lost one half of his body'. Now he was 'in agonies'.[249]

JOHANN PICKLER (1734-1791) was well known in the antiquarian world as a famous stone- cutter; his father had been the same before him. Tischbein was especially impressed with his 'handsome manly build and noble face which charmed everyone; his whole being was calm and his speech very wise'. The German painter often studied and drew his collection of plaster impressions of outstanding antique heads. His talent in carving small heads in hard stone was extraordinary.[250]

Of the various salons one of the best known and most frequented was that of Mme MARIA PIZELLI (1735-1807). Dutens in 1769 described her as known for her 'culture, commonsense, taste, sweetness, modesty, and goodheartedness, with an interesting appearance and an extremely engaging manner'.[251]

JOHANNES REIFFENSTEIN (1719-93) (see ill. overleaf), the Prussian ambassador, was also a leading antiquarian. Our main impressions are owed to Goethe. Reiffenstein organised the young German artists into evening meetings to discuss their development. He was passionate about propagating plants by striking twigs, and also developed

Giovanni Morghen,
Johannes Reiffenstein,
eighteenth century

two methods for helping visitors relax after the rigours of sightseeing: encaustic painting and modelling jewellery in paste. The main product of the former was the already mentioned copy of the Raphael Loggie for Catherine of Russia. In the latter, practised in the old kitchen in Reiffenstein's villa, molten glass paste was poured into a paste mould of the original and fired. On an expedition to Frascati, however, the younger artists made fun of him for his eccentricities. He never tired of recommending that a visitor should not begin with the best art but work up to it gradually, so as not to be disappointed by lesser pieces after seeing the best. Goethe's friend Tischbein was a little less flattering: he was 'an honest man, but had no originality'. He acted like a steward who could not be corrected. He came to Rome as tutor to Count Lynar, and stayed as a guide. He was also a musician and artist, but 'the best thing that he did' was to help Carlo Fea with the Italian translation of Winckelmann's history of art in antiquity.[252]

Another portrait of a musician of the time presented by Burney is of GIUSEPPE SANTARELLI (1710–90), castrato and musicologist. He had 'the most taste of anyone I have yet conversed with in Italy' and was preparing an account of church music. He explained to Burney that the beauty of Allegri's *Miserere* 'arise[s] more from the manner in which it is performed than from the composition'. This same judgement, intriguingly, had been offered by the Mozarts. The choir in the pope's chapel consisted of eight trebles, eight contraltos, eight tenors and eight basses, all dressed in purple, but the music here, Santarelli said, was beginning to decline, because of the high salaries paid in the opera houses and the low esteem in which music was held by the 'first dignitaries of the church'. He was extraordinarily helpful and generous to Burney.[253]

One of the most notorious figures of the time was Baron PHILIP STOSCH (1691-1757), antiquarian and spy on behalf of Hanover on the Jacobites. Montesquieu told the story of an Englishman who spoke badly of the Pretender, who demanded punishment. Stosch claimed French protection for the offender and warned of English retribution

Pier Leone Ghezzi, The Congress of Antiquarians (detail), 1725, showing Baron Stosch (seated foreground) with his famous owl perched behind him and his secretary at the table behind him

against Italians in England. Keysler told of Stosch's blocking of a move by the Pretender to Lungara, where he would be less in the public eye, by threatening the pope with unspecified English retaliation. It was Stosch's private habits which attracted attention: 'His apartment is not the neatest I have seen. His constant companion in it, some time since, was a young boor [the animal, not the human variety], but having presented this to a young English gentleman, it has been succeeded by several owls.' Asked about their dirty habits, he explained that, since he was a hypochondriac, these birds, 'still more dull and saturnine' than he, restored his spirits!²⁵⁴

Cardinal PIERRE TENCIN (1679-1758) was long a leading French player in the highest politics. When Polignac came to Rome he was warned against having much to do with the Pretender, but he was amazed to see that Tencin never left his side. He, Gualtieri and Hay were the only three people trusted by James. Polignac told that Tencin bought his promotion from Hay. De Brosses in 1740 found him most gracious: 'he begged us to look on his house and table as our own; and only regretted that, owing to the great number of people he had to lodge, he could not furnish us with rooms… Surely never was there such a charming person'!²⁵⁵

SOURCE NOTES

1. *Protestants.
2. Dupaty, 163; Smith, 2.299.
3. Keysler, 2.382; de Brosses, 148-9; Staszic in Bilinski, 194.
4. de Brosses, 140-1.
5. Jones, 54, 61, 67, 69.
6. Vigée le Brun, 124-5.
7. Smollett, 223.
8. Smollett, 223; Knight, 105.
9. Keysler, 2.149; Smollett, 223; Knight, 105.
10. Keysler, 2.262, 303, 376; Richard, 166.
11. Montesquieu, 736, Archenholz, 2.49, Keysler, 467, Moore, 487, Arnauld, 293, Starke, 338; Herder, 187; Miller, 3.25.
12. The evidence for Ficoroni's guiding Addison and Spence is, interestingly, not in their standard accounts, but in a letter of Spence's, quoted in his *Observations*, ed. J. Osborn, Oxford 1966, para 1365.
13. Smollett, 224; Jones, 53; Beckford, 230; Arnauld, 3.253; Meyer, 206f.
14. Dupaty, 130.
15. Wright, 1.251; so Montesquieu, 797, although he placed Daniel second and Domenichino third, and omitted Sacchi, and Silhouette, 131, 151; Burney, 131, 151; Smith, 1.344; Arnauld, 3.293.
16. Herder, 193, 194; Moszyński, 210; Pöllnitz, *Lettres*, 2.251, 245.
17. Goethe, 148, 150; Gray, 425; Montesquieu, 708.
18. Starke, 1.333.
19. Jones, 68, 75, 87, 88; Herder, 279, 293; Stolberg, 378.
20. Montesquieu, 707; de Brosses, 183; Meyer, 218; Sharp, 43; Miller, 3.74; Smollett, 224-5; Knight, 179. For lists of the English aristocracy at Rome in 1778, see Jones, 70; for English artists in 1776, Jones, 53; and in 1791, Gray, 369f.

21. Walpole, 209; Richard, 162; de Brosses, 206; Vigée le Brun, 132f.

22. Goethe, 414; Stolberg, 432. For German artists at Rome in 1783 see Meyer, 124; Goethe, 423.

23. Nugent, 3.212-270.

24. Northall, 127, 376.

25. Montesquieu, 690; Keysler, 2.335; Silhouette, 1.238.

26. Meyer, 88; Silhouette, 1.222-4; de Brosses, 216; Volkmann, 2.34f.; Coyer, 1.162; Smollett, 236; Moszyński, 208; Labat, 3.124f.; Staszic in Bilinski, 194.

27. Montesquieu, 691; de Brosses, 217; Smollett, 237; Berkeley, 232; Smollett, 236; see also Volkmann, 2.65, Smith, 1.350; Silhouette, 1.234; Volkmann, 2.65; Coyer, 1.186.

28. Volkmann, 2.75f.; Keysler, 2.268; Richard, 345.

29. Wright, 206; Richard, 330; Goethe, 142.

30. Pöllnitz, Lettres, 2.161; Montesquieu, 688; Keysler, 2.273; Richard, 332; Sharp, 54; Smith, 2.197; Smollett, 237.

31. Archenholz, 2.51f.; Riesch, 2.98; Wright, 1.206; Smith, 1.344; Hervey, 3.195.

32. Arnauld, 3.284; Smith, 2.257.

33. Caylus, 191; de Saint-Non, 137f., 143; de la Platière, 5.305; Burney, 142; de Sade, 292, 293; relics: de Blainville, 2.560; so Caylus 190, Berkeley, 245, Burney, 142, de Sade, 296; chaises: Keysler, 2.195, Berkeley, 245, de Sade, 296. de Brosses, 272, de Sade, 296.

34. Keysler, 2.245; so Richard, 420, Burney, 132; de Sade, 201; Caylus, 185; de Brosses, 246; de Saint-Non, 136; de la Platière, 5.303; so Stolberg, 375; Hervey, 3.199; Berkeley, 228.

35. de Blainville, 2.572; Keysler, 2.221; de Brosses, 272; Richard, 416; Burney, 141; de Sade, 231-2.

36. de Sade, 219-20; ibid., 221-2.

37. de Sade, 266; ibid., 207; de Blainville, 3.72; de Brosses, 196; Smith, 2.166.

38. Montesquieu, 711; de Sade, 216; Smith, 2.172; Montesquieu, 690; de Sade, 275-7; de Sade, 299-300.

39. de Sade, 215-6; ibid, 278; de Brosses, 194, Caylus, 182; de Sade, 270; ibid., 282.

40. Berkeley, 238; de Sade, 244-5; ibid., 247; ibid., 239.

41. Montesquieu, 690; Smith, 2.161; Aracœli: de Blainville, 2.481; Montesquieu, 702-3; de Brosses, 239; Meyer, 145; Concezione: de Brosses, 163; de Sade, 245-7; Pembroke, 275; Minerva: de Blainville, 3.54; de Brosses, 195; Smollett, 256; also de Sade, 252; Pace: de Sade, 302; Goethe, 434.

42. Smollett, 220; de Sade, 195-8; Smith, 2.23; de Blainville, 2.456.

43. de Sade, 260; ibid., 306-7; Berkeley, 244; de Saint-Non, 145; Coyer, 169; de Sade, 204; Riesch, 2.222; Dupaty, 272; Smith, 2.157.

44. de Brosses, 239; de Sade, 309; de Blainville, 2.568; de Sade, 228; again he described also the lower levels. Caylus, 186; Wright, 1.243.

45. Montesquieu, 697; Keysler, 2.247; de Brosses, 225-6; Smollett, 256-7; de la Platière, 5.400; Goethe, 432-3; Stolberg, 405.

46. de Blainville, 2.570f.; Labat, 3.323; Richard, 440; Boswell, 66-7; de Sade, 223; Pembroke, 278.

47. de Sade, 229-30; de Blainville, 3.1; Smith, 2.159; de Sade, 259; Caylus, 192; Berkeley, 244; de Brosses, 245; de Sade, 289; de la Platière, 3.260.

48. de Blainville, 3.38; Montesquieu, 670; de Brosses, 151-2; de Sade, 249.

49. de Blainville, 2.541f.; Keysler, 2.319; Pembroke, 270-1; de Brosses, 269; Hobhouse, 181.

50. Goethe, 159-60.

51. Berkeley, 237; Spence, 344-5; Goethe, 162.

52. Hervey, 2.557; Caylus, 189; de Blainville, 2.326; Mozart, 126; Berry, 1.106-7; Smith, 2.263; Gray, 59-60, so Walpole, 210; Smith, 2.267; de Saint-Non, 141; Mozart, 127; Keysler, 2.122, see also Duclos, 212f.; Vigée le Brun, 128-9.

53. Dupaty, 298-9; Goethe, 348; Meyer, 184f.

54. Grosley, 2.105.

55. Goethe, 142-3.

56. de Brosse, 270-2.

57. Gray, 385.

58. Thompson, 1.160; so, much shorter, Pöllnitz, Lettres, 2.197.

59. de Brosses, 201; Keysler, 2.342.

60. de Brosses, 195; Keysler, 2.341; Smollett, 258.

61. de Blainville, 3.82, with full lists of
antiquities and paintings; Caylus, 188;
Berkeley, 235; Breval, 2.302; further list
of antiquities, Wright, 1.289; Keysler,
2.343-9; de Brosses, 164-5; de Saint-Non,
150; Smollett, 257; Burney, 152-3; de Sade,
326-36; de la Platière, 5.335; Smith, 2.214.
The tortured history of the Barberini is
not easy to find (the *Dizionario biografico degli italiani* is interested only in the
famous members). Their days of glory,
power and wealth were, of course, the
preceding century, with Urban VIII and
his two brothers, and this continued with
the next generation providing two cardinals. The title prince of Palestrina was
added in 1630, but Maffeo (d. 1685) was
succeeded by Urbano (1664-1722), whose
son Matteo died in 1703, aged four. The
heiress of the family was thus Camilla
(1716-1797), who married Giulio Cesare
Colonna (1702-1787), Their son, Carlo
Maria (1735-1819) must be the prince
whom the eighteenth century visitors
complain of. Religious importance was
all very well, but generation after generation one male was left to carry on the
family, a highly dangerous ploy, which
produced the inevitable result.
62. de Blainville, 3.85f.; Berkeley, 233; Keysler,
2.350f.; Thompson, 159; de Brosses, 154;
Smollett, 257; de Sade, 321-6.
63. de Blainville, 3.69; de Brosses, 200;
Keysler, 2.353.
64. de Blainville, 2.458; Wright, 1.296;
Richardson, 282f.; Keysler, 2.377; de
Brosses, 156.
65. Addison, 473-4; (for the Raphael compare the *Madonna with Christ, four saints
and four angels* in the Pitti); de Blainville,
2.432f, see also Keysler, 2.378.
66. Breval, 2.307; Wright, 1.305; de Brosses,
185. The only *Pietà* ascribed to Guercino
is now in Rennes.
67. de Saint-Non, 147; Smollett, 257; Burney,
131; de Sade, 340-3. The only genuine
Magdalen by Correggio is in London, but
did not come via the Colonna collection,
but there are many copies, one of which
is in Rome.
68. Riesch, 2.127f; Stolberg, 310, 430.
69. Burney, 148. Magdalen was a very popular

subject with Titian. There is none now
in the Doria collection, but a fine one
painted for Urbino now in the Pitti.
70. de Sade, 333-6. – The only *Prodigal Son*
known by Guercino is now in San Diego.
71. Smith, 2.224.
72. de Blainville, 3.65f; Wright, 1.282;
Silhouette, 1.247, so Thompson, 1.156; de
Brosses, 202f; Smollett, 255; Burney, 134;
Miller, 3.85; Moore, 2.10; Dupaty, 178;
Goethe, 161, 346.
73. Blainville, 3.54f, also Wright, 1.302;
Richardson, 153f; Keysler, 2.389f; de
Brosses, 197-8. The only portrait of Julius
II by Raphael is in the Uffizi, and the
only Judgement of Solomon by Poussin is
in the Louvre, but neither had belonged
to the Giustiniani.
74. de Saint-Non, 151; de Sade, 336-40. Only
copies are now known of Caravaggio's
Crowning with Thorns, in Vienna and
Florence.
75. Goethe, 159, 382; Smith, 2.218.
76. Wright, 1.299; Keysler, 2.392. – Of
Caravaggio's Scourging, there is only a
copy at Macerata. There are some three
Dürers of Mary and Christ surviving, but
the description here is too summary to
identify it.
77. Breval, 2.310; Wright, 1.317; Keysler,
2.393; de Brosses, 251.
78. Keysler, 2.393.
79. de Blainville, 3.79f, much the same in
Wright, 1.308f; Breval, 2.301, so Keysler,
2.353; Berkeley, 232; de Brosses, 192. –
There is a roundel with the Madonna,
Christ (but lacking St John) and two
saints in Berlin.
80. de Brosses, 267-8; Goethe, 130-1; Smith,
2.229.
81. Goethe, 364; Stolberg, 383.
82. de Blainville, 2.445; Keysler, 2.401; de
Brosses, 268. – Domenichino's *Adam and
Eve*: there is one surviving painting of this
title, which belonged to the Barberini,
now in a private collection in Brasil.
Otherwise there is the *Expulsion from the
Garden* now in Grenoble, but that was in
the Colonna collection in 1783. Poussin's
Samson crushing the Philistines: perhaps
Joshua against the Amorites (Pushkin
Museum, Moscow). There is no *David*

with the head of Goliath now listed among Poussin's paintings.

83. Keysler, 2.401 and 1.402.

84. There are versions of del Sarto's *Mary and Elizabeth* in the Louvre, Munich and Florence, but none via the Spada collection.

85. Keysler, 2.402; Miller, 3.90; Breval, 2.269.

86. Montesquieu, 669; de Brosses, 195.

87. Pöllnitz, *Lettres*, 2.179; Sharp, 62; Berkeley, 226; Montesquieu, 693; Breval, 2.282; Silhouette, 1.218; de Brosses, 224; de Saint-Non, 142; West in Galt, 105f; Coyer, 166; Boswell, 70, 89; Smollett, 252-3; Moore, 2.15f; Riesch, 2.95; Dupaty, 203; Goethe, 363; Stolberg, 2.432.

88. Riesch, 2.90f; Meyer, 105f; Moszyński, 208; Goethe, 422; Archenholz, 2.74.

89. Starke, 2.2.

90. Montesquieu, 696; de Brosses, 222; Reynolds, *Letters*, 30; Breval, 2.279; Wright, 1.261; Volkmann, 2.102f; Richard, 358; Smollett, 251; de la Platière, 5.317; Moszyński in Bilinski, 185; Goethe, 146, 376, 380; Smith, 2.57; Stolberg, 439.

91. Montesquieu, 687-8; de Brosses, 219-21; much the same in Volkmann, 2.111f; Reynolds in McIntyre, 50, 56; de Saint-Non, 139; Richard, 365; Smollett, 251; Burney, 147; Tischbein, 135; Moszyński in Bilinski, 186; Vigée le Brun, 122; Wright, 2.7f.

92. Montesquieu, 692, 705; de Brosses, 223; Richard, 360; Goethe, 393-4.

93. Berkeley, 225; Thompson, 1.151; de Brosses, 249-51 (Richard, 384, also describes the T-shaped arrangement of the library); Smollett, 258; Burney, 143, 145; Björnstahl, 2.260f, 3.52f; Herder, 193.

94. de Brosses, 193.

95. de Blainville, 2.461.

96. ibid.

97. Northcote, 39.

98. Burney, 148; Miller, 3.130; de la Platière, 5.340; Archenholz, 2.89; Goethe, 483; Riesch, 115f.

99. Berkeley, 242-3; Richardson, 305; Montesquieu, 664; de Brosses, 269; Miller, 3.134; de Sade, 320-1; Pembroke, 277-8; Stolberg, 444.

100. de Blainville, 3.30f; Caylus, 186-7; Berkeley, 227, 229-30; Dyer in Longstaff,

267; Montesquieu, 710; de Brosses, 154-5; Smollett, 234-6; Miller, 3.145f; Jones, 93, 91; Pembroke, 276-7; Riesch, 2.105f; Meyer, 218f; Berry, 1.68; Stolberg, 351.

101. Montesquieu, 684-6; de Brosses, 226; Goethe, 361.

102. de Sade, 198-9; Smith, 2.243.

103. de Blainville, 3.25; de Brosses, 167-8; de Sade, 272-3; Pembroke, 278; Riesch, 2.159; Smith, 2.234f; Stolberg, 326f.

104. Montesquieu, 739; Burney, 133. – Ingamels, 1014, calls this the palazzo Rafaele between the villa Medici and villa Borghese!

105. Addison, 466; Room 1: a Seneca, an Amazon, Agrippina the Younger, Hadrian, Antoninus Pius, Marcus Aurelius, Brutus, Plenty, Commodus on horseback; Room 2: Antinoüs, Venus Erycina, satyr drawing thorn out of Silenus' foot, Ceres, Silenus on an ass, a green porphyry table (the only one in Rome); Room 3: a table of oriental stone, Brutus and Porcia, head of Cæsar; Room 4: busts of Cicero, Tiberius, L. Verus; Room 5: vase of jasper, statue of Agrippina, Domitia, Thalia, a gladiator, and a sarcophagus; Room 6: bust of Serapis, Hadrian, Antoninus Pius, Marcus Aurelius, Caracalla, Faustina the Younger, Geta, statues of Verus, three children asleep. Blainville, 2.554. Smaller selections: Wright, 1.337; Richardson, 177f; Riesch, 2.151f. – Pembroke, 274; Goethe, 485.

106. de Blainville, 3.26f; Berkeley, 237-8; Breval, 2.309; similarly Wright, 1.327-31; few details in Montesquieu, 670; de Brosses, 152; de Sade, 240-3; much more selective Riesch, 2.177.

107. Pöllnitz, *Lettres*, 2.159; Caylus, 187; Berkeley, 235; Miller, 3.134; de Sade, 209-10; Pembroke, 262.

108. de Blainville, 3.20; de Brosses, 270; de Sade, 248; de la Platière, 5.342; Riesch, 2.182; Smith, 2.233.

109. Tischbein, 125.

110. Richard, 212; Dupaty, 184; Montesquieu, 707; Walpole, 213-214; Montagu, 211; de la Platière, 83f; Moszyński, 211; Montesquieu, 669.

111. Montesquieu, 707; Goethe, 153, 155; de Brosses, 248-9.
112. Gray, 364-5; Dyer in Longstaff, 266; Arnauld, 254-5.
113. Gibbon, *Memoirs*, 134.
114. Addison, 459; Hobhouse, 179; Addison, 477.
115. Goethe, 168, 421.
116. de Blainville, 2.502; de Brosses, 241; Sharp, 53; Boswell, 63-4; Miller, 3.26; Smith, 280; Stolberg, 325; Moore, 1.443; Meyer, 151; Dupaty, 152; Volkmann, 2.521-2.
117. Addison, 480; de Sade, 314; de la Platière, 2.240; Riesch, 252; Hobhouse, 192; de Blainville, 2.492; Volkmann, 2.516; de Sade, 213.
118. Miller, 3.26; de Brosses, 242; Volkmann, 2.525; Grosley, 2.12; Riesch, 2.52; Archenholz, 2.27; de Brosses, 162-3; de Sade, 269; de la Platière, 2.242; de Sade, 269; Wright, 2.253; Breval, 2.268; de Sade, 307.
119. Breval, 2.294; Berkeley, 240.
120. Addison, 478; Breval, 2.66; Richardson, 310; de Brosses, 189; Meyer, 158; Hobhouse, 185.
121. de Blainville, 2.504; Breval, 2.298f cf. Lanciani, *Storia*, 6.29; Montesquieu, 693; de Brosses, 252-3; Boswell, 65; de Sade, 315-7, so Knight, 70; Hobhouse, 215; Starke, 1.344.
122. de Blainville, 2.467; Breval, 287; Pöllnitz, *Lettres*, 2.193; Smollett, 253-4; Labat, 3.309; Smith, 2.3; de la Platière, 5.325.
123. Breval, 2.293; Wright, 1.327; Moore, 1.444; Stolberg, 338.
124. This figure comes from the Chronographer of 354. Seating is now calculated at c. 50,000 (Claridge, 278).
125. de Blainville, 2.532f; Pöllnitz, *Lettres*, 2.196; Thompson, 1.138; de Brosses, 243; Walpole, 13,210; Volkmann, 2.165; Boswell, 64; Smollett, 241; Moore, 1.416; Beckford, 230-1; Dupaty, 299, 231; Moszyński in Bilinski, 189.
126. de Brosses, 244. – Domus Ciceronis: this was located at the foot of the Palatine near the temple of Jupiter Stator (i.e. Castor) by Fulvio and Marliani, but by most other antiquarians on the Palatine. See F. Nardini, *Roma antica*, 1665, 4th

edn, 1819, 3.199. – de Blainville, 2.535; de la Platière, 5.232.
127. Addison, 480; shamelessly plagiarised by de Blainville, 2.535; so Thompson, 1.125; de Brosses, 243; Barthelemy, 110, François Blondel, *Cours d'architecture*, Paris 1675-83; de Sade, 227-8; Dupaty, 228.
128. Berkeley, 233; Thompson, 1.122; de Brosses, 160-1; Volkmann, 2.317; de Saint-Non, 135; Smollett, 239; de Sade, 255f; Jones, 93; Archenholz, 1.231; Smith, 1.340; Stolberg, 1.424.
129. de Blainville, 3.43; Caylus, 191; Berkeley, 240; Grosley, 2.5; de la Platière, 5.287; Hobhouse, 235; Moszyński in Bilinski, 188; Goethe, 361.
130. Addison, 478: coins of 172-3 refer to *Religio Augusti*, Claudian, *sext. cons. Hon.* 339f; Berkeley, 242; Richardson, 311; Montesquieu, 706, so Keysler, 2.458; de Brosses, 155-6; Jones, 71; de Brosses, 157; de Sade, 244.
131. de Brosses, 163.
132. De Blainville, 2.245; Silhouette, 1.208f and Montesquieu, 702; West in Galt, 114; de la Platière, 5.324; Starke, 357.
133. Walpole, 213.
134. Berkeley, 240; de Brosses, 244; de Sade, 226.
135. Caylus, 184; Breval, 2.259; Thompson, 1.129; Smollett, 244; Starke, 360.
136. Berkeley, 237; Breval, 2.261; Stolberg, 1.306.
137. de Blainville, 2.513; de Sade, 265.
138. Berkeley, 246; Knight, 52; Archenholz, 2.163; Riesch, 2.146.
139. Berkeley, 231; de Blainville, 3.43; Breval, 2.248; Goethe, 383; Stolberg, 422; de Brosses, 165; Berry, 2.66; Goethe, 168.
140. Berkeley, 241-2; Montesquieu, 671; Smollett, 232.
141. de Blainville, 3.17; Caylus, 183; Berkeley, 244; Keysler, 2.180; de Brosses, 269; de Sade, 204; Keysler, 2.195.
142. de Blainville, 2.295; Caylus, 185; Berkeley in 1717 seems to say the same, 227; de Brosses, 247; Smollett, 248; de Sade, 201.
143. de Sade, 219.
144. de Blainville, 3.21; de Sade, 274. More puzzling is de Sade's reference to a nearby almost complete circular temple, with six niches. Lanciani's *Forma Urbis*

shows here the round temple of Venus in the Sallustian Gardens, but it is known only to Pirro Ligorio!

145. de Blainville, 2.470f; Caylus, 181; Breval, 2.287f; Silhouette, 1.200; Thompson, 1.128; de Brosses, 237-8; Volkmann, 2.479f; Smollett, 254-5; Burney, 137-8; Miller, 2.406; Riesch, 2.57-68; Goethe, 422; Smith, 2.202f; Stolberg, 334, 366f.
146. Grosley, 2.34f.; not known to Lanciani, *Storia*.
147. Addison, 467-8.
148. Addison, 462; illustrated in Lanciani, *Storia*, 2.93; de Blainville, 3.68.
149. Addison, 469.
150. Addison, 468; the name is not known to Lanciani's *Storia*.
151. de Sade, 261, not apparently in Lanciani, *Storia*, 6; Jones, 62; Berry, 1.95.
152. Labat, 3.329; Montesquieu, 686; Thompson, 1.120, still cited 120,000, as Duclos, 113; Moore, 1.399, 440; de la Platière, 5.112; Dupaty, 247; Bonstetten, 304.
153. de Brosse, 229; Walpole, 208, 214; Sherlock, 32-3; Gray, 373-4; Montesquieu, 676.
154. Labat, 3.68; lights: Coyer, 1.198, de la Platière, 5.107; Sherlock, 33.
155. Smollett, 226; de la Platière, 5.73; Archenholz, 2.14.
156. de Brosses, 147.
157. de Brosses, 215.
158. Goethe, 447-8; Miller, 3.35.
159. Jones, 54.
160. Ferber, 186f; Smith, 2.296.
161. de Blainville, 3.8, 58; Montesquieu, 797, 736; de Brosses, 146, 163; Riesch, 2.42; de Sade, 275; Duclos, 63; Goethe, 432.
162. Hervey, 3.189f; de la Platière, 5.113; Meyer, 205; Dupaty, 295f; Archenholz, 2.125.
163. de Blainville, 3.56; Labat, 3.277; Pöllnitz, *Lettres*, 2.243; de Brosses, 198; Tischbein, 216; de Blainville, 2.452; Berkeley, 231; Keysler, 2.297; Burney, 129; Pöllnitz, *Lettres*, 2.146; Duclos, 36; de Brosses, 139.
164. Pöllnitz, *Lettres*, 2.151; Thompson, 1.163; Wright, 1.274; Montesquieu, 670, 691; de Brosses, 150-1.
165. de Blainville, 2.414-6; Keysler, 2.217; Spence, 331-2; de Brosses, 143; Sherlock, 49; Goethe, 373.

166. Archenholz, 2.124.
167. Duclos, 65; Coyer, 286; de la Platière, 5.12; Dupaty, 249, 271; Moszyński, 207.
168. Archenholz, 2.132; Hervey, 3.177; ibid., 3.200; Archenholz, 2.152; Staszic in Bersano-Begey, 15.
169. Labat, 3.290; Merville, 2.60f; Hervey, 3.209.
170. Montesquieu, 677; Richard, 5.90, 238; Duclos, 126; Meyer, 158f; Archenholz, 1.245; Goethe, 145; Stolberg, 341; Hervey, 2.522f; Jones, 63, 67; Hervey, 3.231f; Burney, 143; Labat, 3.96-100; Staszic in Bersano-Begey, 23.
171. de Blainville, 23.40; Spence, 115. He was, in fact, heavily reliant on Conyers Middleton, *A letter from Rome*, 1729. Gray, 353.
172. Pöllnitz, *Lettres*, 2.327; Keysler, 2.139; de Brosses, 205-6; Richard, 104f; de la Platière, 5.22.
173. Montagu, 212, 215; Hervey, 2.522; Staszic in Bilinski, 195.
174. Labat, 3.87; Sharp, 204f; de Brosses, 230-1; Duclos, 203; Richard, 217; Labat, 3.92f; Richard, 219.
175. Montesquieu, 668, 669, 672, 678, 752; Duclos, 120; Richard, 220-3; Moszyński, 210; de la Platière, 5.24; Duclos, 117, 124; Riesch, 1.232f; de Blainville, 3.9.
176. Montesquieu, 667; lottery: Merville, 2.68; Moszyński, 205-6; Goethe, 346, 361.
177. Montagu, 212; de la Platière, 5.105f; Grosley, 68f.
178. Pöllnitz, *Lettres*, 2.259; Mozart, 127; Silhouette, 1.263; Richard, 5.68-9; ibid., 5.119.
179. Pöllnitz, *Lettres*, 2.206, 214; Walpole, 208-9; Richard, 5.126; Stolberg, 340; Meyer, 179; Jones, 55-56.
180. de la Platière, 5.77; Jones, 55; Dupaty, 286; Archenholz, 2.168; Richard, 114; Herder, 96; Montesquieu, 701; Merville, 2.53; Boswell, 54.
181. Labat, 3.208; de Brosses, 174-5; ibid., 141.
182. Labat, 3.273f; Keysler, 2.318; Richard, 272; Staszic in Bilinski, 193; Berkeley, 248; Miller, 3.101; de Brosses, 152-3; Björnstahl, 2.248.
183. Björnstahl, 2.273. See this fourteenth letter of Björnstahl (260f) for a general account of Roman libraries. Labat, 3.114;

de Brosses, 196; Richard, 468; de Sade, 254-5.

184. Merville, 2.79; Coyer, 1.199; Archenholz, 2.114f; Berry, 1.108; Goethe, 444-5; Staszic in Bersano-Begey, 13.

185. de Brosses, 192; Goethe, 381; de Sade, 309-11; Goethe, 480, 492.

186. Pöllnitz, *Lettres*, 2.151, 156-7; ibid., 2.246; de Brosses, 228-9. None of these women can be found in the *Indice biografico italiano* (fiche); Richard, 143; Moore, 1.384f; de la Platière, 5.55; Sherlock, 51-2; Stolberg, 304, 432; Moszyński, 207.

187. Deutsch, 16-23; Mozart, 131; Burney, 131. References consulted, without success, include *Dizionario biografico degli italiani, Indice biografico italiano* (fiche), *Dizionario enciclopedico universale della musica e dei musicisti*, K. Kutsch and L. Riemer, *Grosses Sängerlexikon*. – Burney, 138-9; ibid., 151, 153; Goethe, 476; Vigée le Brun, 130.

188. Richard, 175; Archenholz, 2.149, 182, Goethe, 365, 369.

189. Berkeley, 245; Montesquieu, 679-80; Pöllnitz, *Lettres*, 2.241; Spence, 342-3; de Brosses, 157-8; Hervey, 498f; Coyer, 192-5; Jones, 57; Smith, 2.55; Goethe, 465 and 366, 157.

190. Goethe, 466; Gray, 63. 'La Diamantina' is known only by this nickname: listed as such in Margaret Campbell, *The great violinists*, London 1980, 84, and Henry Roth, *Violin virtuosos*, Los Angeles 1997, 309.

191. Pöllnitz, *Lettres*, 2.244, 251; Richard, 210-2; Archenholz, 1.232f; Moszyński, 207; Dupaty, 248.

192. de Blainville, 2.483f.

193. Merville, 2.100f; ibid., 2.119f.

194. Merville, 2.425f. In the conclave of 1721 there were four 'parties': the 'Clementines' led by Albani; the 'Zelanti' under Fabroni; the Imperialists; and the Bourbons. There were some thirty papabili – a very high number. Cardinal Althan for the Emperor vetoed Paolucci. Conti was a serious contender from mid April. He was elected on the 75th ballot! See Pastor, 34.6f.

195. Montesquieu, 744-6. In the conclave of 1724 there were fifty-three electors.

Olivieri was thought to be too pro French. Piazzi was destroyed by the Albani. Orsini was a 'neutral' candidate. There are extraordinary accounts of the Imperial envoy Count Kaunitz climbing up and kneeling on a sill with his head through a window to communicate with Cienfuegos. Pastor, 34.98f.

196. Dyer in Longstaff, 267.

197. Pöllnitz, *Lettres*, 2.164f. In the conclave of 1730, there were 55 electors. There was no dominant party, and many were undecided; there were thirty papabili. Imperiali was vetoed by Spain. Corsini was supported by France and thought certain by mid May. Davia was favourite in June. Next came Corradini, but he was opposed by the courts. Hence the return to Corsini. Pastor, 34.303f. – Keysler, 2.114f.

198. Pöllnitz, *Lettres*, 2.217f.

199. Ibid., 2.301.

200. de Brosses, 158-9.

201. de Brosses, 274-5.

202. Walpole, 215-7; ibid., 220; Gray, 68; Duclos, 74. There were 56 participating cardinals in the conclave, divided into two main parties: the 'young' cardinals appointed by Clement XII, led by Neri Corsini, supported by France and Austria, and the 'older' cardinals led by Annibale Albani and supported by Spain. Ruffo was an early favourite (vetoed by France and Germany), then Porzia in April (who was one vote short), then Ferrao in June and Aldrovandi in July and August. Four cardinals died: Ottoboni, Altieri, Porzia and Cenci. Pastor, 35.1f.

203. Spence, 331-2.

204. Duclos, 48f.

205. Duclos, 75f.

206. Grosley, 118.

207. Hervey, 2.564; ibid., 3.122f

208. Ibid., 3.287, 301.

209. Albani. One would think naturally of Alessandro, cardinal since 1721 and dean of the cardinal deacons, in which capacity he crowned Clement XIII, XIV and Pius VI. His nephew, Giovan Francesco, however, cardinal since 1747, was the dean of the college. Pastor, however,

assigns no special role to either of them in this conclave (38.11).

210. Dutens, 1.259f.

211. Dutens, 270f; Mayer, 53f.

212. Moore, 1.452f.

213. Moore, 1.399f.

214. Jones, 68-9.

215. Ibid., 73.

216. Archenholz, 2.176f.

217. Starke, 1.114f.

218. Labat, 3,154f.

219. Montesquieu, 665; 667; 674-5; 739; 702. Keysler, 2.112f; Pöllnitz, Lettres, 2.182f; ibid., 205; Silhouette, 1.252f; de Brosses, 209.

220. Pöllnitz, Lettres, 2.311; Silhouette, 1.256; de Brosses, 172-4, 199, 208.

221. Spence, 337.

222. Richard, 46, 156, 198; Duclos, 133.

223. Björnstahl, 2.221f; Moore, 2.21f; West in Galt, 131f; Moore, 2.25f.; Archenholz, 2.137.

224. Meyer, 179; Plümicke, 232f; Stolberg, 339; Starke, 1.178f; Moore, 2.48f.

225. Grosley, 2.24; West in Galt, 103; Burney, 132-3; Dutens, 1.254f; Hartig, 207; Genlis, 170.

226. de Brosses, 211.

227. de Brosses, 231-2.

228. Burney, 149; Archenholz, 2.110f; Tischbein, 205-7.

229. de Brosses, 176-7.

230. Miller, 2.189f; Hartig, 193f; de la Platière, 5.64; Genlis, 167-70; Dupaty, 290-1; Archenholz, 1.242; Herder, 175.

231. Archenholz, 2.85.

232. Moore, 1.381, 391, 416, 444; Jones, 56.

233. Walpole, 208; de Brosses, 172; Duclos, 133.

234. Walpole, 215.

235. Knight, 206-7.

236. Wright, 1.235, 292, 343, 350; de Brosses, 184; ibid., 249. On Ficoroni, see Ridley.

237. Jones, 71.

238. Berkeley, 226.

239. Archenholz, 2.102; Goethe, 138, 345, 347.

240. Goethe, 422-3.

241. Pöllnitz, Lettres, 2.229f; Montesquieu, 699, 741f, 757; Keysler, 2.148f; de Brosses, 178-9; Gray, 69; Spence, 342; Montagu, 227, 231, 234; Sharp, 195, 215.

242. de Brosses, 181-2; Gray, 59; 69; Montague, 227-8; Miller, 2.198; Smith, 2.47.

243. Jones, 56, 59, 67, 69-70; Goethe, 407; Gray, 377.

244. Goethe, 375-6 and 472; Herder, 294; Vigée le Brun, 122.

245. Burney, 139.

246. Boswell, 66, 68; Burney, 154.

247. Jones, 74-5.

248. de Blainville, 2.391; Walpole, 214.

249. de Brosses, 175-6; Hervey, 287-91. Passionei had been papal nuncio in Vienna (1731-1738). Here he met Italy's foremost historian of the eighteenth century, Pietro Giannone (1676-1748), and inexorably goaded the Inquisition to pursue him across Europe as a heretic. For his zeal, in 1738 he was recalled to Rome, created cardinal, and appointed prefect of the Vatican library.

250. Tischbein, 214.

251. Dutens, 251.

252. Goethe, 138, 367, 393-5; Tischbein, 211.

253. Burney, 136, 139f, 144. On the Mozarts and the Miserere, see above, p. 51.

254. Montesquieu, 680-1; Keysler, 2.151f.

255. Montesquieu, 742; de Brosses, 172.

LIST OF POPES

REGNAL NAME	BIRTH NAME	DATES OF REIGN
Innocent XII	Antonio Pignatelli, OFS	12 July 1691 to 27 September 1700
Clement XI	Giovanni Francesco Albani	23 November 1700 to 19 March 1721
Innocent XIII	Michelangelo dei Conti	8 May 1721 to 7 March 1724
Benedict XIII	Pietro Francesco Orsini, OP	29 May 1724 to 21 February 1730
Clement XII	Lorenzo Corsini, OFS	12 July 1730 to 6 February 1740
Benedict XIV	Prospero Lorenzo Lambertini	17 August 1740 to 3 May 1758
Clement XIII	Carlo della Torre di Rezzonico	6 July 1758 to 2 February 1769
Clement XIV	Giovanni Vincenzo Antonio Ganganeli, OFM Conv.	19 May 1769 to 22 September 1774
Pius VI	Count Giovanni Angelo Braschi	15 February 1775 to 29 August 1799
Interregnum	——————————	29 August 1799 to 14 March 1800

Opposite: Giovanni Battista Nolli, Map of Rome *(detail), 1748*

LIST OF ILLUSTRATIONS

Frontispiece: Jacob More, *A distant view of Rome across the Tiber*, c. 1774; Wikimedia

p. vi: Hubert Robert, *Hermit in the Colosseum*, 1790; Dallas Museum of Art

The eighteenth century

p. 2: Anon., *Lady Mary Wortley Montagu, in Turkish dress*, c. 1717-8; Royal Collection

p. 5: Charles Cochin, *Charles de Brosses*, eighteenth century

p. 7: Elizabeth Vigée-Lebrun, *Self-portrait*, after 1782; National Gallery

p. 8: Johann Tischbein, *Goethe in the campagna*, 1787; Städel Museum

p. 15: Pier Leone Ghezzi, *Dr James Hay as a 'bear leader'*, 1737; British Museum

p. 16: Domenchino, *Communion of St Jerome*, 1614; Pinacoteca Vaticana

p. 17: Andrea Saschi, *San Romualdo*, 1631; Pinacoteca Vaticana

p. 21: Katherine Read, *English Gentlemen in Rome*, c. 1750; Yale Center for British Art

p. 26: Thomas Jones, *Elegant Figures on a Hillside*, 1776-1783; location unknown

p. 27: Giambattista Nolli, *Map of Rome* (detail), 1748

p. 29: Guercino, *St Petronilla*, c. 1623; Musei Capitolini

p. 38: Guido Reni, *St Michael*; 1635; S Maria della Concezione

p. 39: Michelangelo, *The Risen Christ*, 1519-21; S Maria sopra Minerva; photographer unknown

p. 41: Bernini, *Ecstasy of St Teresa*, 1647-52; Capella Cornaro, S Maria della Vittoria

p. 44: Michelangelo, *Moses*, 1513-15 (photographed by Jörg Bittner Unna, 2011); S Pietro in Vincoli

p. 46: Daniele da Volterra, *Descent from the Cross*, 1541; S Trinità

p. 52: Louis Desprez, *Papal benediction*, 1770s; location unknown

p. 55: Joseph Wright (of Derby), *The Annual Girandola at Castel Sant'Angelo*, c. 1776; Walker Art Gallery

p. 59: Giudo Reni, *The Penitent Magdalen*, 1633; Barberini, now Corsini

p. 61: Giuseppe Vasi, *Palazzo Borghese*, 1754; J. Paul Getty Museum

p. 62: Domenichino, *Sibyl*, 1616-17; Galleria Borghese

p. 63: Domenichino, *Diana and the hunt*, 1616-17; Galleria Borghese

p. 64: Giuseppe Vasi, *Palazzo Colonna*, 1754; J. Paul Getty Museum

p. 65: *The Apotheosis of Homer* (photographed by Marie-Lan Nguyen, 2011); British Museum

p. 67: Giuseppe Vasi, *Palazzo Farnese*, 1754

p. 69: *The Giustiniani Minerva*

(photographed by Tetraktys, 2010); Museo Chiaramonti

p. 71: Giuseppe Vasi, *Palazzo Massimo*, 1754; J. Paul Getty Museum

p. 72: '*Clytie*', now identified as *Antonia*; British Museum

p. 73: Giuseppe Vasi, *Palazzo Odescalchi*, 1754; J. Paul Getty Museum

p. 74: Giuseppe Vasi, *Palazzo Quirinale*, 1754; J. Paul Getty Museum

p. 75: Giuseppe Vasi, *Palazzo Rospigliosi*, 1754; J. Paul Getty Museum

p. 76: Guido Reni, *Aurora before Apollo's chariot*, 1614; palazzo Rospigliosi

p. 78: *The Laocoön*; Museo Pio-Clementino

p. 79: *The Apollo Belvedere* (photographed by Livioandronico2013, 2014); Museo Pio-Clementino

p. 80: *The Belvedere Antinoüs* (photographed by Jean-Pol GRAND-MONT, date unknown); Museo Pio-Clementino

p. 81: *Belvedere Torso* (photographed by Yair Haklai, 2009); Museo Pio-Clementino

p. 89: Antonio Capellani-Francesco Piranesi, *The hemicycle of the Villa Albani*, 1780

p. 90: *The Aldobrandini Wedding*; Biblioteca Apostolica Vaticana

p. 91: Alessandro Specchi, *Villa Borghese*, 1699; Princeton University Library

p. 92: *The Borghese Gladiator* (photographed by Ryan Baumann, 2014); Louvre

p. 93: *Dying Seneca* (photographed by Marie-Lan Nguyen, 2007); now Louvre

p. 94: Bernini, *David*, 1623-4 (photographed by James Anderson, 1845-55; J. Paul Getty Museum); Galleria Borghese

p. 95: Bernini, *Apollo and Daphne*, 1622-5 (photographed by James Anderson, 1845-55; J. Paul Getty Museum); Galleria Borghese

p. 99: Giuseppe Vasi, *Villa Ludovisi*, 1761; J. Paul Getty Museum

p. 100: Francesco Piranesi, *Orestes and Electra*, engraving dated 1783; Museo di Roma

p. 101: *The dying Gallic couple* (photographed by Marie-Lan Nguyen, 2006); Museo di Roma

p. 103: Giuseppe Vasi, *Villa Medici*, 1761; J. Paul Getty Museum

p. 104: *The Arrotino* (photographed by Sailko, 2013); Galleria degli Uffizi

p. 105: *Niobe and child*; Galleria degli Uffizi

p. 106: G. B. Piranesi, *Villa Pamphilii*, 1776; Yale University Art Gallery

p. 115: Gian Paolo Panini, *The Forum*, 1747; Walters Art Museum

p. 116: G. B. Piranesi, *The Arch of Titus*, 1748-78

p. 117: Giuseppe Vasi, *The Arch of Severus*, 1752; J. Paul Getty Museum

p. 118: G. B. Piranesi, *Basilica of Maxentius*, 1757; J. Paul Getty Museum

p. 119: Giuseppe Vasi, *The Forum Boarium*, 1754; J. Paul Getty Museum

p. 121: Giuseppe Vasi, *The Column of Trajan*, 1752; J. Paul Getty Museum

p. 122: François Boucher, *Imaginary Landscape with the Palatine Hill from Campo Vaccino*, 1734; Metropolitan Museum of Art

p. 125: Gian Paolo Panini, *The Colosseum*, 1747; Walters Art Museum

p. 126: Giovanni Volpato, *The arena
of the Colosseum*, 1780; British
Museum

p. 128: Abraham Ducros, *Arch of
Constantine*, c. 1790; location
unknown

p. 129: Canaletto, *The Pantheon*, 1742;
Royal Collection

p. 132: Giovanni Paolo Panini, *The
Lottery in Piazza di Montecitorio*,
1743-4; Metropolitan Museum of
Art

p. 133: Giuseppe Vasi, *The Hadrianeum*,
1752; J. Paul Getty Museum

p. 134: G. B. Piranesi, *The Quirinal
Horsetamers*, 1750; Yale University
Art Gallery

p. 136: Abraham Ducros, *Baths of
Caracalla*, 1780s; Metropolitan
Museum of Art

p. 137: Filippo Juvarra, *Baths of Diocletian*, c. 1710

p. 139: G. B. Piranesi, *Santa Costanza*,
1748-88; University of Tokyo

p. 141: G. B. Piranesi, *Columbarium of
the Arruntii*, 1757

p. 143: *Seated Agrippina* (photographer
and date unknown); Musei Capitolini

p. 151: G. B. Piranesi, *View of the Foun-
tainhead of the Acqua Paola on
Monte Aureo*, 1751; Yale University
Art Gallery

p. 152: Giuseppe Vasi, *Piazza Giudea*,
1754; J. Paul Getty Museum

p. 153: Gian Paolo Panini, *Piazza
Navona*, 1756; Niedersächsisches
Landesmuseum Hannover

p. 156: Gaspar van Wittel, *The Tiber near
the Porto di Ripa Grande*, c. 1711;
Accademia di San Luca

p. 161: G. B. Piranesi, *The Gothic Arch*,

from *Carceri d'invenzione* (*Imaginary Prisons*), c. 1750; Metropolitan
Museum of Art

p. 167: Giovanni Paolo Panini, *The
Piazza Farnese Decorated for a Celebration in Honor of the Marriage
of the Dauphin*, 1745; Chrysler
Museum of Art

p. 175: Jacques-Louis David, *The Oath of
the Horatii*, 1786; Louvre

p. 181: Giovanni Paolo Panini, *Musical
feast given by the cardinal de La
Rochefoucauld in the Teatro Argentina in Rome in 1747 on the occasion
of the marriage of Dauphin, son of
Louis XV*, 1747; Louvre

p. 186: Alessandro Specchi, *The catafalque for James II in S. Lorenzo
in Lucina*, 1701; Getty Research
Institute

p. 196: Bartolomeo Pinelli, *A nocturnal
burial in the Protestant cemetery*,
1831; Stadtschloss (Weimar)

p. 199: Elias Christoph Heiss, *Clement XI*, date unknown; location
unknown

p. 199: Pietro Bracci, *Benedict XIII*, date
unknown; location unknown

p. 200: Agostino Masucci, *Clement XII*,
date unknown; private
collection

p. 200: Pierre Hubert Subleyras, *Benedict XIV*, 1746; Metropolitan
Museum of Art

p. 202: Anton Mengs, *Clement XIII*,
1758; Ca' Rezzonico

p. 203: Christopher Hewetson, *Clement
XIV*, 1773; Victoria and Albert
Museum

p. 203: Pompeo Batoni, *Pius VI*, 1775;
National Gallery of Ireland

p. 206: Etienne Poussin, *Cardinal*

Alessandro Albani, 1764; British Museum

p. 208: Pompeo Batoni, *Self-portrait*, 1773-4; Galleria degli Uffizi

p. 209: Pierre Savart, *Cardinal de Bernis*, 1778; Universitätsbibliothek Leipzig

p. 212: Robert Fagan, *Portrait of himself and Italian wife Maria*, 1803; Hunt Museum

p. 215: Alexis Simon Belle, *James Stuart, 'The Old Pretender'*, 1715; National Portrait Gallery

p. 221: Angelika Kauffman, *Self-portrait, 1770-5*; National Portrait Gallery

p. 226: Giovanni Morghen, *Johannes Reiffenstein*, eighteenth century; Winckelmann-Museum

p. 227: Pier Leone Ghezzi, *The Congress of Antiquarians* (detail), 1725; Die Albertina

Back matter

p. 236: Giovanni Battista Nolli, *Map of Rome* (detail), 1748; Bibliothèque nationale de France

Illustrations on Frontispiece and pp. 5, 7, 8, 27, 29, 41, 46, 55, 62, 63, 67, 95, 115, 125, 139, 153, 156, 175, 181, 196, 202, 203 (right), 208, 215 and 221 courtesy of Wikimedia; on p. vi courtesy of Dallas Museum of Art; on pp. 2 and 129 courtesy of the Royal Collection; on pp. 15, 72, 100, 126 and 206 courtesy of the British Museum; on p. 17 courtesy of the Pinacoteca Vaticana; on pp. 18, 52, 89, 105, 137, 141, 199 (left), 212 and 227 courtesy of the collection of the author; on

p. 21 courtesy of Yale Center for British Art; on p. 26 courtesy of myartprints. co.uk; on pp. 38 and 116 courtesy of wikiart.org; on p. 39 courtesy of roameternalcity.wordpress.com; on p. 44 courtesy of Jörg Bittner Unna (Wikimedia user); on p. 59 courtesy of studyblue.com; on pp. 61, 64, 71, 73, 74, 75, 94, 99, 103, 117, 118, 119, 121, 133 and 152 courtesy of the J. Paul Getty Museum; on pp. 65, 93 and 101 courtesy of Marie-Lan Nguyen (Wikimedia user 'Jastrow'); p. 76 courtesy of alchetron.com; p. 78 courtesy of imgur.com; p. 79 courtesy of Livioandronico2013 (Wikimedia user); p. 80 courtesy of Jean-Pol GRANDMONT (Wikimedia user); p. 81 courtesy of Yair Haklai (Wikimedia user); p. 90 courtesy of Biblioteca Apostolica Vaticana; p. 91 courtesy of Princeton University Library; p. 92 courtesy of Ryan Baumann (Flickr user); p. 104 courtesy of Sailko (Wikimedia user); pp. 106, 134 and 151 courtesy of Yale University Art Gallery; pp. 122, 132, 136, 161 and 200 courtesy of the Metropolitan Museum of Art; p. 128 courtesy of thegiftsoflife. tumblr.com; p. 143 courtesy of spencer alley.blogspot.com; p. 167 courtesy of the Chrysler Museum of Art; p. 186 courtesy of the Getty Research Institute; pp. 199 (right) and 200 courtesy of papalartifacts.com; p. 203 (left) courtesy of the Victoria and Albert Museum; p. 209 courtesy of Universitätsbibliothek Leipzig; p. 227 courtesy of the Albertina; p. 236 courtesy of the Bibliothèque nationale de France

NOTE ON LEADING ILLUSTRATORS
OF ROMAN TOPOGRAPHY
(EIGHTEENTH CENTURY)

Gian Paolo Panini (1691-1765): born at Piacenza, he moved to Rome in 1711, and began decorating palaces, before turning to *vedute*, as well as commemorating events, and doing portraits, and illustrating 'galleries'. (*Grove Dictionary of Art*, 24.9-11)

Giovanni Battista Piranesi (1720-1778): born at Venice, and trained as an architect, he came to Rome in 1740, and studied briefly with Vasi and worked with the cartographer Giovanni Battista Nolli. He was amazingly prolific; works included *Vedute di Roma* 1748-78 (135 plates), *Antichità romane* 1756 (217 plates) and *Della magnificenza ed architettura de'Romani*, 1761. (*Grove Dictionary of Art*, 24.841-7)

Alessandro Specchi (1668-1729), a Roman architect and engraver, who studied with Fontana. Author of *Quarto libro del nuovo teatro de palazzi di Roma*, 1699. (*Grove Dictionary of Art*, 29.373)

Giuseppe Vasi (1710-1782): born at Corleone, Sicily, he came to Rome in 1736 as a subject of the kingdom of Naples. He was briefly teacher of Piranesi, and is unjustly overshadowed by him. His most famous work is *Delle magnificenze di Roma antica e moderna* (10 vols), 1747-1761 (250 plates). (*Grove Dictionary of Art*, 32.70)

Gaspare van Wittel (Vanvitelli) (1652/3-1736): born at Utrecht, he was in Rome by 1675. He is a leading vedutist, and his exquisite watercolours portray much more than the customary riuins: he was mostly interested in modern Rome. (*Grove Dictionary of Art*, 33.268-70.) See Giuliano Briganti, *Gaspar van Wittel*, Milan 1996.

SOURCES

Addison, Joseph: *Remarks on Italy* in *Works*, ed. Richard Hurd, 6 vols, London 1890, vol. 1

Archenholz, Johann Wilhelm, *A picture of Italy*, trans. Joseph Trapp, 2 vols, London 1791

Arnauld, Vincent: *Souvenirs d'un sexagenaire*, 4 vols, Paris 1833

Barthelemy, Jean Jacques: *Voyage en Italie*, Paris 1801

Berkeley, George: *Journal in Italy*, in *Works*, ed. A. Fraser, 4 vols, London 1901

Berry, Mary: *Extracts from the journals and correspondence of Miss Berry*, ed. Therese Lewis, 3 vols, London 1865

Bersano-Begay, Marina: *Il viaggio in Italia di Stanislao Staszic*, Torino 1935

Bilinski, Bronislaw: *Figure e momenti polacche a Roma*, Wroclaw 1992

Bjornstahl, Jacob: *Lettere ne' suoi viaggi stranieri*, 6 vols, Poschiavo 1782-7

Blainville, —: *Travels through Holland, Germany, Switzerland, and other parts of Europe, especially Italy*, trans. George Turnbill and William Guthrie, 3 vols, London 1843

Bonstetten, Charles Victor de: *Voyage sur le scène des six derniers livres de l'Énéide*, Geneva 1805

Boswell, James: *Boswell on the grand tour*, ed. F. Brady and F. Pottle, Yale 1955

Breval, John, *Remarks on several parts of Europe*, 2 vols, London 1726

Brosses, Charles de: *Selections from the letters of de Brosses*, trans. R. Sutherland, London 1897

Burney, Charles: (Journal) *Music, men and manners in France and Italy 1770*, ed. H. Edmund Poole, London 1969

Caylus, comte Anne Claude: *Voyage d'Italie*, ed. Amilda Pons, Paris 1914

Claridge, Amanda: *Rome, an archaeological guide*, Oxford 1998

Coyer, Gabriel: *Voyages en Italie*, 2 vols, Paris 1775

Deutsch, Otto: *Handel, a documentary biography*, London 1955

Dictionary of national biography, 2nd ed. 60 vols, Oxford 2004

Dictionnaire de biographie française, Paris 1933-

Dizionario biografico degli italiani, Rome 1960-

Dizionario enciclopedico universale della musica e dei musicisti, ed. Alberto Basso, 16 vols, Torino 1983-9.

Duclos, Charles: *Voyage en Italie*, 2nd edn, Paris 1791

Dupaty, Charles: *Travels through Italy in a series of letters in the year 1785*, London 1788

Dutens, Louis: *Mémoirs d'un voyageur qui se repose*, 3 vols, London 1806

Ferber, Johann Jacob: *Travels through Italy in the years 1771 and 1772*, trans. R. Raspe, London 1776

Galt, John: *The life and studies of Benjamin West compiled from materials furnished by himself*, London 1817

Genlis, Caroline comtesse de: *Mémoires*, Paris 1878

Gibbon, Edward: *Letters*, ed. Jane Norton, 3 vols, London 1956

—*Memoirs of my life*, ed. Georges Bonnard, London 1966

Goethe, Johann Wolfgang: *Italian journey*, trans. W.H. Auden and Elizabeth Mayer, London 1962

Gray, Robert: *Letters during the course of a tour through Germany, Switzerland and Italy in the years 1791 and 1792*, London 1794

(Grosley, Pierre Jean): *New observations on Italy and its inhabitants written in French by two Swedish gentlemen*, trans. Thomas Nugent, 2 vols, London 1769

Grove Dictionary of art, ed. Jane Turner, 34 vols, London and New York 1996

Hartig, Franz conte de: *Lettres sur la France, l'Angleterre et l'Italie*, Geneva 1785

Herder, Johann Gottfried: *Briefwechsel mit seiner Gattin*, Giessen 1859

Hervey, Christopher: *Letters from Portugal, Spain, Italy and Germany in the years 1759-61*, 3 vols, London 1785

Hobhouse, Benjamin: *Remarks on parts of France, Italy etc. in the years 1783, 4 and 5*, Bath 1796

Indice biografico italiano (fiche)

Jones, Thomas: *Memoirs*, London 1951 (= Walpole Society, 32)

Keysler, Johann Georg: *Travels through Germany, Bohemia, Hungary, Switzerland, Italy and Lorrain*, 4 vols, 3rd ed., London 1763

Knight, Lady Philippina: *Letters*, London 1905

Ingamells, John (ed.): *A dictionary of British and Irish travellers in Italy 1701-1800*, Yale 1997

Labat, Jean Baptiste: *Voyage en Espagne et en Italie*, Paris 1730

Lanciani, Rodolfo: *Storia degli scavi di Roma*, new ed., 6 vols, Rome 1989-2002

Longstaff, W.: 'Notes on the life and writings of John Dyer the poet', *Patrician* 4 (1847), 264-8

McIntyre, Ian: *Joshua Reynolds*, London 2003

Merville, Michel Guyot de: *Voyage historique en Italie*, 2 vols, Hague 1719

Meyer, Frederik Johann: *Voyage en Italie*, Paris 1802

Miller, Lady Ann: *Letters from Italy*, 3 vols, London 1776

Moore, John: *View of society and manners in Italy*, 2 vols, London 1781

Montagu, Lady Mary Wortley: *Complete letters*, Oxford 1966

Montesquieu, Charles de Secondat, baron de: *Oeuvres complètes*, 2 vols, Paris 1949 (Pleiade ed.)

Moszyński, August: letters in Andrea Busiri Vici, *I Poniatowski e Roma*, Florence 1971, 204f. See also Bilinski

Mozart, Wolfgang Amadeus: *Letters*, ed. Emily Anderson, London 1985

Northall, John: *Travels through Italy*, London 1766

Northcote, James: *Life of Sir Joshua Reynolds*, 2 vols, London 1818

Nugent, Thomas: *The grand tour*, 4 vols, London 1749

Pastor, Ludwig: *The history of the popes*, 40 vols, London 1938-67

Pembroke, Henry Herbert 10th Earl of: *Letters and diaries*, London 1939

Platière, Jean Marie Rolande de la: *Lettres écrites de Suisse, d'Italie, de Suède et de Malte*, 6 vols, Amsterdam 1780.

Pöllnitz, Karl Ludwig: *Lettres*, 3 vols, London 1747

—*Mémoires*, 2 vols, 5th ed., London 1747

Reynolds, Joshua: *Letters*, ed. John Ingamells and J. Edgecombe, Yale 2000

—See also McIntyre, Northcote

Richard, Jérôme: *Description historique et critique d l'Italie*, 6 vols, Dijon 1766

Richardson, Jonathon: *An account of the statues, basreliefs, drawings and pictures in Italy*, London 1722

Ridley, R. T., *The prince of antiquarians: Francesco de Ficoroni*, Rome 2017

Riesch, Isaak Wolfgang: *Observations faites pendant un voyage en Italie*, 2 vols, Dresden 1781

Sade, Donatien Alphonse François de: Rome in *Oeuvres complètes*, vol. 16, Paris 1977

Saint-Non, Jean Baptiste Richard, abbé de: *Panoptikon italiano*, Rome 1986

Sharp, Samuel: *Letters from Italy*, 3rd ed., London 1767

Sherlock, Martin: *Letters of an English traveller*, London 1780

Silhouette, Etienne: *Relation d'un voyage de Paris en Espagne, Portugal et Italie*, 4 vols, Paris 1770

Smith, James Edward: *Sketch of a tour on the Continent in the years 1786 and 1787*, 3 vols, London 1793

Smollett, Tobias: *Travels through France and Italy*, London 1949

Spence, Joseph: *Letters from the Grand Tour*, Montreal 1975

Starke, Marianne: *Travels in Italy between the years 1792 and 1798*, 2 vols, London 1802

Stolberg, Count Friedrich Leopold: *Travels through Germany, Switzerland, Italy and Sicily*, trans. Thomas Holcroft, 2 vols, London 1796

Thompson, Charles: *Travels*, 3 vols, Reading 1744

Tischbein, Johann Heinrich: *Aus meinem Leben*, Berlin 1922

Vigée le Brun, Elisabeth: *Souvenir of Mme le Brun*, 2 vols, London 1879

Volkmann, Johann Jacob: *Historische-Kritische Nachrichten von Italien*, 2 vols, Leipzig 1770

Walpole, Horace: *Correspondence*, ed. W. Lewis, Oxford 1937- , vol. 13

Wright, Edward: *Some observations in travelling through France, Italy etc. in the years 1720, 1721, 1722*, 2 vols, London 1738

First published 2019 by
Pallas Athene (Publishers) Ltd,
Studio IIA, Archway Studios
25-27 Bickerton Road, London N19 5JT
For further information on our books please visit
www.pallasathene.co.uk

 pallasathenebooks   PallasAtheneBooks

Pallas_books   Pallasathene0

ISBN 978 1 84368 139 7

Printed in England